Structuralism and Marxism

Structuralism and Marxism

by

ADAM SCHAFF

Member of the Polish Academy of Sciences

PERGAMON PRESS

OXFORD · NEW YORK · TORONTO · SYDNEY · PARIS · FRANKFURT

U. K.	Pergamon Press Ltd., Headington Hill Hall, Oxford OX3 0BW, England
U. S. A.	Pergamon Press Inc., Maxwell House, Fairview Park, Elmsford, New York 10523, U.S.A.
CANADA	Pergamon of Canada Ltd., 75 The East Mall, Toronto, Ontario, Canada
AUSTRALIA	Pergamon Press (Aust.) Pty. Ltd., 19a Boundary Street, Rushcutters Bay, N.S.W. 2011, Australia
FRANCE	Pergamon Press SARL, 24 rue des Ecoles, 75240 Paris, Cedex 05, France
FEDERAL REPUBLIC OF GERMANY	Pergamon Press GmbH, 6242 Kronberg-Taunus, Pferdstrasse 1, Federal Republic of Germany

First edition 1978

British Library Cataloguing in Publication Data

Schaff, Adam
Structuralism and Marxism.
1. Structuralism – Addresses, essays, lectures
I. Title
149' .9   B841.4   77–30331
ISBN 0 08 020505 4

Printed in Great Britain by William Clowes & Sons Limited London, Beccles and Colchester

Contents

Foreword

The present book despite its title forms a coherent whole.

The first essay is an introduction to the set of problems discussed here and explains the concept of structuralism as an intellectual trend which is homogeneous, on the one hand, but internally differentiated, on the other. The second is a critical analysis of what is called Marxist structuralism in France, and the third takes up the philosophical issues in Chomsky's generative grammar. The link between these three essays is my zeroing in on the philosophical aspects of structuralism.

The form of essays has been dictated by practical considerations. In view of the immense variety of the trends and currents which are now being termed structuralist and the number of issues within each of such trends and currents it is extremely difficult, if not impossible, to include the whole set of the problems related to that intellectual current in a single book, if one is to avoid vulgarization. The form of essays makes it possible to analyse the selected issues in depth and, at the same time, to combine them into a whole on the basis of certain problems common to all of them, which it has been my intention to do.

The essays included in this book are concerned with selected issues whose importance in philosophy needs no explanation. The absence of other issues, no less important – such as an analysis of the structural approach of the Prague school of linguistics, which in the 1930s originated the triumphant march of structuralism; the closely related anthropological structuralism of the Lévi-Strauss school, which was decisive for the success of structuralism in France; the specifically French structuralism associated with the names of Foucault, Barthes and others; and above all the analysis of the anthropological trend initiated by Claude Lévi-Strauss, a trend that has found wide repercussions in Poland – is explained by the fact that such a vast range of problems cannot reasonably be handled in a single book, both because of the amount of work it would require and the practical limitations of book size. It is my intention to discuss the problems of the anthropological structuralism of Lévi-Strauss in the near future.

My focussing in the present book on the problems of what is termed Marxist structuralism was due to my conviction that a critical analysis of this trend is of topical interest. In my opinion, the trend is extremely harmful to the further development of Marxist philosophy because the vagueness of the concepts it uses may result in much ideological confusion, which can, even now, be noticed in 'Romance' countries in Europe and in Latin America.

ADAM SCHAFF

Structuralism as an Intellectual Current

It would be trivial to say that structuralism has become an intellectual fashion. The intensity of that fashion, it is true, varies from country to country and from one intellectual milieu to another, but it is indisputable that the phenomenon is universal.

For all its apparent triviality, this statement implies two theses which, according to one interpretation, are not only not trivial, but false.

First, if we say that structuralism has become an intellectual fashion, which is true, this statement could be interpreted in the sense that people have only now realized the theoretical and methodological importance of using the concept of structure in science. And this is utterly false. For while structuralism was not 'in' 40 or 50 years ago, the concept of structure was intellectually so significant that not only did those research methods which availed themselves of the concept mark notable successes in chemistry, biology, psychology, and linguistics, but the concept itself found in the 1930s the following general philosophical appraisal, formulated by J. Metallmann, the Polish philosopher and methodologist of natural science, in his *venia legendi* lecture:

> In recent decades we have been witnessing an extraordinary phenomenon. A concept whose first applications go back to the first half of the 19th century has become, gradually but systematically, naturalized in a growing number of fields, from natural science, at first, to the humanities and the social sciences later on. From its rather modest role of a concept useful in chemistry, the concept of structure has grown so important, and has covered so vast a range of phenomena, that its increasing significance is probably comparable only to that of the concept of *evolution* in the late 19th and the early 20th century. [1]

And he concludes thus:

> It has not been too common, in the history of human thought, for a concept viable in an increasing number of specialized disciplines to attain great significance in philosophical investigations. The concept of structure does in fact seem predestined to become a focal one and to play a primary scientific and philosophical role in contemporary thought. [2]

1

Secondly, the statement on structuralism as a present-day intellectual fashion is not to be interpreted so that its significance in science is denied (although the term *fashion* often has a derogatory sense). At least, such an assessment is not to be understood as an explanation of the popularity of a given intellectual trend. The fact that structuralism has become fashionable does not in any way explain its popularity, but, on the contrary, calls for an explanation.[3] The point is to know why one trend has grasped human minds, and the other has not; why one intellectual current has become fashionable, and the other has not. The cause of such a fashion is no less interesting and no less important for an analysis of the issues involved.

We shall accordingly make such an endeavour by beginning with an apparently simple, but in fact very intricate, problem: What is structuralism?

What is Structuralism?

The question itself can be understood in various ways, but its most obvious interpretation is that it calls for a definition of the term. And at this very moment troubles arise.

The fact is that we have to do with a large number of theories which either explicitly stress their allegiance to structuralism in their respective names (structural linguistics, structural anthropology, etc.) or follow the structural approach in some sense of the term, even though they do not refer to it in their names (cf. organismalism in biology, the interpretation of fables made by Propp in his study of the Russian folklore, etc.). All tentative general definitions must accordingly start from the available data, that is, from the class of those theories which pretend to be structuralist. A real definition should grasp the common characteristics of such theories, characteristics which make them form a specified class which is the designatum of the term *structuralism*. But all such endeavours are doomed to failure because the differences among those theories which pretend to be elements of that class are so great that, despite the frequent use they make of the adjective *structural*, they cannot be covered by any single definition that would be anything more than a collection of generalities. The differences are due not only to the peculiarities of the spheres of research (for instance, Bertalanffy's organismalism and Propp's theory of the fable, the theory of models in mathematical logic and Lévi-Strauss' theory of myths), but also to different approaches to one and the same sphere of research, as is the case of the various trends in structural linguistics. For, contrary to the prevailing opinion that in this field – from which structural trends in the social sciences and the humanities have recently drawn inspiration – the theoretical assumptions, and possibly also the definition of structuralism, are simple matters, the situation is so complicated that the various schools which come into question (there are at least five of them: the Prague school, the Copenhagen school, the British school, the American descriptivist school with the separate school of transformational generative grammar, and the Soviet school) cannot be given one common name of structuralism. After all, this is precisely the milieu in which crushing criticism of structuralism as a void class have originated. For instance, A. Martinet[4] says that the term *structuralism* has become the label of nearly all non-traditional trends in linguistics, while E. Benveniste[5] follows Martinet by saying that the word *structure* is often used to veil profound differences of opinion. The Chomsky school avoids references to structuralism and is even reluctant to admit all kinship with that trend. No wonder then, the situation becomes aggravated and complicated because fields of work are concerned which in fact are very far apart from one another.

For that reason there could be another, although scientifically less reliable possibility to bear in mind: that of taking as the point of difference the concept of 'structure' used each time in any given theory. However, it emerges that even here the situation is no less complicated. Thoroughgoing studies of the concept 'structure'[6] reveal clearly that this is a homonym – with as many meanings as there are theories using it.

The American anthropologist A. L. Kroeber, quoted by Lévi-Strauss, has been most clear in stressing the negative side to this: 'The notion "structure" is very likely just a concession to fashion . . . everything that is not completely formless has a structure . . . the expression "structure" adds absolutely nothing to whatever is in our mind in using it save for an agreeable flavour.'[7]

R. Boudon, already mentioned before, concludes that the notion 'structure' is a class of homonyms[8] and that in view of this fact no inductive definition of it is possible.

R. Bastide, in the already mentioned collection of articles, the outcome of a special scientific colloquium under the auspices of UNESCO, comes to a similarly negative conclusion: 'Words as current as *group, class, power,* and *structure* now do not have two, three, or four meanings, which would be normal, but as many of them as there are authors — meanings which are irreducible to any common denominator, and are even quite autonomous.'[9]

It is not my task here to analyse the concept of structure: it serves my purpose to stress the ambiguity of that term, which does not let us state unambiguously that a person is a structuralist because the term *structure* occurs in his theoretical considerations. One comment on the ambiguity of the term *structure* seems to be relevant here, because the conceptual confusion in that case results in particularly damaging theoretical complications, and also because — despite its essential significance for our considerations — it has been discussed in the literature of the subject on exceptional occasions only (one such laudable exception being the quoted comment by E. Benveniste, *'Structure' en linguistique,* in the collection of papers edited by R. Bastide).

I refer here to the ambiguity of the term *structure* as it relates to the term *system.*

The original meaning of the term *structure* was 'a structure of something', in the sense of 'the way something is constructed' or 'the relations which holds among the elements of a given whole'. That meaning of the term is also connected with its etymology: in Latin, *structura* comes from *struere,* 'to build'. Now, in this case we have to make a clear distinction between a system and its structure. The term *system* is used with reference to a whole that consists of elements which bear to one another such a relation that a change in the position of one of them results in a change in the position of the remaining ones. The way in which those elements are interconnected within a given system, i.e. the totality of the relations among them, is termed the *structure* of that system. These two terms are thus inseparable from one another, and that in a very peculiar manner: there is no structure without a system to which it refers, but there is also no system without an appropriate structure, which follows from the very definition of the term *system.* That organic relationship, however, is not identity; on the contrary, we have to do with two different terms with different meanings, terms which accordingly can be neither identified nor confused.

It is remarkable that the founders of the school from which the fashion for structuralism has originated, namely the founders of the Prague school of structural phonology, realized that perfectly well, and the appropriate terminological distinction was made in their works with exceptional clarity and precision. This was also connected with the theoretical foundations of their trend, foundations which can be reduced to two basic concepts: a *system* of a language, and its *structure*, the latter being based on the (principally) binary oppositions of phonemes.

As has been noted by Benveniste in his paper cited above, De Saussure in his *Cours de linquistique générale* did not use the term *structure* at all, but only the term *system* (although he is recognized as the spiritual father of structural linguistics).[10] It was only the Prague Circle which introduced the term *structure* in the sense of relations among the elements of the system of a language, that is, among phonemes (or, strictly speaking, pairs of phonemes).[11] In this case the term *structure* is evidently used in the sense of the *structure of a system*. This is also the sense in which it was used by the founders of structural phonology, e.g. N. Troubetzkoy, who in his well-known paper 'La phonologie actuelle' (1933) referred to *the structure of system* and stressed the contrast between structuralism and the atomistic approach to problems which had marked traditional methodology.[12]

The trouble is, however, that next to its basic meaning, *the structure of something*, the term *structure* also functions as a synonym of the term *system*, and hence denotes *something which has a specified structure*. Ambiguity is common in natural languages, and it was only the cat in *Alice in Wonderland* who handled the problem without difficulty; she claimed that she just paid the words more. Human beings are much more clumsy when coping with the problem, and they usually have to pay for that with additional logical confusion and obscurity of formulations. This is especially the case when, as in the present-day literature on structuralism, the term *structure* is used in both meanings which are sometimes confused in one and the same sentence. This results in a complete mix-up of concepts and the undermining of the very foundations of the structuralist idea, which in its every variation must have at its disposal the concept of system and that of its structure in the sense of interconnections and relationships among the elements of that system.

This is only an additional, though, in my opinion, very important, argument in favour of the claim of such authors as R. Boudon, who says that the use of the term *structure* in a given theory does not entitle us to call it structuralist, for that term is a collection of homonyms each of which has a different meaning in nearly every theory and for nearly every author. If the term *structuralism* were to depend on the use of the word *structure* in a given theory and to be based in each case on its different interpretation, then *structuralism* would mean something else in each case, and there would be no grounds for any single definition of that trend. The word stands for many different theories and trends, its uses vary from theory to theory, and the striving for its general definition is accordingly illusory. The worst happens when that illusion that results from a hypostasis (if there is a name, then there must be the object it denotes) is due to ordinary ignorance. Unfortunately, in the case of intellectual fashions this is an effect of pseudopopularizations and, in fact, vulgarizations. Such phenomena thrive in an atmosphere of a sociopsychological trauma, as is the case of France, especially when it comes to what is called Marxist structuralism, but that is a separate subject.

Are we therefore to jump to the radical conclusion that *structuralism* as a general term denotes an empty class? That there are various theories which claim to be called structural, but each of them is so different from the remaining ones that they have nothing in common, and that to speak about a structural trend in present-day science is merely to fall victim of an illusion?

Such a conclusion would not only be radical, but obviously wrong as well. It would not follow from what has been said so far, namely that the term *structuralism* does not denote any single and homogeneous trend, and that various theories which claim to be structural do not have, next to their distinctive features, common elements that can make us refer to a certain intellectual trend. If such features do exist, even in a number of the theories that come here in question, then they can be extrapolated so that we arrive not at a definition of something which does not exist in the sense of any homogeneous theory, but at pointing to the essential characteristics of an intellectual trend, which is more productive for an analysis of trends in science than definitions which are sterile in their vague generalities. Such statements as those by Metallmann, cited earlier, and by

Troubetzkoy, made in the same year, statements which are *sui generis* illustrations of the general consensus on the issue, prove that such an endeavour is not doomed to failure, because features characteristic of a given intellectual trend can be found even in those spheres of research which are remote from one another.

We shall try to make such an extrapolation while neither pretending to offer a complete analysis of the problem nor striving to provide evidence for every thesis by quoting data from the disciplines involved. Time-consuming as it is, this is relatively easy to do, but it would make the text difficult to read; while I consider such a manner of writing useful in certain cases, it would not serve its purpose here in view of the tasks I have set myself. My point is to offer an analysis of the ontological and gnosiological foundations of structuralism and to explain, in this connection, why researchers have turned their interest toward synchronic analyses. All other issues will be treated as auxiliary, even if reference to them proves indispensable (this applies, above all, to the explanation of the basic concepts).

Examining the theses advanced by the various theories which claim to be structural, and the ways in which the problems investigated in those theories are approached, provides – in my opinion – grounds for extrapolating at least four features that are common to such theories.

1. The primary principle of all those trends which may conventionally be termed structural (we take here into account both natural and social science and cultural anthropology) is to approach the subject matter of research as a specific whole which dominates all its elements. This approach has developed as the opposition to the method which may conventionally be called atomistic and which starts from studying things and phenomena either in disregarding more comprehensive wholes or by treating them as independent parts of an aggregate which is nothing else than the sum of its elements. In the integrated approach the whole in question is treated as a system, i.e. as a whole in which its elements are interconnected so that the structure of the whole determines the position of every element, and a change in the position of any element results in a change in the positions of the remaining ones, and hence in a change of the system. This approach thus stresses both the dependence of the elements on the system of which they are parts, and the fact that a whole is something more than the sum of its elements, and hence something more than an ordinary aggregate.[13]

The above description is, of course, schematic and simplifies the problem in the spirit of ideal types. This is, however, not only admissible, but even necessary if the problem is to be presented clearly. While in research practice the demarcation line is not so sharp as it would appear from the analysis of the ideal types, and while the atomistic trend is not always indifferent to the links between things and phenomena under investigation, on the one hand, and more comprehensive wholes, on the other, etc., yet even if these reservations are made the differences remain objective and qualitative (and not merely quantitative) in nature. This is why they can be used as the basis for suitable distinctions and for the typology resulting from them.

2. The second feature of those trends which are classed as structural cannot be separated from the act of treating the subject-matter of research as a system. That second feature consists in the principle, universally adopted in those trends, that every system has a specified structure, and that the task of science is to find what that structure is.

This formulation implies certain general gnosiological assumptions, namely that both a given system and its structure are objective in nature, and that the task of scientific cognition is to disclose, or, in other words, 'to reflect', them. Without going into details, which would exceed the limits of this essay, I have to state plainly what my position in this controversy is, the more so since in the literature on the subject we also find other formulation (cf. R. Boudon's study of the concept of structure, cited above). While being intentionally brief in my formulations, I must state, in order to avoid misunderstandings, that when I speak about the objective nature of systems and structures I mean only that what is disclosed in the process of cognition is not just *any* systems and/or structures; that cognition maps something which exists objectively. I do not thereby deny the active role of the cognizing subject as I do take into account the whole gamut of subjective factors, and not merely the knowledge that results from scientific cognition.

The statement that a system must have a structure may be taken to be analytic, since it follows from the interpretation of the term *system*. It might, therefore, seem trivial, but it only appears to be such. This is so because, as we have said after R. Boudon, the term *structure* is a set of homonyms (or, in plain English, is ambiguous); but it is also a set of synonyms because those different meanings have counterparts in synonymous words. Special attention must be drawn in this connection to the meaning of the word *organization*, because *structure*, in one sense of the word, means the same as *organization*; we can accordingly speak synonymically about the structure of a system and the (inner) organization of a system. We have said, 'in one sense of the word', thus stressing the fact that the term *structure* is a set of homonyms, and hence the word has other meanings as well. The point here is that *organization*, in the strict sense of the term, refers to an outcome of purposeful human activity. Thus *the structure of a system* is synonymous with *the organization of a system* only if the system in question is a result of purposeful human activity. Hence a machine built to serve a specified purpose and any relatively separated social whole, such as a family, a firm, a class, can be called a system with a specified organization (structure) in the literal sense of the term *organization*, but such a system as the organism of an animal can be said to have an organization only in the figurative sense of that word. This is stressed here not for pedantry alone: this is a problem to which we shall have to revert in our further discussions of tentative structural interpretations of Marxism, be it alone for the fact that appropriate analyses are to be found in the book of a forerunner of present-day endeavours. I mean here A. Bogdanov and his fundamental work on tectology, interpreted by him as a general theory of organization.[14] As is known, Bogdanov's ideas were taken up by Bukharin, especially with reference to the theory of equilibrium and its disturbances. When Marxist circles, especially in France, are now trying to interpret Marxism in terms of structural analysis, passing over the works of these authors in silence is just incomprehensible.

3. The third feature common to all those theories which in some way are inclined toward structuralism is their interest in the laws which most often are called coexistential, or morphological, or structural. I mean here the laws of science which describe certain regularities that are common to, or universal for, a given class of things or phenomena, with the proviso that these regularities are not in the sphere of changes, and hence are not casual, but in the sphere of *coexistence* of things, or phenomena, or their properties. Such studies, which result in the formulation of coexistential laws, mean a static approach to facts. Whatever exists is in some kind of motion, and hence the static approach always is an idealization which assumes that the time factor $t=0$. We thus have to do with an idealization

which treats facts as it were in a time section (the formulation *time section* is metaphorical and alludes to the term *anatomical section*; an anatomical section, which shows, for instance, the structure of the tissues of a muscle, also is an idealization as it eliminates — this time not conceptually, but with an anatomist's knife — all other aspects of the organism in question from the sphere of our interest by assuming that t=0). But it is only in this way that we can come to know that aspect of reality and its characteristic coexistential (morphological) regularities, which are objective in nature, and are thus not an arbitrary construct of the cognizing mind. The process of idealization, without which it would not be possible to acquire the knowledge of such regularities, is not specific to coexistential laws, and hence it does not discredit such laws in any way. For if that idealization which reduces the time factor to zero, or, in other words, disregards motion (i.e. the dynamic aspect of facts), is required to formulate coexistential laws, then in turn the formulation of dynamic, causal laws requires disregarding the structure of things and the coexistential laws.

There is no doubt that causal (dynamic, genetic) laws have been discussed in the literature of the subject more often and in greater detail, be it alone because of the domination of genetic studies in the last hundred years. It does not follow therefrom that the causal laws are the only type of scientific laws or that they are dominant in science. Not only in natural science in its stage marked by interest in systematics (especially at the turn of the eighteenth century), but also — and perhaps even especially — now, both in natural and in social science, the study of the structure of reality, and hence the study of coexistential (morphological) regularities, has won such significance that it has equalled in importance, as J. Metallmann wrote in his paper mentioned at the beginning of this essay, the concept of evolution as it dominated nineteenth century science.

It is true that literature on coexistential laws is still much poorer than on causal (dynamic) laws; it may even be said to be quite poor. This scantiness of comments on one of the focal issues of structuralism does not do credit to the ability of its followers to grasp theoretical problems, especially if we consider how much has been written on structuralism and related issues.

I am concerned here with the problem as we see it now rather than with its history. If we go back far enough we find statements related to that problem in Aristotle's works, and historians of philosophy could certainly point to many other sources which would prove that many thinkers in the past had been aware of the importance of the issue. But the first advanced analysis of the problem of coexistential laws is to be found in *A System of Logic* by John Stuart Mill (cf. Chap. XXII, 'On the Principles of Coexistence Which Are Not Dependent on Causality'). This is not a coincidence: Mill simply gave a theoretical generalization of what the great systematists in natural science, such as Linné, had done in practice. When Mill made a distinction between the coexistence of effects of a given cause or various coexisting causes (Chap. XXII, Sec. 1), which he considered trivial from the point of view of science, and the coexistence of properties of things, which defines a genus independent of a cause (Chap. XXII, Sec. 2), coexistence which is specific law of nature (Chap. XXII, Sec. 3), then he in fact merely gave a theoretical form to what the systematists had done in practice.[15]

It is characteristic that the prolific outburst of research based on an analysis of systems, and hence their structures as well (research which is structural in this sense), in so widely different disciplines as mathematics, chemistry, biology, psychology, linguistics, economics, anthropology, sociology, etc., has seen so few reflections on laws of coexistence. Goethe is a notable exception, even though his poetic genius has obscured his achievements in science, one of them being his theory of morphological type as a structural law. He developed it as a result of his own methodological reflections on the distinction between dynamic laws and synchronic structural laws.[16] Such a degree of comprehension of the focal issue of the structuralist trend cannot be found later even in L. von Bertalanffy, for all his philosophical inclinations.

In recent times, reflections on that subject can (very rarely) be found in works by researchers concerned with the methodology of physics. This applies in particular to *Foundations of Science* by Norman Robert Campbell and to *What Is Science?*, a more popular book by the same author. While he denies the causal laws their dominant role in science, Campbell claims that there are laws about the properties of a given system, and hence structural laws, which he calls *laws of properties of substance.* He says that

> Nevertheless, there is one particular form of relation involved in laws which can be distinguished from others, and on which emphasis may be laid once more. This relation is that which characterizes what we have called the law of

the properties of a substance, or a kind of system, the law, namely, which asserts that there is such-and-such a substance or such-and-such a kind of system, steel or magnets, for example.[17]

Mario Bunge in his *Causality* also stresses the existence in science of laws which are other than causal, namely morphological laws, which correspond to what we have termed coexistential laws (or: laws of coexistence).[18]

But, as far as I know, the most comprehensive analysis of morphological (coexistential) laws has been given by J. Metallmann in his fundamental work *Determinizm nauk przyrodniczych* (Determinism in Natural Science), published in Cracow in 1934, which unfortunately is little known outside Poland because of the language barrier. Its comprehensive Chapter VII is concerned with coexistential laws; the English equivalent of its title is *qualitative determinism*, and the meaning of this term is explained by Metallmann in one of the introductory comments.

The chapter is about the laws that pertain to properties of things. Metallmann says that:

> Properties, however, also are elements of nature. The need may, or even must, arise to define them unambiguously. Causal laws do not serve that purpose. Hence, if next to such four-dimensional factors as processes there are also in nature such independent elements which cannot be specified by reference to four co-ordinates, and hence to any co-ordinate, then next to laws that enable us to define and predict processes science must formulate laws that would enable us to define and predict such unchanging factors as properties. *I would term such laws qualitative or morphological.* They would consist of elements which are outside space—time. Such laws will never enable us to define changes, as causal laws never enable us to define properties.[19]

In a comprehensive footnote to this paragraph Metallmann, while rejecting the suggestion by C. Stumpf (formulated in his *Zur Einleitung der Wissenschaften* in the Proceedings of the Prussian Academy of Science, 1906) that such laws be called structural, adds the following explanation:

> I think that the term *morphological* must be preserved next to the term *qualitative* in order to emphasize that we mean relationships between properties, or characteristics, and hence 'qualities', but not as opposed to quantities. . . . *Qualitative* accordingly does not mean here *non-quantitative*, but indicates reference to *properties*, which, as we shall see, can, and very often are, defined quantitatively, as are also relationships between them.[20]

While defending the significance of laws of coexistence Metallmann also firmly dissociates himself from the positivist illusion that there are 'bare' facts. On the contrary, he says that a fact without a theory has no scientific value and that it becomes a scientific fact only as a result of a rationalization. He likewise opposes the classification of sciences into descriptive and explanatory, since those which are called descriptive offer explanations, too. This is why, if there are laws of nature which are neither causal nor statistical, then the difference is not in the fact that those other laws are not explanatory and do not enable us to make predictions, but in the fact that they do so otherwise. 'What then is the difference between them? The subject-matter. The laws which we refer to here have permanent coexistence of properties as their subject matter.'[21]

Science looks both for permanent coexistence of properties and for causal changes. This is proved by the strivings of systematists from Aristotle to Linné, strivings which were not abandoned even at the time when the idea of evolution was triumphant (compare, for instance, Lamarck's systematics). This is the role of classification in science.

Penetrating analysis of various disciplines, both in natural science and in social science and anthropology, has resulted in Metallmann's conclusion that causal regularities are not only the unique, but not even the most frequent subject matter of research. Coexistential (morphological, structural) regularities are not only more frequent than the causal ones, since they underlie all classification in science, but they also have enormous heuristic significance.

We have discussed the problem of coexistential (morphological, structural) laws at some length since they are the theoretical prime mover of all structuralist trends. Science is interested not in singular things and facts as such, but always in classes of things and facts. In other words, in science we always look for laws, and the claim that some disciplines are idiographic as they describe singular facts is groundless, because it disregards, to say the least, the generalizing function of all classifications and systematizations. In any case, when science is concerned not with the origin but with the structure of facts it also has discovery of laws in view, such laws being in this case those of structure, and hence those of coexistence. Without that there is no structuralism in any sense of that ambiguous term. Without comprehending the nature of the laws of coexistence we cannot understand any theory that pretends to be structural in nature. Stressing the role of the laws of coexistence is common to the *whole* structuralist trend. And this brings us to the issue of the static, synchronic approach to facts as characteristic of the entire structuralist trend, of structuralism as an intellectual current.

4. It has been said earlier that coexistential laws are idealizations based on the assumption that the time factor t=0. It does not follow that a person who studies facts from the synchronic point of view because he is interested in structural laws has to deny, or at least to underestimate, the importance of the diachronic viewpoint. It is true that in the case of certain variations of structuralism which function, contrary to their own principles and claims, as a philosophy and an ideology, we have in fact to do with neo-Eleatism.[22] But we should not identify certain radical philosophical standpoint, resulting from the emphasis on the new aspects of research, with structuralism as such. We should not make our position in the discussion excessively convenient, losing thereby the possibility of noticing what is both new and valuable in the structuralist programme. The fact is that not only have the structuralists seen the significance of diachronic research, but they have recommended it.[23] In my opinion, the point is that the recommendation of synchronic research does not exclude the acceptance, and even recommendation, of diachronic research; these two methods are not mutually exclusive, but *complementary*.

He who calls for the study of coexistential (structural) laws and, for that purpose, disregards the dynamic aspect of facts and its laws (and this approach is characteristic of all variations of the structural trend), thereby neither denies that facts are dynamic in nature (which would be sheer madness in view of the present state of science), nor claims that only the static (synchronic) method of research is significant in science; he merely stresses the importance of the study of structures (in this sense the term *structure* refers to the totality of relations that hold among the elements of a given system). In the case of this moderate interpretation of the call for synchronic analyses and the search for coexistential (structural) laws we may add (which has often been done by the various representatives of structuralism) that an exact knowledge of what changes and develops, that is, an exact knowledge of the system under investigation and of its ‘structure is a necessary condition of any studies of the dynamic aspect of facts, i.e. of historical or genetic studies. This is dictated by common sense which tells us that the synchronic and the diachronic method are complementary not only in the sense that they give a complete picture of facts only when put together, but also in the sense that they depend one on the other. Our genetic studies can succeed on the condition that we know the structure of a given subject matter of research, and we arrive at that knowledge by finding the appropriate coexistential (structural) laws; and vice versa, a profound knowledge of the origin and history of a system enables us to succeed in investigating its structure.

We cannot interpret the motion and dynamics of a system as the sum of its states at rest without being trapped by antinomies which have been prefectly well known since the activity of the Eleatic school; on the contrary, we do not run such risks if we interpret rest (in the sense of a relative rest) as a momentary state in the process of motion. If we approach the problems of dynamic (causal) and static (coexistential) laws in an analogous manner, then by interpreting the coexistential laws properly we can treat them as idealizational models of sections of the phenomena under investigation (as we have said earlier, idealization here consists in our treating the time factor so that $t=0$).

With all these comments and reservations, intended to prevent us from simplifying our approach to the requirements of structuralism (the more so as some of the current theories called structural imply such simplifications), we may say that all the variations of that trend concentrate on a synchronic study of the structure of specified systems which fall within the scope of their interest.

We have thus, as has been announced, arrived not at a definition of structuralism, which has proved a futile task, but at listing certain elements which are necessary for a given theory, while its specific features are respected, to be classed as structuralist in the broadest sense of the term.

We have singled out four such elements: (1) approaching the subject-matter of research as a whole which has the nature of a system; (2) defining the goal of research as the discovery of the structure of a given system; (3) striving to discover those structural (coexistential) laws which are at work in a given system; (4) studying a given system from the synchronic point of view, so that the time factor is eliminated from the idealizational model of that system (the assumption being that $t=0$).

We now return to the issue raised at the outset. It has been said that the spreading of the structuralist tendencies in the latest period of the history of science cannot be explained merely by reference to fashion; on the contrary, the fact that structuralism has become 'in' should be explained and given a satisfactory interpretation. What then are the causes of the spreading of structuralism as a theory and as a method? Are the factors involved merely subjective, or are they objective laws of the development of science?

There is no doubt, when it comes to the answer to this question, that both subjective and objective factors are involved. The term *fashion* as such suggests subjective factors above all, and they are most frequently discussed in connection with structuralism. The objective ones are mentioned less often, and yet they are, in my opinion, essential for the understanding of the problem. This is why they will be the starting-point of our future analysis.

The Ontological and Gnosiological Foundations of the Structuralist Trend

The problem raised above is meaningful only if we adopt the standpoint of cognitive realism, that is, the theory of cognition which treats cognition as a specific mapping of reality that exists objectively, and hence independent of, and outside of, all consciousness. In the case of the subjective approach the problem vanishes, for if cognition makes use of arbitrary constructions, then we have to ask only about the choice to be made from among such possible constructions, but each of them is admissible and the issue comes to an end once we make our choice. The problem arises only if we accept the fact that the choice is not arbitrary, and we therefore ask the question 'why?', in the sense of 'on what grounds has our choice been made?'

This is why, at the outset of our analysis, we have to state which philosophical trend in ontology and gnosiology is taken as our standpoint. This is indispensable to make matters clear, so that our opponent can clearly see where our paths part as far as the assumptions made in our controversy are concerned (which usually means the end of the road, because in philosophical controversies we most often are not in a position to indicate a crucial experiment, and verification may prove an infinite process) or else that he can accompany us on our path.

Our analyses of the issue are based on the acceptance of materialism in the ontological sense of what we mean by reality, and of cognitive realism in the gnosiological sense. Thus, by taking reality to be material, and hence as having an objective existence, we treat it as a whole which is in a state of eternal motion and change. These are the initial points, which may be interpreted as our assumptions with reference to further considerations.

There is no doubt that material reality, which is in a state of eternal motion and change, can and should be investigated from the point of view of the regularity of its dynamics. (The term *regularity* is intended to mean something which is characteristic of the process of change; the term *law of science* is to mean the formulation of that regularity in the language of science at a given stage of its development.) It is accordingly understandable that, when investigating the dynamics of reality, scientists formulate the laws of that dynamics usually in the form of causal laws.

But reality, while being in a state of eternal motion and change, is not an amorphous stream of events. On the contrary, motion and change result in states of a relative equilibrium of relatively isolated systems which are parts of what we call the world. We refer to *equilibrium* in the sense of specified durability of links among elements of the world (e.g. a crystal or a human organism); we refer to *relative* equilibrium in the sense that (i) it is not eternal, but lasts for a given period of time only; (ii) it applies only to a certain set of elements (a relatively isolated system), because we disregard its links and interactions with other relatively isolated systems. These relatively isolated systems, which are in a state of relative equilibrium, have an objective existence, and hence are a potential subject-matter of cognition. When it comes to cognition, it is important to discover and formulate not only the laws of motion and development which govern a given subject-matter of research (i.e. its development, dynamic, causal laws), but also the structural laws which govern such relatively isolated systems in a state of a relative equilibrium. It is obvious that if the world is in a state of incessant motion and change while some of its parts are in a state of relative equilibrium, then it is not only legitimate to search for the laws of both types: we obtain the full picture of the world by treating these two types of laws as complementary. As has been already said, if we want to study laws of development (i.e. genetic, causal laws) of something, then we must know what that something is, i.e. we must know its structural (coexistential, morphological) laws. Such knowledge of the origin and development of the objects we investigate but some knowledge is necessary if we are to be able to distinguish elements of the world. Hence the knowledge of coexistential, morphological laws, even though acquired not through scientific reflection, but as a result of practical activity, is the oldest in the history of mankind: man displays such knowledge by being able to distinguish one plant from another and one animal from another, that is, to split the world around him into its elements by means of his practical ability to distinguish objects marked by the coexistence of certain properties.

In this sense, man has been a structuralist since the very beginning of his manhood. This formulation, intentionally exaggerated, has a grain of truth in it. At least, it shows convincingly that there is something trivial in the theses of structuralism, be it even interpreted so simply. This is not intended to discredit structuralism, for the fact of the need to study the structure of the systems in the world around us finds its ontological and gnosiological justification, does not discredit it, but, on the contrary, stresses its objective significance. The point is only that the issue should not be limited to a vaguely general requirement which, in fact, borders on triviality; by making it more precise we should shed more light upon that type of structural research which is suitable in a given case. It is only by doing so that we pass from a vague philosophical statement to theoretical and methodological theses which deserve being called structural.

To illustrate this, let us refer to linguistic structuralism of the Prague school of phonology. Structural phonology uses two basic concepts: system and structure. Language is a system of sound units which it handles in a certain way, which means, among other things, that the place of each such unit (phoneme) is determined by the whole, which is something more than just the sum of those units, as it also covers the relations that hold among the said units. The structure of the system is the totality of those relations which, in the theory of structural phonology, are of a special kind: they always consist in oppositions (mainly binary ones) and hence any given value is an attribute not of a unit, a phoneme as such, but of that opposition within a pair of phonemes without which no sound unit has a value.

It follows that neither the frequency with which the term *structure* is used, nor the rejection of diachronic research in favour of synchronic studies, nor any other vulgarized form of paying ransom to structural analysis (including the endeavour mechanically to transfer the achievements of the structural method, which mark progress in a specified field of knowledge, e.g. phonology, to other spheres of knowledge, which require their own solutions) justify the labelling of a theory as structural. The only legitimate procedure is a qualified application of the general principles of structuralism, namely an application which enables us to translate the trivial statement that every object and every phenomenon has not only a dynamic but also a synchronic (and hence static) aspect into the language of specified methodological indications applicable to a given structure. This is, of course, a radical requirement, which visibly reduces the possible classes of structuralism. But here it is merely a marginal note, because we are now interested in another problem: how much that which has been said above enables us to comprehend the turn toward structuralism, the structuralist 'fashion' which is beyond dispute and which we try to understand and to interpret. Here is a sample of such an interpretation.

The world is a flow of motion and change, with states of relative equilibrium in its elements. Hence the objective bi-aspectuality of the world and the duality of the regularities which are observable in it: the world is both dynamic and static, changing and (relatively) unchanging, and thus governed by dynamic (causal) laws and by synchronic (coexistential, morphological) ones. The formula used here is not *either . . . or . . .* (in the sense of Latin *aut . . . aut . . .*), but *both . . . and . . . .* This is why, as we have said, only the method of complementary analysis of these two aspects of the world, only the picture obtained by the superposition of these two ways of seeing the world, give us the proper perspective of cognition. This, however, results in certain complications in the process of cognition.

Theoretically, it may be said that a researcher, by having in view that complementarity of the ways in which he sees the world and the corresponding research methods, should always use both methods of investigation and strive for their specific synthesis in the knowledge which he acquires. But in practice the development of scientific cognition does not follow such a path of peaceful synthesis, and that for at least two reasons.

First, scientists have not always been in a position to engage in such reflection and metatheoretical self-consciousness. This has become possible, and even trivial, only in recent times as a result of the adequate development of science and related experience.

Secondly, and no less importantly in the development of science, a scientist, even if he has adequate methodological self-knowledge, is inclined to concentrate on that aspect of the world which, in a given case, especially attracts his attention; from this there is only a small step to granting his privileged method of research the status of a *de facto* monopoly. The point is that we have to do not only with a subjective factor that could always be reduced to a one-sided commitment on the part of the researcher to the method he prefers to use. The problem is much more deeply rooted in the objective conditioning of the process of scientific cognition. As mentioned above, the two aspects of the world form an organic whole which affects cognition and the requirements with which it is supposed to comply. Complete knowledge of the world assumes the use of both complementary methods of research, and the results are expected to be superimposed upon one another and thus to form a specific synthesis. But the real process of cognition reveals its own regularities in that respect: both levels of research are not only interconnected, but interdependent as well. One cannot carry on genetic studies if the structure of the subject-matter of research has not been investigated satisfactorily; and vice versa, adequate structural research requires corresponding genetic, historical knowledge if the system under investigation is to be known properly. Such a knowledge is evolutionary and subject to gradation: each new stage of cognition at one level must be paralleled by the corresponding stage at the other. Hence progress at both levels takes place alternately: it is not (and cannot be) fully simultaneous in both complementary spheres: adequate knowledge must be accumulated at one level (in practice the process begins with a better knowledge of the structure of the subject-matter of research and its specific coexistential laws) to enable the corresponding process to continue at the other level. Hence we witness periodical exhaustion of the possibilities of progress at one level, as it is restrained by an inadequate scope of knowledge at the other. In such a case researchers show increasing interest in the 'retarded' sphere, because investigations there prove more fertile and more likely to yield valuable results. It accordingly becomes fashionable, not for subjective or snobbish reasons (even though snobbishness may work as a by-product), but because there is an objective need to promote research at that level. It is thus understandable that in the history of science we have to do with a specific sequence of periods marked by the predominance of the one or the other sphere (or level) of research, and with a specific sequence of periodically recurrent interest in the structural (synchronic) and the dynamic (diachronic) approach.

This is the most frequent in the study of animate nature, where the period of emphasis on systematics was followed by genetic and evolutionary research, to be replaced again by a *sui generis* organismalism, interested in structural laws. What I have said above is, self-evidently, a schematic simplification, but the general idea can find illustrations in all spheres of research, with the proviso that the periods which in turn stress interest in structural and in dynamic laws follow one another, as it were, along a spiral line. We could even try to investigate the structure of that process; a tentative interpretation has been given by François Jacob (cf. his *La Logique du vivant*, Paris, 1970).

What we see now, both in natural science and in social science and the humanities, is a specific exemplification of the general principle: the period of a marked dominance of the genetic and historical method has been followed by the growing importance of structural research. If we understand the fact that both methods are complementary to one another, then we cannot have any doubt that this is not any rejection or repudiation of the validity of the genetic and historical method, but a periodic shift of the stress on the structural aspect of cognition. This is also why a criticism of the excessive use of the structural method (in the broadest sense of the term) in research is not intended to deny its validity, but merely to place its present expansion in the proper context and in the proper perspective.

Let us conclude this section by the query: Does structuralism (in the sense explained above) as an intellectual current open any new prospects in research? I think that in the light of what has been said earlier the answer must be in the affirmative. The novelty does not consist in what some structuralists claim, namely that the importance of genetic and historical studies has been negated, and that we witness the victory of an anti-historicism which they allege to eliminate the dynamic approach in research in favour of the static, synchronic one (these are statements which no reasonable scientist can make seriously); it consists in the fact that we are now in possession of adequate methodological instruments which enable us to acquire a much better knowledge of one of the aspects of the world now that we witness a new stage in the development of science. This is not to say that one method of research has ultimately eliminated the other. It is merely that, in the dialectical alternation of thesis and antithesis, in accordance with Hegel's classical schema, a basis has emerged for a new, higher, synthesis of, and new progress in, our knowledge of the world. And if we understand that, then no serious school in science should oppose the successive turn in the method of research, a turn which does not imply the elimination of the complementary method, but merely means an improved structural vision of the world. On the contrary, every school should avail itself of that turn in the way which suits it best. This applies to the Marxist school as well. The conclusion is self-evident, but I mention it here because we are now witnessing a controversy over the relationship between Marxism and structuralism, a controversy which unfortunately does not always comply with the requirements of clarity and precision necessary for a resolution of the controversy that would be to the advantage of science.

The Subjective Factors in the Fashion for Structuralism

I have tried to bring out the objective conditioning of the structuralist fashion not in order to diminish the importance of the subjective conditioning of that phenomenon, but in order not to lose sight of that which is rational and progressive in the structuralist trend by overemphasizing the subjective factor of the problem.

Let us begin with a general issue, which is therefore more important than any factors whose impact is limited to a narrower sphere: in the case of structuralism as a fashion we have to do with a specific intellectual current in the social sciences and the humanities. In natural science the study of structure and coexistential laws is, as we know, nothing novel. Yet no one has ever proclaimed any structuralist revolution or even simply a structuralist turn in natural science, although that type of research has long been common in chemistry, biology, etc. The fact has won publicity, and has even been called revolutionary when, in the recent decades, the humanities and the social sciences have been involved in structuralist research. And here again the point was not that the thing was completely new: *Gestaltpsychologie* introduced a *sui generis* structuralism in the early twentieth century, and Marx used similar research methods in economics and sociology even in the nineteenth century. The vogue of structuralism began in fact with the triumph of structural linguistics of the Prague school, and that for very specific reasons.

The structuralism advanced by the Prague school of phonology became a kind of pattern for the humanities and the social sciences in the 1930s not only because the new research method made it possible to obtain interesting results, but mainly because it in fact revolutionized a branch of the humanities by giving it the shape of an exact discipline which could vie in that respect with natural science. Now we have to bear in mind that this relates to the psychological trauma characteristic of representatives of the humanities and social scientists (a trauma which is rarely recognized by them, and still less frequently mentioned in public) and their longing for equalling natural and exact scientists in the precision and objectivity of results of research. It is true that declarations are often made, with a varying degree of conviction, about the peculiar nature of the humanities and the social sciences, but whenever there is a ray of hope that those peculiarities (which turn out not to be valued so much by the humanists themselves) can be overcome – as was the case when logical positivists advocated the use of the language of mathematical logic and when the expansion of mathematical methods bred expectations that science (and especially the social sciences) could be mathematized – fashions emerged which are telling evidence of that trauma. It is therefore quite understandable that with the appearance of a new structuralist trend, which in addition had the support of objective needs of the development of science, a new fashion came like a storm.

The coincidence of a number of factors was necessary for that fashion to emerge, i.e. for structuralism to be really internalized in the scholarly milieu as the preferred method of research; next to the objective needs of the development of science, mentioned above, and the longing of humanists and social scientists for the precision and empiricism of natural science, there must have been an additional local factor, for otherwise it would be impossible to explain the fact that an intellectual vogue, sometimes in a violent way, swept some countries, while at the same time it left other countries untouched. Such was the case of the logical analysis of the language of science, which was a mannerism of the logical positivists: at one time it dominated Poland completely, whereas France remained indifferent to it. Conversely, existentialism came to sway France after 1945, whereas in Poland it remained – until the end of its domination of France – a peripheral and somewhat exotic object of interest of philosophers.

When we refer to the vogue of structuralism we have to pay attention to the kind of structuralism and to the kind of vogue involved. It is beyond doubt that structuralism in linguistics (in its various versions) is witnessing its triumph all over the world and there is no question of any recession of its influence. If a humanist in Poland were asked about the position of structuralism in Polish science, he would associate that with structural linguistics (in its classical form represented by the Prague school, and possibly with Lévi-Strauss as far as he uses the Prague school method in anthropology) and his appraisal would be positive. But this has very little in common with the vogue of structuralism as we see it in France. But even if in Poland we find some traces of that phenomenon, nothing of that kind can be noticed, for example, in Britain. For the explanation of this fact we have to look for the presence, or absence, of that additional local factor mentioned above. We shall accordingly try to analyse, be it superficially, the specifically French conditioning of the vogue of structuralism as it emerged in France and radiated upon other countries.

In France, to be a structuralist meant, and to a large extent still means today (even though the vogue, like all vogues, has passed its apogee and is ebbing now), to discharge one's intellectual duty. Otherwise one could be considered old-fashioned, outdated, and even, to some extent, *Salonunfähig*. This can be seen from the number of variations of structuralism which proliferate in France (with genuine structural linguistics having the smallest repercussions in the literature of the subject, and being probably the least known of all). Further evidence is provided not only by those of its critics, especially when it comes to the controversy among Marxists over the validity and the interpretation of what is called Marxist structuralism. The intellectual pressure of structuralism is so strong that even its French critics would in other countries be considered its supporters.

The French intellectual milieu is certainly very susceptible to external influence, which it later rather easily rejects. This is a typical manifestation of succumbing to fashion, as in the sphere of dress, hair styles, etc. Perhaps a penetrating study in social psychology would disclose a connection between these two facts in the country which was renowned for being the leader in fashion, at least in women's dress. In the case of intellectual life the idea is alarming, because during a comparatively brief period after 1945 France had been promoting an intellectual fashion for at least the second time: at first it was existentialism, next — which is of interest for us now — it was structuralism. They were not original trends; borrowed from outside, they were being 'sold as second-hand goods' in the form which in both cases provoked protests on the part of the real originators of those trends. This is certainly an interesting social psychological phenomenon. We therefore ask ourselves why this is so, especially when it comes to the vogue of structuralism, with which we are concerned here.

It is characteristic that this problem, although apparently imposed by observable facts, does not seem to have aroused the interest of the French students of the issue. The only interesting endeavour to analyse the problem I have found (perhaps because of my insufficient acquaintance with the literature of the subject) is François Furet's article 'Les Français et le structuralisme';[24] L. Althusser's 'Introduction' to his *For Marx*[25] has served me indirectly as additional data for reflections on the issue. What follows is my own interpretation of the problem.

The radically minded French intellectuals came to be dominated, after 1945, by two philosophical trends which tuned them both ideologically and methodologically, namely by Marxism and existentialism. That neighbourhood resulted not so much in opposition and conflict as in specific interactions, relationships and alliances. That intricate network of connections and mutual influence is best represented personally by Jean-Paul Sartre and Roger Garaudy.

The crisis in the influence of existentialism was clearly due to the spending of the attractive force of its intellectual fashionability. It had appealed to intellectuals by stressing the problems of human individual, its freedom and its creative role in history, problems which had been neglected, or even repudiated, by the dogmatic version of Marxism; on the other hand, existentialism had its weak point in subjectivism that could not satisfy the aspirations of the radicals. In both cases the crisis came in the 1950s. This resulted in a growing intellectual vacuum, and since vacuum tends to be filled (which also holds in the case of intellectual currents), there was a search for the replacement in the form of a new trend. The psychological ground for a new fashion was thus prepared.

And then a new trend appeared, which promised salvation to the ideological refugees of both former camps.

On the one hand, the Marxists, disillusioned by 'ideology' (which in fact was the personality cult in which they believed and which they used to serve blindly) and longing for 'pure' science, saw a vista of a structuralist paradise of objective science. Nothing is more characteristic in that respect than Althusser's 'Introduction' to *For Marx*, usually over-looked but extremely instructive. It is an interesting document of soul searching by those who, after ideological turns and retreats, started longing for something new but were unable to shed their old skin. It is a specific declaration of faith, or, if anyone wishes to put it that way, an ideological last will.

On the other hand, the door to objective science opened to the existentialists, disillusioned by the sterility of subjective speculation on individual freedom.

The proposal was accepted, and the new fashion adopted. The process was all the easier since the proposal was a second-hand offer and was accepted as a specific philosophy and ideology. Structuralism's way in France was paved not by the acquaintance with structural linguistics, as presented in the works of Troubetzkoy and Jakobson, but by what was transmitted by Lévi-Strauss, not even in *Les Structures élémentaires de la parenté*, in which he tried to apply the methods of structural phonology to the study of kinship, but in his more philosophical books, namely *Anthropologie structurale* and *Tristes Tropiques* (*Mythologiques* being later).

The gap was filled, and structuralism was accepted, but − contrary to declarations − as a philosophy and an ideology. The variations of that trend in France are many and differentiated. Lévi-Strauss, Foucault, Barthes, Althusser (and other representatives of 'Marxist structuralism') all differ from one another in their opinion. If we do not want to confine ourselves to vague generalities and total criticism, which would be at variance with the foregoing analysis of the objective conditioning of the vogue of structuralism, we have to analyse each of these variations. From the Marxist point of view it is Louis Althusser and his school of 'Marxist structuralism' who are the most interesting of all. But that requires a separate essay.

NOTES

1. J. Metallmann, 'Problemat struktury i jego dominujçe stanowisko w nauce współczesnej' (The Problem of Structure and its Dominant Position in Con-temporary Science), *Kwartalnik Filozoficzny*, 1933, Vol. XI, No. 4, p. 332.
2. *Ibid.*, p. 353.
3. On this issue see the interesting paper by Günther Kröber, 'Die Kategorie

"Struktur" und der kategorische *Strukturalismus*', *Deutsche Zeitschrift für Philosophie*, 1968, No. 11, pp. 1311 *et passim*.

4. A. Martinet, *Economie des changements phonétiques*, Berne, 1955, Chap. III.

5. E. Benveniste, ' "Structure" en liguistique', in: *Sens et usages du terme 'Structure'* (Ed. R. Bastide), 's-Gravenhage, 1962, p.38.

6. Among the numerous studies in this field I consider two books to be of particular importance: the collected papers edited by R. Bastide and cited in note 5 above, and Raymond Boudon, *A quoi sert la notion de 'structure'?*, Paris, 1968.

7. A. L. Kroeber, *Anthropology*, New York, 1948, quoted after C. Lévi-Strauss, *Structural Anthropology*, Basic Books, 1963, p. 278.

8. R. Boudon, *op. cit.*, p. 19.

9. *Sens et usages du terme 'Structure'*, *ed. cit.*, p. 9.

10. 'La langue est un système qui ne connait que son ordre propre' (*Cours de linguistique générale*, Paris, 1949, p. 43); 'La langue, système de signes arbitraires . . .' (*ibid.*, p. 106); 'La langue est un système dont toutes les parties peuvent et doivent être considérées dans leur solidarité synchronique' (*ibid.*, p. 124).

11. The Theses of the Prague Circle, submitted to the First Congress of Slavonic Philology in 1929 (which were a kind of the manifesto of the Prague Circle), read: 'Il faut caractériser le système phololologique . . . en spécifiant obligatoire-ment les relations existantes entre les dits phonèmes, c.à-d. en traçant le schème de structure de la langue considérée.' 'On ne peut déterminer la place d'un mot dans un système lexical qu'après avoit étudié la *structure* du dit système.' (Quoted after E. Benveniste, *op. cit.*, pp. 34–35.)

12. In view of the general significance of that statement for the understanding of the structuralist approach the formulation deserves being quoted in full: 'La phonologie actuelle est caractérisée surtout par son structuralisme et son universalisme systèmatique. . . . L'époque ou nous vivons est caractérisée par la tendence de toutes les disciplines scientifiques à remplacer l'atomisme par le structuralisme et l'individualisme par l'universalisme (au sens philosophique de ces termes, bien entendu). Cette tendence se laisse observer en physique, en chimie, en biologie, en psychologie, en science économique, etc. La phonologie actuelle n'est donc pas isolée. Elle fait partie d'un mouvement scientifique plus ample.' (N. Troubetzkoy, 'La phonologie actuelle', in: *Psychologie de language*, Paris, 1933, pp. 245–6; quoted after E. Benveniste, *op. cit.*, p. 36.)

13. This singling out a system as a whole which is not just the sum of its elements, but covers the relations between those elements as well, is of special significance in biology (cf. Bertalanffy's organismalism), but can also be found in other structuralist theories, such as structural phonology. Oskar Lange used a different terminology to state the same ideas. He referred not to a system as a whole endowed with special characteristics, but to a whole as a system endowed with special characteristics. See his *Całość i rozwój w świetle cybernetyki* (The Concepts of the Whole and Development in the Light of Cybernetics), Warszawa, 1962, p. 9.

14. A. Bogdanov, *Allgemeine Organisationslehre*, Leipzig, 1924, 1928 (first pub-lished in Russian in 1913).

15. 'But these same considerations compel us to recognize that there must be one class of coexistences which cannot depend on causation; the coexistences between the ultimate properties of things, those properties which are the cause

of all phenomena, but are not themselves caused by any phenomenon, and a cause for which could only be sought by ascending to the origin of all things. Yet among these ultimate properties there are not only coexistences, but uniformities of coexistence. General propositions may be, and are, formed, which assert that whenever certain properties are found, certain others are found along with them. . . . To this we have now to add, that every proposition by which anything is asserted of a kind, affirms a uniformity of coexistence. Since we know nothing of kinds but their properties, the kind, to us, *is* the set of properties by which it is identified, and which must of course be sufficient to distinguish it from every other kind.' (J. St. Mill, *A System of Logic*, London, Longmans, 1865, Chap. XXII, Sec. 2, p. 110.)

16 The subject-matter is interestingly discussed by Andrzej Bednarczyk in his paper 'Johann Wolfgang Goethe — Typ morfologiczny jako wyraz prawidłowości' (Johann Wolfgang Goethe: The Morphological Type as a Manifestation of Regularity), in: *Z dziejów pojęcia prawa w naukach biologicznych* (Issues in the History of the Concept of Law in the Biological Sciences), (ed.) W. Krajewski, Warszawa, 1967.

17. N. R. Campbell, *What Is Science?*, Dover Publ., New York, 1921, p. 56; see also *Foundations of Science* by the same author (Dover Publ., New York, Chap. III).

18. M. Bunge, *Causality*, Harvard University Press, 1959, p. 255.

19. J. Metallmann, *op. cit.*, pp. 277—8 (italics — A. S.).

20. J. Metallmann, *op. cit.*, p. 278.

21. J. Metallmann, *op. cit.*, pp. 281—2.

22. On this issue see Henri Lefebvre, *Au delà du structuralisme*, Paris, 1971.

23. Cf. R. Jakobson, 'Principles de phonologie historique', in: R. Jakobson, *Selected Writings*, 's-Gravenhage, 1962, pp. 202—20.

24. Cf. *Preuves*, 1967, No. 192.

25. L. Althusser, *For Marx*, The Penguin Press, London, 1971 (first published in French in 1965).

On Pseudomarxist Pseudostructuralism

Two issues must certainly be explained: first, why in analysing structuralism I am concerned with the trend I have termed *pseudostructuralism* in the title of this essay; second, since we have to do with a trend connected with French Marxists, why I do this so late, now the trend is practically declining in France. The questions are clearly formulated and apparently simple, but the answers are neither simple nor easy to give. Nevertheless they must be given at the very beginning in order to prepare the proper background for further analysis.

The crux of the matter — to begin with the focal though manifest issue — is in the fact that what is an intellectual game for some (in some milieux, the more a person is non-conventional and even provoking by his paradoxicality, the more he is applauded, be it just for a short time) is a vital issue for others. All the masquerades, all that playing with words 'Marxism is anti-humanism', 'Marxism is anti-historicism', etc., which rather seem to be statements made *pour épater les collegues*, are not amusing, but — in certain political contexts — are outright dangerous. It is common knowledge that the struggle, both in theory and in practice, for the right of citizenship of socialist, and hence Marxist, humanism was a form of struggle against that phenomenon in the life of socialist societies which was called personality cult. Althusser condescendingly admits in his essays that the struggle for socialist democracy and similar 'trifles' explains why the problem of socialist humanism is of such a topical interest for those who live in the socialist countries (which implies that it ceases to be interesting outside those countries). I heard similar statements in a discussion, held several years ago, with some Italian Marxists who at that time were close to the Althusser's school: 'For you (i.e. those who live in the socialist countries) the problems of man are important; we are interested in other issues, namely in fighting the capitalist system, etc.' Not only is this opinion erroneous — the fortunes of the communist movement are indivisible on the global scale, and we bear joint and several responsibilities for all the mistakes we may make — but it is dangerous as well, because it might be used as an argument by those who defend the ideological and political heritage of dogmatism and accordingly see their ideological opponents precisely in those people who proclaim and work out the ideas of socialist humanism. Can there be a better gift for the former than their possibility of referring to a Marxist renowned in the West, a communist and, moreover, a professor in the Ecole Normale Supérieure, who may be claimed 'to know best'? Fortunately, the issue was both too esoteric, and intended for the French milieu, and also too clearly in contradiction with universally accepted Marxist theses, for such an argument to be used in public discussion. But it nevertheless may be used on some other occasion. This is why — be it for political reasons alone — we have to forestall such argumentation by demonstrating that the king has no clothes. This is what I intend to do now.

But if there are such important reasons for taking up the gauntlet, why do I do that only now? Why did I remain silent for so long a time, considering the fact that I read *For Marx* (in its original French version) in 1965 and had become acquainted with the separate essays even earlier, on their appearance in periodicals? What has changed since that time, what has made me react only now, when the highest tide of the structuralist vogue seems to be over?

The explanation is that previously one could assume reasonably that it was a local French vogue which could, and even should, be passed over in silence instead of being publicized. Today, the change of my attitude has been due to three factors.

1. There is no certainty that such and such milieux, guided by considerations of political conflict, would not avail themselves of those arguments in the struggle against socialist humanism, since, as experience has shown, they did not hesitate to seek assistance which was much more ideological in nature and much more dangerous to the future of socialism and Marxism. Such being the case, one cannot hesitate and just wait and see, but has to defuse the potential bomb in advance.

2. We have seen that, contrary to expectations, under certain circumstances local ideological phenomena can spread over other regions and work as sources of contagion. It is true that when we witnessed the high tide of structuralism in the Marxist milieu in France the phenomenon had

practically no effect outside France. Some traces of it could be found in Italy, and that was all. But today, with the ebb-tide in France, the influence of the Althusser group has increased in Marxist milieux in Latin America, and we cannot be sure that this phenomenon would not repeat itself elsewhere.

Why is it so? First of all, the aversion of progressive intellectuals, who just because of their radicalism gravitate towards Marxism, to the dogmatized form of that theory (dogmatized in a certain sense, because what is taken as the dogma is not the ideas of the founders of the Marxist theory, but a specific − sometimes quite erroneous − interpretation of those ideas). What is called Marxist structuralism brought something new and fresh as it grew on the soil of such a rebellion, which was explicitly stated by Althusser in his 'Introduction' to *For Marx*. That trend derived its attractive force from the weakness of the dogmatized version of Marxism, and not from the alleged values of the new version. But this did not play any important role, at least in the first period. Novelty and vogue prevail: they create the illusion of genuine progress, whereas, in fact, we have to do with a regression; they create the illusion of a vast expanse of novelty, whereas, in fact, we have to do with a poor-quality imitation of positivist tendencies which have already been overcome in bourgeois philosophy. And yet, for all these illusions, they keep their ground. Marxist criticism sometimes even makes them gain strength, for that criticism is dismissed as the defensive action on the part of the dogmatists.

There are, of course, people who assess that pseudonovelty reasonably. Henri Lefebvre speaks about a neo-Eleatic approach: 'It is Heraclitus in a new edition, revised and amended by an Eleatic',[1] and his is right. Mikel Dufrenne speaks about logical positivism: 'France has now discovered logical positivism, with a time lag as compared with the Anglo-Saxons',[2] and he is right. In a discussion of Althusser's opinions at the Centre d'Etudes Socialistes Robert Paris said that it was not Marxism, but the opinions of Althusser himself, camouflaged with Marxist phraseology: 'In my opinion, Althusser has little in common with Marxism. . . . I do not blame Althusser for having written what he did, but for presenting what he wrote as a Marxist thing',[3] and he is most emphatically right.

But for other people, especially the outsiders, all that is a novelty, a revelation, admitting fresh air into the stenched room of dogmatized Marxism. The factors mentioned earlier are obviously at work here.

Dissatisfaction with the dogmatized version of Marxism favours all novelty, pseudonovelty included. This applies above all to those who are friendly disposed to Marxism or who consider Marxism to be close to them because of their social condition, but who cannot accept its dogmatic or sectarian version.

In the introduction to the discussion at the Centre d'Etudes Socialistes (see the mention above) reference is made to Althusser's opinions as a renaissance of Marxism. 'We thought that in the critical and problematically "varying" conjuncture of the post-Stalinist period the studies and publications by Althusser and his co-workers in 1962–6 were contributions – whose importance was acknowledged even by those who slandered him – to what could be defined as a renaissance of Marxist vision, clarity, and discipline.'[4]

Jean Conilh, in his article published in the already mentioned special issue of the *Esprit*, dedicated to Althusser's structuralism, described him as the man who frees us from the tedious repetitions made by official commentators and thus restores to Marxism its creative force. 'Althusser suggests us a "symptomatic" reading of Marx's works . . . thus freeing us from the monotonous refrains of official vitality which it seemed to have lost.'[5]

But, in my opinion, pride of place goes to the testimony of a group of young leftists, interviewed by the quarterly *Preuves*. Their statements are symptomatic as they come from people who had good intentions and wanted to be revolutionaries, although, as they themselves admitted, they were not good at theory. Now those leftists, in whose opinion the Communist Party of France did not take the revolutionary standpoint, in the galaxy of great names in the history of revolutions mentioned Althusser in one breath with Marx (Engels was not included in that group), Lenin, Rose Luxembourg, Trotsky, Plekhanov, Kautsky, Mao, Guevara.[6]

This formulation clearly reveals the reasoning adopted in Latin America: since Althusser says something other than the official version of Marxism, he is considered an innovator and accepted.

3. The third factor, apparently striking, is at work too: the point is to save from the inevitable rout of pseudostructuralism for Marxism that which in structuralism interpreted as a specific intellectual current is sensible and methodologically valuable. This is why my intention here is

not only to critically analyse the opinions of representatives of so-called Marxist structuralism as exemplified by Althusser and his co-workers, but also to analyse positively the relationship between Marxism and structuralism.

The introduction to the analysis proper should, in my opinion, not only answer the question, why I have engaged in a discussion with Althusser's views just now, with a large time-lag in relation to the apogee of his influence, but also the question about the origin of his views. Without analysing that, and in particular the political aspect of the issue, we could hardly proceed to discuss other problems. What I mean here is not an answer to the question about the origin of the French vogue of structuralism in general (which I have discussed in the first essay), but about the special case of so-called Marxist structuralism in France. It can, of course, be placed within the general trend, but at the same time reveals specific features which I intend to discuss.

The problem has been raised by many authors who analyse the opinions of Althusser and his followers. For all the differences in their conclusions they all agree on the fact that Althusser's views form a specified ideology. This statement is important for the comprehension of the problem as a whole, but at the same time·it seems paradoxical if we consider that the main point in Althusser's programme is his struggle against ideology — I shall not, for the time being, state with precision what I mean by the term *ideology* — and he is not alone in his awkward and paradoxical situation of a man who has originated something against which he campaigned: he shares in that respect the misfortunes of the logical positivists (the analogies, as we shall see, are not confined to this issue) who had gone to battle under the banner of opposition to all metaphysics and ended in creating a metaphysics of their own.

Jean Paul Sartre is radical in his assessment of the vogue of structuralism in France, and his statement, general as it is, applies to so-called Marxist structuralism as well. In his opinion, it is the last ideological barrier raised by the bourgeoisie against Marxism. 'The point is to create a new ideology, the last barrier which the bourgeoisie is still in a position to raise against Marx.'[7] This is also how Jean Marie Domenach, the editor-in-chief of the *Esprit*, understands the situation; while disagreeing with the way in which J. P. Sartre assesses structuralism, he in fact repeats his argumentation by pointing to the contradiction between the theoretical views of structuralists and their political attitude, that is, a contradiction which is ideological in nature. 'Ultimately, not only man's ability to act, *praxis*, but even the very possibility of events is excluded . . . it seems that structuralists . . . rank order higher than change, and that tendency is common to all positivist trends.'[8]

Henri Lefebvre briefly says the same in his work cited previously, where he describes Althusser's opinion as the neo-Eleatic approach.[9]

The origin of Marxist structuralism, i.e. the origin of the tentative structuralist interpretation of Marxism, has been comprehensively discussed by Lucien Sebag, who certainly originated that idea in France. In his statement, published posthumously by André Akoun, we find several important comments on the subject discussed here. All of them focus on the issue of ideology: that a revolutionary idea may change into an ideology; that mystifying ideologies are perhaps necessary for the attainment of certain goals; that Marxism has changed into an ideology. His reflections culminated in the statement which strikes us by his longing for the scientific approach and by his dislike of ideologies. 'The statements we can afford may reveal certain scientific guarantees, but they lack that supreme scientific guarantee which Marxism claims as a doctrine. This is why the true problem is that of ideology, that is of what we say as people who are members of a certain society, and who tend to transform that society.'[10]

From the genetic point of view, this statement shows the focal issue of the 'structuralist revolution' in the Marxist milieu: an important role was played in it by the frustrations of those who were communist 'believers' and who, like communists all over the world, experienced the shock of the revelations connected with what came to be termed the personality cult.

In no one can all this be found in a clearer and acuter form as in Althusser, and in no one does the frustration factor play such a great role. This is evidenced by his own 'confession of faith' in the 'Introduction' to the collected essays entitled *For Marx*. From a certain point of view — which is decisive for our understanding the origin of Althusser's ideas — that 'Introduction' of 10 pages is more interesting than the rest of the book. In any case, without that 'Introduction' it would be difficult, if not impossible, to understand the book, and especially its main idea: opposing science to ideology. What all that is worth will be said later. At this point we are interested in the motives of the change in attitudes. Let us therefore listen to Althusser's confession in the 'Introduction'.

The 'Introduction' to *For Marx* is a *sui generis* intellectual and ideological autobiography of its author who describes in it — from his contact with Marxism and fascination with the then prevailing opinions to the shock and ideological disillusionment caused by the 20th Congress of the Communist Party of the Soviet Union to the endeavour of transforming Marxism into pure science by the rejection of ideology — not only his own evolution, but also that of the entire generation. Let us follow one by one the main ideas of that autobiography.

The first motif is the encounter by the generation of radically minded intellectuals of Marxism transformed into an ideology. For the time being we still do not ask Althusser what he means by *ideology*; for the time being we listen to his own story. In the post-1945 period the whole generation of young intellectuals was sent to the front-line of the political and ideological battle led by the Communist Party. What campaign was that? Frustration comes to the surface immediately: to defend such undertakings as Lysenko's 'biology' (as Althusser puts it) it was necessary to resort to the leftist formula 'bourgeois science, proletarian science'; 'we had been made to treat science, a status claimed by every page of Marx, as merely the first-comer among ideologies'.[11]

And here is one more reason for nostalgia: 'So we spent the best part of our time in agitation when we would have been better employed in the defence of our right and duty to know, and in study for production as such.'[12]

It turns out that that generation did not know much; they did not even know the works of the mature Marx and were satisfied with the knowledge of the works from his youth (which really was the specifically French situation). And what about the leaders who should have shown them the right path? Were they also ignorant? Why?

Here we find the second important motif of the 'Introduction': the French worker movement lacked theoretical culture. 'In Germany there were Marx and Engels and the earlier Kautsky; in Poland, Rosa Luxembourg; in Russia, Plekhanov and Lenin; in Italy, Labriola, . . . then Gramsci. Who were our theoreticians?'[13] There was no wonder that young people were going astray. That was no coincidence: in all other countries intellectuals were revolutionary-minded because the bourgeoisie was reactionary; in France, it was vice versa: the bourgeoisie was revolutionary and that was why it succeeded in making intellectuals join their side. The worker movement without intellectuals (those who joined it failed to rid themselves completely of the bourgeois ideology) could not develop its own theory. Hence the feeling of a lack of philosophical heritage. 'We had no *maîtres*. There was no lack of willing spirits, nor of highly cultivated minds, scholars, literary figures and many more. But I mean masters of Marxist philosophy, emerging from our own history, accessible and close to us.'[14]

And here comes the third motif: the shock caused by the revelations at the 20th Congress of the Communist Party of the Soviet Union after Stalin's death. This element is widely known in the whole international communist movement. Bitter words were spoken about the past, words which were a consequence of that shock, words comprehensible to every Marxist philosopher who lived at that time.

> There was no way out for a philosopher. If he spoke and wrote the philosophy the Party wanted he was restricted to commentary and slight idiosyncrasies in his own way of using the Famous Quotations. We had no audience among our peers. Our enemies flung in our faces the charge that we were merely politicians; our most enlightened colleagues argued that we ought to study our authors before judging them, justify our principles objectively before proclaiming and applying them. . . . We were politically and philosophically convinced that we had reached the only firm ground in the world, but as we could not demonstrate its existence or firmness philosophically, no one else could see any firm ground beneath our feet – only conviction.[15]

What were the consequences? The people we are speaking about started circulating the slogan of 'the end of philosophy', which referred to certain formulations found in Marx. Some interpreted them as the evanescence of philosophy as a result of its realization in revolutionary action, others, as its dissolution in science. Here we pass to the fundamental issue, because Althusser, when speaking about certain trends characteristic of that period, in fact speaks about himself.

> So we contorted ourselves to give philosophy a death worthy of it: a philosophical death. Here again we sought support from more texts of Marx and from a third reading of the others. We proceeded on the assumption that the end of philosophy could not but be *critical*, as the sub-title of *Capital* proclaims that book to be of Political Economy: it is essential to go to the things themselves, to finish with philosophical ideologies and to turn to the study of the real world – *but*, and this we hoped would secure us from positivism, in turning against ideology, we saw that it constantly threatened 'the understanding of positive things', besieged science and obscured real characteristics. So we entrusted philosophy with the continual critical

reduction of the thread if ideological illusion, and in doing so we made philosophy the conscience of science pure and simple.[16]

This is the fourth motif, extremely important because in these words we discover Althusser himself even though he does not state explicitly whether he is in solidarity with those ideas; in fact we find their traces in his own works. Let us say that plainly: it is a repetition of the positivist confession of faith, it *is* positivism.

For what does Althusser say in the passage quoted above? That those Marxist philosophers who — having developed doubts as to the correctness of that version of Marxism which they had previously accepted without reservation — started proclaiming the programme of the 'philosophical death of philosophy' reduced it to a critique of science ('we made philosophy the conscience of science pure and simple') in order to eliminate ideologies from it.

Some 50 years before Althusser wrote that the programme of the Vienna Circle was shaped (and formulated explicitly in the *Manifesto* published in 1928); it was the exponent of opinions on the tasks of philosophy, opinions held mainly by representatives of natural science gathered in that Circle. The essence of the programme was the battle against metaphysics and the elimination of the latter by the logical analysis of the language of science. That analysis was the only residue of the functions of philosophy 'purified' in that way.

Both trends show far-reaching analogies of motivations and programmes.

First, in both cases the intention is to keep positive disciplines free from 'impurities'; such impurities are called metaphysics in one case and ideology in the other, but the apprehensions and attitudes are essentially the same.

Second, in both cases we have to do with the revival of the old positivist claim about the end of philosophy. In one case, the goal was to put an end to traditional philosophy as metaphysics, and to restrict the functions of philosophy to the logical analysis of language, which analysis was supposed to enable us to reject metaphysical statements as meaningless, since they could be neither confirmed nor disproved, and were not tautologies in the logical sense of the term, either. In the other case, the same thing was postulated with reference to ideology, philosophy being assigned the role of the guardian of scientific conscience ('the conscience of science pure and simple'), since philosophy is permanently to purify science from ideological admixtures.

These analogies are accompanied by essential differences. The positivist adherents of the Vienna Circle were pedantically precise in thinking, and regardless of whether we agree with them or not we have to admit that they constructed their system with clarity and precision, and knew how to state precisely which statements are to be considered manifestations of metaphysical meaninglessness and rejected following the logical analysis of language. The advocates of so-called Marxist structuralism, propagated by Althusser and his group, are marked by a lack of precision and semantic culture. The cause of this is to be seen in the provincialism of French philosophy rightly criticized by Althusser (I have to admit that without that criticism of his I would not dare to use such an argument), provincialism which accounts for the fact that France has remained unaffected by logical positivism. In such an atmosphere of philosophizing it is possible to use ambiguous concepts without even trying to give them precision and without realizing the resulting danger of logical slips. As an example, we may mention the use of the term *ideology*, fundamental for the argumentation of the Althusser school, which makes both that term and the whole discussion based on it to be completely vacuous, which I shall analyse in detail later. It is only in such an atmosphere that the use of the Hegelian language is still obligatory, which in Althusser's case renders all criticism of Hegel's works 'rebellion on one's bended knees'.

In view of these comments, which shed additional light upon the origin of Althusserism, it is easy to note that the analogy with logical positivism is that of the merits of the issue, while the difference is that of form. It is not to be wondered, therefore, that the 'Introduction' to *For Marx* reveals further factual analogies that prove a strange congeniality of opinions. For who repudiates philosophy and calls for its elimination (*qua* metaphysics or *qua* ideology) he obviously cannot hold the history of philosophy in esteem: philosophy interpreted in such a manner cannot have any history. Kazimierz Ajdukiewicz, one of the eminent representatives of logical positivism (although he differed notably from members of the Vienna Circle), used to say that the history of philosophy is the history of human stupidity. It must be added here that that was, in a sense, a declaration of philosophical faith, because Ajdukiewicz had a profound knowledge of the history of philosophy, the latest period included. And this is what we read in the 'Introduction' to *For Marx*, again in the same style which makes it difficult to grasp whether reference is made to the author himself or to others: 'According to this reading, there could no longer be any question of a history of philosophy; how could there be a history of dissipated phantasms, of shadows traversed? The only history possible is that of reality. . . . Marx said so himself in *The German Ideology*: "Philosophy has no history." '[17]

I claim that, for all the difference in the points of departure of the conceptions of philosophy in logical positivism and in Marxist structuralism, this agreement, too, is evidence of something essential: the agreement on the opinion that all philosophy must be eliminated, and a new one must be formulated. This opinion has not been worded so bluntly or so openly by any representative of either trend, but since it follows logically from the premises they have adopted, it *ought* to be formulated.

This is how we reach the fifth and the last motif in Althusser's 'Introduction' to *For Marx*: Marxist philosophy must only be constituted (not developed, not completed or transformed, but just constituted!):

> After all, it is never possible to liberate, even from dogmatism, more than already *exists*. . . . The end of dogmatism puts us face to face with this reality: that Marxist philosophy, founded by Marx in the very act of founding his theory of history, has still largely to be constituted, since, as Lenin said, only the corner-stones have been laid down; that the theoretical difficulties we debated in the dogmatist night were not completely artificial – rather they were largely the result of a meagerly elaborated Marxist philosophy. . . .[18]

It is a correct demand – if it is properly interpreted. But what is the interpretation involved? What is it that Althusser demands: a further development of Marxist philosophy or its *constituting*? If it is only to be constituted, what are the directions for that operation? These are questions on which we shall concentrate when we later proceed to analyse Louis Althusser's philosophical views.

Why am I concerned just with Althusser's philosophical views if it is common knowledge that the advocates in France of the structuralist interpretation of Marxism represent various trends? I do so because Althusser represents that trend which is the most influential of all, the trend which has had most publicity and the largest number of followers. It is true that the new orientation was initiated by Lucien Sebag, but he met his tragic death as a young man, and his book on Marxism and structuralism cannot today be treated as representative. It is otherwise in the case of Maurice Godelier who, while confining himself to the field of economics and anthropology, was the first to formulate many ideas, and formulated them otherwise than Althusser did later. This is why I shall occasionally refer to Godelier's views, but I will deliberately limit those references to make my arguments clear. An analysis of Godelier's views, close to, but different from, those of Althusser's (and certainly less radical than the latter's) would require a separate study.

As I have said earlier, these preliminary remarks are intended to describe the origin of so-called Marxist structuralism in order to make it easier for the reader to grasp my later comments. I have in this connection mentioned two problems, or rather two groups of problems: present-day philosophical ideas in France and recent frustrations of some Marxist intellectuals in that country.

Readers, for instance, in Poland and in English-speaking countries may find this 'key' to the first group of problems to be particularly important. In Althusser's case we have to do with a specific syndrome: the dominance of the Hegelian language in philosophy plus the ignorance of certain trends in contemporary philosophy and logic plus the lack of responsibility (resulting from the two preceding factors) in using philosophical language, which is manifested in his lack of concern about the precision and semantic clarity of formulations. A philosopher trained in a country which has had any variation of analytic philosophy (this is why I have mentioned Poland and English-speaking countries) would find it hard to believe — regardless of what his own philosophical opinions might be — that a present-day philosopher can ignore (or pretend to ignore) logical positivism, and that he can write hundreds of pages on such concepts as *ideology, science, humanism* and *historicism* without realizing their ambiguity and without posing himself the question in what sense he is using them. A philosopher from the said area would find it difficult to believe that there are still philosophers who use the Hegelian language in their works, even if they criticize Hegel, and he would find it even more difficult to *understand* that language if he were himself not an expert on Hegel's works. I have used the word *understand* in its most ordinary, and not metaphorical, sense (it is often used in the latter by various philosophers: if a philosopher says that he does not understand what another philosopher says, he usually means that he understands him perfectly well, but does not agree with him). I mean here a very simple thing, which has nothing to do with 'philosophy'. One can use the same words which one's interlocutor does, and yet fail to comprehend the latter's statements if the words in question are ambiguous and the senses in which they are used have not been fixed; this applies in particular to those cases in which a person uses words in meanings which had been current at one time, but came to be changed later. I have experienced that myself when reading Althusser. When I found the statements that Marxism is anti-humanism, anti-historicism, anti-empirism, etc., I had either to assume that what he wrote simply does not make sense, since what he wrote is at variance with obvious facts, or to guess that he used those words in specific senses which differ from those in current usage. I chose, of course, the latter solution as I know Althusser to be an educated person. This is a much more general issue: an outsider, for whom what Althusser writes is often incomprehensible, will just be baffled if he lacks the key that would enable him to look for explanations in the right places. This is what my foregoing explanations are intended to do.

When it comes to the second group of problems – frustrations of some Marxist intellectuals in France – the matter is simpler, but no less important for the understanding of Althusser's works, I have mentioned that in general terms in my first essay, but I think that the problem must be discussed here in greater detail. Now, one cannot understand Althusser's opinions out of their situational context which in his case is the behaviour of a faithful and pious adherent of a specified version of Marxism who has become disillusioned with the object of his faith, but cannot, or does not want to, break with it and accordingly tries to give it the sense which is the exact opposition of that adopted earlier. This is typical of those whose frustration results in a heresy. Althusser is not an apostate, he does not renounce his faith as such; he is a typical heretic who, while retaining the object of his faith, changes its articles so that they become their own opposition, and at the same time tries to demonstrate that that is the true faith. The trouble with Althusser is that – as one of his critics has said – he has something to say, but he makes it the point to sell that as Marxism. Althusser's attitude is nothing extraordinary; on the contrary, it is typical of those who suffer from ideological frustrations, and it is interesting for us just because it is typical: it applies to a whole milieu, and not just to a certain individual. This also explains the strong response which the vogue of structuralism has evoked in a certain milieu,

and in particular it explains so-called Marxist structuralism. The fashionable battle-cry 'Down with ideology, long live science!' has little — if
anything — to do with structuralism as a theory and a method, but is
comprehensible from the psychological point of view, and hence it is
attractive for the members of a milieu which is linked by certain common
experiences.

It may be said that any person who reads Althusser's texts and
understands them must realize the actual state of things. And it probably
really is so. But, when writing about those things I have the duty to
facilitate the understanding of those facts by pointing to the psychological
background of those views of his which I analyse. To do so I have to cover
by my analysis those texts of his which usually escape reader's notice
because he acquires merely superficial knowledge of those works or even
skips them over, despite the fact that — as is the case especially of the
'Introduction' to *For Marx* — they call for special attention.

A few words more about the further course of the analysis to be given
below.

Practically every problem raised by Althusser in his works requires a
critical analysis both from the general philosophical point of view and, in
particular, from the standpoint of Marxist philosophy. This imposes the
necessity of carrying out two mental operations: selecting the problems to
be discussed, in order not to lose important issues in a mess of less
significant details; arranging the problems logically, which determines the
order in which they are to be discussed and links them into a coherent
whole. It is obvious that those operations, regardless of my endeavours to
be objective, will not be free from the subjective factors, which will be
reflected in my evaluations and the way I see the problems in question.
This is a rather trivial statement: were it otherwise, no difference of
opinion on a system of views would be possible. I could also add here why
the said whole is constructed as it is and what are my reasons for selecting
and ordering the issues as I have done. That, however, would take too
much space; moreover, my reasons for adopting such and such solutions
will become manifest in the course of my analysis which is split into five
sections: *Ideology versus science; Anti-empiricism or idealism?; Anti-
historicism or eleatism?; Anti-humanism or anti-Marxism?; One Marx or
two Marxes?*

Ideology versus Science

Opposing ideology to science and fighting ideology while apotheosizing science is the focal issue in Althusser's system of thought. This is why I commence my analysis by discussing that problem, since in Althusser's system everything else is subordinated to the dichotomy based on the following principle: what is ideological is erroneous, mystified, and should be rejected; what is scientific is automatically identical with objective truth (and, of course, is given a halo of positive emotional evaluation). The modifiers *ideological*, as something cognitively bad, and *scientific*, as something cognitively good, occur very often in works by Althusser and his followers. Althusser's programme could be described briefly as a crusade against ideology in Marxism in the name of a purely scientific nature of Marxism, which is not refuted by the fact that on some occasions Althusser says that ideology is 'eternal' and derides the myth of 'pure' science. This proves that there are contradictions in Althusser's views, but does not cancel his basic claim that Marxism must be defended as science by having ideology eliminated from it.

It has been said earlier what are the psycho-political origins of that dislike of ideology. We have to do with people who at one time became disillusioned with the ideology of the communist movement and are reacting to their shock by repudiating *all* ideology, by trying to overcome it and to engage in 'pure' science. By the way, those French Marxists who sought escape from ideology in structuralism were original only in the choice of the course they took. They were neither the only ones nor the first ones to react to their disillusionment by aversion to all ideology and by trying to escape it by declaring adherence to those who engage in 'pure' science. As a telling example we can quote the discussion on ideology and science, held in Poland after the political changes in October 1956, a discussion whose political background and scientific tenor were analogous to the situation in the Marxist milieu in France.

Althusser emphasizes at the outset his predilection for precision of terms to be used and even warns the reader of the difficulties he (the reader) will have to cope with in this connection.

> The reader should realize that I am doing all I can to give the *concepts* I use a strict meaning, and that if he wants to understand these concepts he will have to pay attention to this rigour, and, in so far as it is not imaginary, he will have to adopt it himself. Need I remind him that without the rigour demanded

by its object there can be no question of *theory*, that is, of theoretical practice in the strict sense of the term?[19]

This is a correct and laudable intention, for, as Francis Bacon says, 'Truth emerges more readily from error than from confusion.'[20] There is really no greater sin against science than vagueness and opacity, because we can discuss errors, whereas opacity undermines all scientific discussion and drives it into a blind alley. Yet, contrary to his declarations, this greatest sin against science invalidates Althusser's analyses.

Since I do not want to be suspected of partiality I suggest that we look at the facts. The reader, in order to see what the truth is, must endure a number of quotations. It will be, of course, only a selection of some passages on ideology, but a representative one. When reading those passages which at least imply tentative definitions the reader should bear several things in mind:

that Althusser is a Marxist, and a learned one at that, who certainly knows that Marx and Engels defined ideology as false consciousness;

that Lenin, on the contrary, spoke not only about opposing proletarian ideology to bourgeois ideology, but also referred to Marxism as scientific ideology;

that Althusser, as a member of a communist party, has heard something about ideological struggle and the battle-cry of the victory of Marxist ideology, to which he contributes actively by being a party member;

that Althusser is a professor of philosophy at the Ecole Normale Supérieure, the most renowned French university school in the field of the humanities, and hence certainly is familiar with the contemporary literature on the theory of ideology, in particular with books by sociologists of knowledge, above all those by Karl Mannheim, who concentrated his attention on problems of ideology.

Let us, then, listen to Althusser. We shall, of course, expect him to adopt an attitude toward the apparently contradictory statements of his masters whom he avows as such, and toward the views of sociologists of knowledge, of whom Mannheim explicitly refers to Marx; and also to try to define his own standpoint, to state what he means by the ambiguous term *ideology*, and, of course, consistently to use the term so defined, i.e. without being in contradiction with his own definition of that term. I shall endeavour to grasp Althusser's ideas by following his analyses in the order they occur in his works, my intention being to avoid my own subjective approach in ordering his ideas by my own criteria. The necessary selection consists in my quoting those passages in which *different* concepts and definitions of ideology occur explicitly or implicitly. The fact that they are many and they differ from one another just confirms the thesis that Althusser does not use the term unequivocally.

> I should add that if it is not so much the immediate content of the objects reflected as the way the problems are posed which constitutes the ultimate ideological essence of an ideology, this problematic is not of itself immediately present to the historian's reflection, for good reason: in general a philosopher *thinks in it rather than thinking of it*, and his 'order of reasons' does not coincide with the 'order of reasons' of his philosophy. An ideology (in the strict Marxist sense of the term – the sense in which Marxism is not itself an ideology) can be regarded as characterized in this particular respect by the fact that *its own problematic is not conscious of itself.*[21]

1. This is somewhat intricate, but this is due to the language of philosophizing, to which we have to get used. If we number Althusser's definitions of, or comments on, ideology, then under No. 1 we make this entry: An ideology is characterized by the fact its own problematic is not conscious of itself. Let us also note that Althusser believes to have explained with this formulation the meaning of the word *ideology* 'in the strict Marxist sense of the term'.

> For the world of the German ideology was then *without any possible comparison the world that was worst crushed beneath its ideology* (in the strict sense), that is, the world farthest from the actual realities of history, *the most mystified, the most alienated world that then* [in the 1830s and 1840s – A. S.] *existed* in a Europe of ideologies.[22]

2. We make the second entry with the following idea (or quasi-definition): An ideology is what does not coincide with the actual realities of history, what is mystified, what is alienated.

> ... there is no *pure* theoretical practice, no perfectly transparent science which throughout its history as a science will always be preserved, by I know not what Grace, from the threats and taints of idealism, that is, of the *ideologies* which besiege it; we know that a 'pure' science only exists on condition that it continually frees itself from the ideology which occupies it, haunts it, or lies in wait for it. The inevitable price of this purification and liberation is a continuous struggle against ideology itself, that is, against idealism.[23]

3. This time it is stated plainly and clearly – which is not to say correctly – that ideology = idealism.

> The act of abstraction whereby the pure essence is extracted from concrete individuals *is an ideological myth.*[24]

4. Since on the preceding page Althusser comes out against the empiricist ideology 'which has allowed him [Marx – A. S.] to maintain that a scientific concept is produced exactly as the general concept of fruit "should be" produced, by an abstraction acting on concrete fruits',[25] we can make the next entry stating that ideology consists in shaping a specified idea of abstraction, namely the idea which explains general concepts by a specified mental operation on individuals.

> ... the concept 'socialism' is indeed a scientific concept, but the concept 'humanism' is no more than an *ideological* one.
> Note that my purpose is not to dispute the reality that the concept of socialist humanism is supposed to designate, but to define the *theoretical* value of the concept. When I say that the concept of humanism is an ideological concept (not a scientific one), I mean that while it really does designate a set of existing relations, unlike a scientific concept, it does not provide us with a means of knowing them. In a particular (ideological) mode, it designates some existents, but it does not give us their essences.[26]

5. Ideology as opposed to science consists in designating a certain reality, but does not enable us to know it; it designates a reality, but does not give us its essence.

While, so far, we have been extracting quasi-definitions implied by loose comments on ideology (even those comments being something exceptional among the numerous ones in which the words *ideology* and *ideological* occur merely in a derogatory sense), we now pass to the only one (over hundreds of pages) tentative of a semantic analysis of the concept *ideology*. It is self-evident that we shall pay special attention to that tentative made by Althusser.

It is true that he begins with a negative statement: 'There can be no question of attempting a profound definition of ideology here',[27] but he nevertheless does make such an attempt. In fact, it is rather a series of various attempts, and we shall accordingly review them one by one.

> It will suffice to know very schematically that an ideology is a system (with its own logic and rigour) of representations (images, myths, ideas or concepts, depending on the case) endowed with a historical existence and role within a given society. Without embarking on the problem of relations between a science and its (ideological) past, we can say that ideology, as a system of representations, is distinguished from science in that in it the practico-social function is more important than the theoretical function (function of knowledge).[28]

6. Ideology is a system of representations (interpreted as something which under specified conditions means either images, or ideas, or concepts) which really exist in a given society and has an historical role in it. Moreover, an ideology differs from science in that its practico-social function is more important than its function of knowledge.

But this tentative definition is followed, on the next pages, by an even more striking one, because, apart from everything else, it contains, 'in the name of true Marxism', an open polemic with the well-known opinion of the Marxist classics who by an ideology used to mean 'a false consciousness'. This is what Althusser has to say on the issue:

> It is customary to suggest that ideology belongs to the region of 'consciousness'. We must not be misled by this appelation which is still contaminated by the idealist problematic that preceded Marx. In truth, ideology has very little to do with 'consciousness', even supposing this term to have an unambiguous meaning. It is profoundly *unconscious*, even when it presents itself in a reflected form (as in pre-Marxist 'philosophy'). Ideology is indeed a system of representations, but in the majority of cases these representations have nothing to do with 'consciousness': they are usually images and occasionally concepts, but it is above all as *structures* that they impose on the vast majority of men, not via their 'consciousness'. They are perceived − accepted − suffered cultural objects and they act functionally on men via a process that escapes them. Men 'live' their ideologies as the Cartesian 'saw' or did not see − if he was not looking at it − the moon two hundred paces away: *not at all as a form of consciousness, but as an object of their 'world'* − as their *'world'* itself.[29]

7. Ideology is a system of representations which:

(a) in the majority of cases have nothing to do with 'consciousness'; ideology is 'profoundly unconscious';

(b) are images, occasionally concepts, but above all structures, and impose on the majority of men, but not via their 'consciousness';

(c) are cultural objects which are perceived, accepted, suffered, and act functionally on men via a process that escapes them;

(d) are 'lived' by men, but not as a form of consciousness, but as an object of their 'world'.

We shall revert to the analysis of this definition, but already at this moment it is necessary to point to its originality. For we have here to do either with a discovery that would deserve a Nobel Prize (e.g. images and concepts somehow exist outside human consciousness; likewise, structures act upon human beings not via their consciousness; ideologies as cultural objects which exist outside human consciousness and are 'lived' by them), or with a typical 'philosophical' language which tries to hypnotize by the sound of words, like Heidegger's notorious formulation *das Nichts nichtet*, which at one time was ridiculed by Carnap. It is also worth mentioning that the opinions presented in the passage quoted above are in a glaring contradiction with Marx's classical formulation in the 'Preface' to *A Contribution to the Critique of Political Economy*, where Marx refers to the various ideological forms in which people come to realize social conflicts, and hence forms which pass through their consciousness.

But this is not all. The five pages of Althusser's text include two other definitions of ideology, stated explicitly.

8. Ideology is false consciousness. Of course, Althusser, who negates the role of consciousness, does not use that term here, either, but he says what was said by Marxist classics. He uses the example of the bourgeois ideology of freedom to demonstrate by the play on the word *freedom* (freedom for capitalists and freedom for all people) that ideology mystifies both those who are exploited and those who exploit them.[30]

9. '. . . *ideology (as a system of mass representations) is indispensable in any society if men are to be formed, transformed and equipped to respond to the demands of their conditions of existence.*'[31]

The novelty in this definition consists in ideology being interpreted as a system of mass representations, and not that of individual ones.

In connection with these tentative definitions it is worth noting some comments made by Althusser on ideology in a classless society, comments which add complications to the picture which is already not too clear.

It is said there that 'Only an ideological world outlook could have imagined societies *without ideology* and accepted the utopian idea of a world in which ideology (not just one of its historical forms) would disappear without trace, to be replaced by *science*'.[31a] Further, it is claimed that '*historical materialism cannot conceive that even a communist society could ever do without ideology*'.[31b] Finally, that ideology is not just a myth fabricated by the ruling class to fool those it is exploiting, which accordingly could disappear with the disappearance of classes, that ideology is indispensable in any society if men are to be formed, and that 'In a class society ideology is the relay whereby, and the element in which, the relation between men and their conditions of existence is settled to the profit of the ruling class. In a classless society ideology is the relay whereby, and the element in which, the relation between men and their conditions of existence is lived to the profit of all men.'[31c]

These are correct statements as far as they concern the thesis that ideology is an indispensable element of public life in every social formation, but in view of the definitions of ideology quoted above the thesis makes us wonder: Why is such a system of 'representations' (the term *representation* also being a puzzling one from the point of view of the accepted scientific terminology), which is mystified, alienated, dissociated from the realities of human life, false, existing outside human consciousness and 'profoundly unconscious', etc., why is such a system indispensable in public life in *any* social formation? Would ideology in a communist society be the same thing it is in a capitalist one (i.e. a set of mystified, alienated, false, etc., 'representations') and would the mere change in the social formation make such a vacuous and anti-scientific something work not in a mystifying manner, but to the profit of all? Or is perhaps something wrong with Althusser's definition of ideology, a definition which mystifies the actual state of things and prevents us from understanding what ideology really is?

We have so far been using only the data provided by *For Marx*. *Reading Capital* does not contribute anything new in that respect. On almost every page Althusser uses the terms *ideology* and *ideological* simply as derogatory words, but in fact, when we consider his various definitions of the term *ideology*, as cited above, we do not know which of them he means in a given case, and what he wants to say by using the word. For instance, '. . . there is nothing in true history which allows it to be read in the ideological continuum of a linear time that need only be punctuated and divided. . . .'[32] Or, '. . . the mere existence of an emptiness in the system of concepts of historical materialism is enough to establish in it immediately the fullness of a philosophical ideology, the empiricist ideology. We can only recognize this emptiness by emptying it of the obviousnesses of the ideological philosophy of which it is full.'[33] It is not worthwhile quoting other examples: the word *ideology* just reflects the vacuous verbosity of the 'structuralist' phraseology.

But *Reading Capital* offers the tenth definition of ideology as suggested by Althusser, which deserves being recorded here as a matter of order.

10. Those theses which are due to non-cognitive considerations are ideological in nature.

> In other words, the whole history of Western philosophy is dominated not by the 'problem of knowledge', but by the ideological *solution*, i.e. the solution imposed in advance by practical, religious, ethical and political 'interests' foreign to the reality of the knowledge, which this 'problem' *had to* receive.[34]

> Indeed, it is a peculiarity of every *ideological* conception, especially if it has conquered a scientific conception by diverting it from its true meaning, that it is governed by 'interests' beyond the necessity of knowledge alone.[35]

This concludes the review of those data which enable us to grasp what Althusser does, or does not, mean by the term *ideology*. This listing of quotations and comments may seem both pedantic and intended to ridicule him, but the ambiguity of that term as used by Althusser makes such pedantry inevitable if we are to give a true picture of his ideas. Otherwise we would face the grave danger of misunderstandings, because any person who confuses one of the meanings of that term as found in Althusser's works with his general conception of ideology may easily be led completely astray. As an example we can quote Alfred Schmidt's paper *Der strukturalische Angriff auf die Geschichte*,[36] where he confines himself to discussing Althusser's comments (as described above) on the indispensability of ideology in all social formations and criticizes him for overestimating the role of ideology, which turns everything upside-down.

I have made earlier a distinction between the standpoint of Althusser and that of Godelier, but nevertheless both of them are anti-ideologically minded. Godelier uses the word *ideology* as a derogatory term much less frequently, and the meaning of that term, as occurring in his works, is more stable and much less ambiguous than it is in Althusser's writings. His most explicit definition of the term *ideology* is to be found in his discussion with Maurice Cavening: '. . . all fantastic ideas of reality, that is, in fact, all unrealized ignorance of reality, that is, all ideology.'[37]

He, however, fully shares Althusser's faith in the magic force of the dichotomy 'ideology versus science' within the Marxist theory.

Let us now proceed to analyse that dichotomy. We have so far focused our attention on the meaning of the term *ideology* as occurring in Althusser's works. And how does he understand the term *science*? After all he opposes science to ideology, and this opposition plays a very important role in his conception. And yet it is difficult to answer the above question because over hundreds of pages of his writings we cannot find any trace of an analysis of the concept *science*. Ideology, as we have seen, is honoured by a number of tentative, implicit or explicit, explanations of the meaning of that term. In the case of the term *science* Althusser must have thought that there was no point in taking the trouble to define it as it is comprehensible without any analyses. There is hardly anything more misleading than such a belief, which is shown by the existing literature of the subject. Vague comments on *theory* and *Theory* do not contribute anything: in making them Althusser uses the modifier *scientific*, but leaves it unexplained. The consequences can be seen in *Les Cahiers du Centre D'Etudes Socialistes*, dedicated to the fourth discussion on 'Science and ideology'. It could be said that Althusser is not responsible for the vagueness and lack of clarity of what his followers and critics said in that discussion, but that would be wrong: a master who introduces new ideas is responsible for their clarity. But regardless of the confusion reflected in that discussion and of its markedly anti-Marxist points (e.g. rejection of the theory of reflection, rejection of the criterion of truth, anti-empiricism, etc.) it is a fact that its participants realized the necessity of formulating the fundamental question 'What does *science* mean?', a question Althusser did not take the trouble to pose at all.[38]

We have started our analyses from Althusser's initial thesis on the basic opposition between ideology and science. That thesis results in the requirement that Marxist philosophy be constituted as science by being purified from ideology, to which — in Althusser's opinion — Marx and Engels had succumbed, too, and that even in their mature period of activity.

As we realize the difficulties encountered on that point by present-day literature concerned with the science of science we pose the question: What does Althusser mean by science? In turns out that he does not raise the issue at all and ignores the discussions taking place nowadays.

We ask further: What does Althusser mean by ideology, which he has so mishandled emotionally? It turns out again that he ignores the existing literature of the subject, and he uses the term, which after all is so fundamental in his reasoning, in so many meanings that it is quite to the point to say that we cannot grasp what he is talking about. For if, according to the list of meanings we have given above (and which is by no means complete), in Althusser's approach *ideology* means:

   views which are not based on the knowledge of the problems to which
      they refer;

mystified and alienated views which are at variance with historical realities;

idealism, abstraction which interprets general concepts as mental operations which start from individuals;

views which signify reality but do not provide means by which men are to know it, and which do not disclose the essence of reality;

a system of representations which actually exists in a given society;

a system of representations whose practico-social function dominates their cognitive function (contrary to what occurs in the case of science);

a system of unconscious representations;

structures which impose on a majority of men not via their consciousness;

culture objects which act on men in a way which escapes control by the latter;

something which men live as an object in their 'world';

false consciousness;

mass representations;

views dictated by 'interests' outside the sphere of knowledge;

if, accordingly, the term *ideology* has so many meanings (the occurrence of each of these meanings has been illustrated by an appropriate quotation), then it does not mean anything, it is a sound which serves to convey certain emotions, but is vacuous from the cognitive point of view. The term *ideology* performs a magic function here, is a kind of exorcism, but being so ambiguous it is useless from the scientific point of view.

To make matters worse, Althusser makes contradictory statements about ideology, such as:

it is a system of representations which are unconscious and it is false consciousness;

science must reject ideology which 'besieges' it and ideology is an indispensable element of social life in every social formation.

In his various definitions he also says many strange things which show that he at least does not use precisely defined concepts. What does it mean that ideology is a system of representations which include images, myths, ideas and concepts? When has the term *representation*, which stands for a well-defined category in the sphere of psychology and gnosiology, come to mean the same as concepts and myths? And what does it mean that ideology is a system of representations, but such representations which in a majority of cases do not have anything to do with consciousness?[38a] What a striking discovery this is: unconscious representations! Moreover, they are usually images and concepts (unconscious images and concepts? Are we to believe in the existence of ideal entities outside consciousness and at the same time to accept that as the materialist view?) but above all structures which impose on a majority of men but not via their consciousness (this is not idealism, this is simply mysticism). Further, they are culture objects which exist outside *consciousness* and which men 'live' as their 'world'. If this is not objective idealism, then we have to conclude that philosophical terms do not have any sense at all. Let us note as a point of order that each of Althusser's tentative definitions can be subject to such a purifying operation.

I do not claim that Althusser is an idealist or spiritualist, or, for that matter, that he wants to be an idealist; this is certainly not the case. But I do claim that he uses the language of philosophy in an irresponsible manner, that he writes without paying attention to what he writes and without realizing what he wrote. And in the case of a philosopher this means wrong-doing, for a philosopher uses general concepts, which cannot occur without a language; to use Althusser's manner of writing, the material of a philosopher's 'theoretical practice' is words, which always generalize. This applies to every sphere of science, and philosophy — which I understand to be not rhetorics, but a specialized sphere of science — is exposed to a great danger because of the way in which it uses general terms and of the risk of abuse of language. This is why every philosopher, and not simply a representative of a variation of analytic philosophy, is responsible for the use of the language of philosophy and must be very well disciplined on that point; he must have semantic culture and strive for the precision of the words he uses because words *always* are ambiguous. For, to paraphrase the words of Francis Bacon cited earlier, it is not so much an error in cognition which is dangerous, since an error can be corrected, as the opacity of thoughts, which usually blocks cognitive reflection and hinders, or just prevents, the correction of an error. This is why philosophers can sow confusion in human minds by abusing language, that is, by using it irresponsibly. Socrates was accused of sowing confusion in the minds of young people and was sentenced to drink hemlock. That was wrong, because Socrates taught precision in thinking and in the use of language. Althusser is lucky enough not to have lived in ancient Athens.

Blaming Althusser for the opacity of his concepts, for using the term *ideology* without stating with precision what he is writing about does not settle the issue. The crux of the matter lies in the fact that Althusser, while pretending to be the spokesman of Marxism – and Marxism 'in the strict sense of the word' at that – passes by the focal difficulty which we have to face in the case of Marxism. Let us leave aside for a moment both Althusser and our problems connected with comprehending the term *ideology* as he uses it, and let us turn to the Marxist classics to see in what sense the term *ideology* occurs in their works.

For Marx and Engels, from their early writings to *The German Ideology* to the end of their lives (cf. Engels's work *Ludwig Feuerbach*) *ideology* used to mean *false consciousness.* Althusser's attack (allegedly structuralist in nature) on the treatment of ideology as a form of social consciousness is, as we have said, at variance with Marxism, which is proved by the above-mentioned passage in the *Preface to A Contribution to the Critique of Political Economy*, and hence in a work whose place, in the works of the mature Marx, after the notorious 'break' is not questioned even by Althusser himself. That 'false consciousness', which as a result of being conditioned by the class interests of the bourgeoisie describes social relations in a totally distorted way, may take on various forms: false opinions held by an individual, false consciousness of a class, or false consciousness of an entire epoch. It is thus an expanded and differentiated conception. Its best analysis in the Marxist literature of the subject has been given by Jerzy Szacki,[39] and it is to be regretted that, because of the language barrier, that excellent work, published in a Polish sociological periodical, is not known to specialists in other countries.

But if we take the works by Lenin, who of course knew perfectly well the standpoint and the formulations of Marx and Engels on ideology – the standpoint which by definition linked the concept of ideology with the class status of the bourgeoisie and accordingly, also by definition, classed Marxism as a non-ideology – we find there not only statements about 'bourgeois ideology and proletarian ideology', but also about 'Marxist ideology' and 'scientific ideology'. This holds both for Lenin's early works,[40] and his excellent study from the period of his maturity, namely *Materialism and Empiriocriticism.*[41]

This new interpretation of the term *ideology*, certainly a different and broader one, has been adopted not only by contemporary language, in which people speak about 'bourgeois ideology' and 'proletarian ideology', 'religious ideology' and 'lay ideology', 'conservative ideology' and 'liberal ideology', etc., but also by the everyday language of the present-day workers' movement, and the communist movement in particular; people speak without any embarrassment (and what would Althusser, as a member of the Communist Party of France, say to that?) about the struggle against the bourgeois ideology in the name of the victory of the ideology of the working class, the scientific ideology, i.e. Marxism.

The question arises — regardless of Althusser's anti-ideological crusade — what are we to do with that distinct difference between the meaning of the term *ideology* as used by Marx and Engels and that which is current now in the worker movement and has been taken over from Lenin?

Let us begin with contemporary language, because we are not concerned with history alone, and Althusser's dichotomy 'ideology versus science' claims to be valid today.

As it is used today, the word *ideology* is extremely ambiguous. Arne Naess[42] has carried out an empirical study of its meaning in present-day language and discovered over thirty *groups of meanings* of that term. This is why there is also a great variety of definitions of the term *ideology*, and that according to its sense adopted by a given author. Jerzy Wiatr in his study on ideology[43] gives the following typology of those definitions: *genetic* definitions, which stress the genetic links between the position of a social group and its consciousness; *structural* definitions, which stress the occurrence in a given formulation of valuating judgements or directives for action, and hence not just only theoretical descriptive statements; and *functional* definitions, which stress the functional ancillary nature of given opinions with respect to the interests and, accordingly, the actions of specified classes and groups. Within each of these classes of definitions it is possible to find differences, and even oppositions, of opinions according to the meaning which the term *ideology* is given.

I am personally in favour of a mixed genetic-functional definition, which grasps the meaning of the term *ideology* thus: 'An ideology is a system of opinions which, being based on a selected system of values, conditions human attitudes and behaviour that refer to accepted objectives in the development of a society, a social group, or an individual.'[44] But, for instance, when it comes to the class of functional definitions, we can assume after Mannheim that an ideology serves the interests of conservative classes only, while a utopia serves the interests of progressive classes; we can also, which is my viewpoint, treat the term *ideology* as the name of any system of opinions which originates with the class interests of the group it serves, and which points to the socially accepted objective of that group.

There may be, and there are in fact, very many such differences in the current usage of the word *ideology*: in no case may we now narrow down its meaning to the young Marx's conception of 'false consciousness'. All this is due to the fact that the word *ideology*, like any other word in human language, has its own history, lives its own life and changes together with the life of a given society. This is what any linguist knows only too well: that words change their respective meanings in various ways, that their meanings become broader or narrower, that they change their emotive tinge from a positive to a derogatory one, and vice versa, that respectable words become disreputable or obscene ones, and vice versa, etc. These are ordinary developments, and we would have to consider it a miracle if the word *ideology*, so closely linked with public life and its fortunes, remained exempt from that general regularity. Of course, it is *not* exempt from it, and we cannot ignore that fact for doctrinal reasons, just as we cannot ignore the way language is used, and we cannot afford to contribute to possible divergences between current language and the language used by theorists who cling to old linquistic usage. Such things, it is true, do happen even to very respectable authors (let György Lukács be an example), but their imitation is not recommended. For understanding and analysing the standpoint of Marx and Engels and the terminology they used on this issue, and disregarding the evolution of language and changes in meanings of expressions, changes which accompany the evolution of views on social issues, are two different things.

If we want to understand the terminology used by Marx and Engels we have to go back to the history of the term *ideology*.[45] Coined by Condillac and adopted by the physiocrats, especially by Destutt de Tracy, as the name of the most general science of ideas, it had at first an emotionally neutral connotation, different from the later one, which was closely linked with social issues and had a specific emotional tinge — an understandable effect of the social conflicts which that evolved meaning came to imply. The change was brought about, contrary to expectations, not by a theorist, but by Napoleon I, a man dedicated to practical activity. As is often the case with politicians, he did not like theorists for they hindered his actions, the more so as they opposed his policies. 'Ideologists', i.e. 'ideology', were his *bête noire*. Could there be a better way of attacking them by those in power than to ridicule them and to discredit their standpoints and values, especially if courtiers were willing to take the hint from above? It is an old truth that it is educated men of vision who are hated most by ignorants. And could there be a better way of ridiculing and discrediting the 'ideologists' than by blaming them for being dissociated from practical problems, dreamers and utopians who fail to see facts, in a word — although Napoleon did not use that expression — for having a 'false consciousness'? In this way, Napoleon added one more victory to his military successes, the smashing of feudal Europe and giving it a new shape through his civil code: he gave birth — although few people realize that — to the stereotype of an intellectual who is dissociated from practical problems, an 'ideologist' who as a dreamer fails to see facts and says things that do not make sense, a person who may, and even should, be slighted. This fact must be borne in mind: the derogatory tinge of the term *ideology* emerged as a result of the reactionary trends in Napoleon's policies.

When Marx and Engels engaged in the spiritual conflicts of the 1840s the words *ideology* and *ideologist* had an established connotation and were a permanent element of the heritage of the Napoleonic epoch. The original meanings of those words were completely driven out of circulation. It is obvious that Marx, when engaging in a battle with his former friends, the Young Hegelians — who were, in fact, dissociated from practical issues and absorbed in speculations, and whose philosophical sententiousness hampered revolution since they confined themselves to interpreting the world instead of changing it (for which Marx blamed them in his *Theses on Feuerbach*) — willingly made use of the then current terms *ideology* and *ideologists*. Marx explained 'the German ideology' genetically by pointing to its class substratum and did that to formulate the basic ideas of historical materialism. 'The German ideology' was a class-conditioned 'false consciousness', which interpreted social facts as it were in the camera obscura, that is, upside-down. It was obvious to Marx and Engels that ideology was by definition proper to the bourgeoisie, whose class interests made it falsify — through the intermediary of ideologists — actual social relations, and mystify them in the interest of the propertied classes. Following that interpretation (claiming that ideology originates from the interests of the ruling classes, which it serves) the term *ideology* received a specified genetic-functional definition: *ideology* means *bourgeois ideology*, and hence those views which reflect the interests of the working class as the revolutionary class cannot obviously be termed *ideology*.

But social life continued to evolve, the class struggle was gaining in intensity, becoming, among other things, an ideological struggle, and all this bred new needs, also in the field of language, which must provide names for new things and facts. Views which are genetically connected with class interests and serve the latter by guiding social actions are not specific to the bourgeoisie and the ruling classes; they can also be found in the revolutionary worker movement, where they become more and more precise as the Marxist theory develops and the class struggle waged by the proletariat intensifies.

People act as members of society and strive to attain specified objectives in social life. They see those objectives in various ways, according to what they consider good, i.e. according to what they consider worthy of attainment through their social actions, and that in turn depends on the system of values they accept. The Marxist theory explains the differences and changes in views in those matters by the impact of class interest on human views, attitudes (in the sense of readiness to action) and social actions. Such views, genetically conditioned by class interests, and the resulting attitudes and actions are ancillary to what follows from those class interests and socially accepted objectives of actions: they inspire to action and help carry plans into effect.

What has been said above applies not only to individuals, but also to those groups of individuals which form classes based on common interests. Regardless of the differentiation of individual interests and motivations we can extrapolate that which is the common interest of a given class, and that community of interests explains the community of the accepted system of values and the resulting community of accepted objectives of social actions.

But, as we have said, this is not specific to the bourgeoisie. At a certain level of class development, when a class becomes conscious of its interests and objectives, when — as Marx says, using the Hegelian language — it turns from a 'class in itself' into a 'class for itself', in which process *consciousness* plays the decisive role, this is specific to, and necessary for, the working class as well. It may be that the process is suprahistorical in nature and holds for social life *in every* system. Althusser is right — although this is at variance with his way of thinking — when he says that ideology is an indispensable element of social life in every formation, communism included. It would be even correct to state that in the communist system those views and attitudes which we term *ideology* will play a more important role than they do now, because communism will be the system in which people will overcome the spontaneity of social development and will consciously shape social life in the way they will consider desirable since they will have a better knowledge of the laws that govern social life.

But is it legitimate to use the term *ideology* in this broader sense?

Lenin answered that question in the affirmative as he referred without hesitation to proletarian ideology, to the Marxist theory as the scientific ideology, etc. And his is the only correct stand. Ideology occurs here as a general concept that covers various subordinated ones, such as bourgeois and proletarian ideology, religious and lay ideology, conservative and progressive ideology, unscientific and scientific ideology, etc. Otherwise each of those subsystems would have to bear a name of its own, and in addition we would have to invent a term for the class of those subsystems. Instead of exerting one's ingenuity to find an artificial terminology it is much better to accept the existing one.

Let us stop for a moment at the concept of scientific ideology, which in the light of Althusser's conception seems to be a contradiction in terms, and yet is current in contemporary Marxism, which Althusser wants to represent. As we know, the definition of ideology contains a genetic element: it refers to the class interests which breed given views and attitudes. But our question about the origin of a given ideology is not limited to asking about *what* class interests, interests of *what* class gave birth to that ideology, but covers the issue of cognitive data on the basis of which that ideology developed. This is so because the system of values and the choice of objectives of social actions, which *every* ideology must include, can be based on various assumptions, such as a religious faith, socially accepted superstitions, pseudo-scientific theories like Nazi racialism, but it can also rest on the foundation of a *scientific* analysis of social facts. A social ideology can be constructed on the base of Nazi racialism and the theory of the master race, but it can also be rested on the Marxist analysis of the laws of social development. In both cases we have to do with ideologies, but they differ from one another not only in their origin and class function, but also – in close connection to the former element – in the respective intellectual assumptions to which they refer: in the former case such assumptions are unscientific (or, to put it strictly, anti-scientific), in the latter, scientific in nature. If a person, as Althusser does, blocks by definition the path to the comprehension of that state of things (which is just trivial if we view the problem rationally, without mystifying it), then he additionally proves that his theories and research methods are quite useless. For these are clearly designed to serve as an adequate analysis of facts, and not lead to their mystification and camouflage.

The conception of scientific ideology, which has emerged and acquired its legitimate status in the Marxist theory (as we shall see later, Althusser's pseudo-Marxism deviates from Marxism not on this point alone), necessitates a discussion of the problems of science and scientific approach. I shall take up two issues. First, the theory of ideology as formulated by Karl Mannheim within his sociology of knowledge. I wrote extensively about Mannheim's idea and its relation to Marxism in my *History and Truth*.[46] While I refer those readers who are interested in the issue to this book I wish to dwell here on one point, which is important for our analysis.

As is known, Mannheim based his sociology of knowledge (which fact he stated explicitly), and in particular his theory of ideologies, on the Marxian theory of base and superstructure and on the young Marx's concept of ideology as false consciousness.

On the other hand, it is not commonly known that Mannheim based his idea also on another premiss, namely the theory of truth interpreted as absolute truth. What is not absolute truth, and hence all-comprehensive and unchanging, is falsehood. Since the thesis on the social conditioning of cognition, which follows from the Marxian theory of the effect the base has on the superstructure, implies that cognition is absolute not as a single act and/or product – except, as Engels said, for trivial cases – but only as an endless process, hence any given case of cognition is restricted to its system of reference (Mannheim did not formulate the final conclusion, as had once been done by Kazimierz Twardowski,[47] that it is accordingly a falsehood). Mannheim thus came to face the collapse of relativism, for the denial of objective truth and the necessity of adopting the theory of plurality of truths was a disaster. Mannheim tried to save his ideas by the conception of relationism, a recalculation of perspective, and the assigning to the intelligentsia, or the intellectuals, a status of being above the classes and thus being free, in their cognition, from class conditionings. In the theory of ideology, in which we are here interested most, Mannheim tried to radicalize the Marxist theory by blaming Marx for not having applied his correct theses on the social conditioning of cognition to his own theory. The Marxist theory, being socially conditioned, also is a partial, and not absolute, truth. And since everything is grey in the dark, Marxism must share the misfortunes of all views and theories, which are limited by their respective social conditionings. In other words, since Nazism is an ideology and Marxism is an ideology, and every ideology is class-based genetically and functionally, Nazism and Marxism have the same cognitive status as they both are ideologies. This is a nonsense, which is due to the incomprehension of the concept of scientific ideology, as explained above.

Mannheim's opinion was in fact such, at least by implication. Althusser's ideas are its analogue, and since he approves Mannheim's reasoning he wants to deny facts, namely to deny that Marxism is an ideology, and hence, that it is a scientific ideology. The error of both Mannheim and Althusser consists in their failure to grasp the differences in the social conditioning of cognition, differences which depend on the class involved in a given case; their error also consists in denying the obvious fact that the construction of ideologies is affected not only by the class interests engaged in a given case, but also by the intellectual stuff of which a given ideology is constructed. The two elements are interconnected (class interests affect the fact whether and how far scientific data are taken into account in such constructions) but not identical. Thus the problem of scientific ideology is a fairly independent one, which takes us to the second aspect of the issue.

That second aspect is that the problem of science and the scientific nature of given views emerge -- in connection with the survival of the idea of scientific ideology -- as relating to the meaning of the words *science* and *scientific*. As mentioned earlier, Althusser fails to notice any problem here and freely handles these terms as if they did not require any explanations and were quite comprehensible just on the strength of their being in opposition to the term *ideology*. This is wrong not only because if one does not understand the meaning of the term *ideology* — which is true in Althusser's case — one cannot claim to understand the word *science* just by opposing it to the former: by opposing a certain term to another, whose meaning one does not understand, one can only obtain a term which is equally incomprehensible or ambiguous. In the case under consideration, however, we face an additional difficulty: should we even give a precise meaning to the term *ideology* and understand that term well, this would not automatically entail our correct understanding of the terms *science* and *scientific*, as they are not in a simple opposition to the term *ideology* (cf. the case of 'scientific ideology'), and require a separate analysis. Althusser's care-free approach to that issue — very intricate, as can be seen from the literature of the subject, both comprehensive and infrequently controversial — is just astounding.

From that comprehensive literature of the subject[48] I select a study by the Polish author Stanisław Kamiński, because it is specially dedicated to the concept of science and a recent one at that. I begin by quoting his statement which seems to fit our analysis perfectly well.

> The predicates *science* and *scientific* are used proudly in discussions. We brandish them vigorously in edifying polemics, but what we mean by them often is vague and obscure, and can be grasped intuitively rather than defined precisely. This gives rise to a paradoxical situation, or rather a serious logical defect: the term is used to denote the domain in which exactitude and precision, required on an increasing scale, are specially prized values, but it is itself far from meeting those requirements. Hence the unending controversies over the problem whether, in a given case, cognition is scientific or not. The concept of science also poses many questions which prove the far-reaching misunderstandings as to the nature and content of that concept.[49]

What has been said in the above quotation describes well the general situation concerning the issue we are now discussing, and in particular the situation in the Althusser school, which does brandish vigorously the term *science* in the discussions in which its members take part.

When following S. Kamiński's carefully documented information on the existing definitions of the term *science* we find at least nine different *groups* of meanings of that word, groups which form only a general typology and comprise a multitude of shades of meaning. That variety sometimes makes logicians and methodologists of science quite sceptical about the possibility of defining the term *science* with precision and in an all-comprehensive manner. As an example we can quote so eminent an expert in that field as Tadeusz Kotarbiński, who suggests outright that science be defined as the totality of those disciplines which are taught at universities. This is why Kamiński himself, while answering in the affirmative to the question about the possibility of defining science (by the way, his own tentative definition is far from being satisfactory), ultimately suggests that we should define the various aspects of science, and not science in general.[50]

In my opinion, the difficulties are due to the fact that Kamiński, while making distinctions among the various meanings of the term *science* which result from the choice of the aspect in which the student of the problem sees science (as cognition or as subject-matter), does not seek any other way of defining that which we call science. The point is to seek the solution of the problem not in defining the phenomenon called science, which in fact has extremely many aspects and is very difficult to grasp in a single definition be it for this reason alone, but in the *method of scientific thinking*, a method which, regardless of the variety of acts of cognition, languages, objects studied, etc., which are covered by the term *science*, can be extrapolated as common to all of them. Like in all similar cases, we obtain a very general formulation, which is, however, not a vague platitude, and which enables us to distinguish that thinking which we call *scientific* from that which we call *non-scientific* (the same distinction being applicable to the products of thinking).

I have here in mind the following methodological principle. Thinking that claims the status of being scientific must satisfy at least four conditions: intersubjective observability; communicability; verifiability; methodical presentation of problems. While the first two requirements (that what a person says when he claims the scientific status both of his act of cognition and the result of that act should be directly or indirectly observable by others next to the person who makes the statement, and that what has been observed should be communicable to others in a way which is comprehensible to them, since otherwise we have to do with a mystic experience, but not with science) are self-evident; the other two involve various difficulties. But these are due merely to the complexity of the procedure used. The long controversies within the school of logical empiricism have contributed much to the analysis of the problems of verification and falsification, which have proved much more difficult to solve and much more intricate that it had seemed at first. And although we had to abandon the original radicalism of requirements (for which great credit is due to Popper), even today cognition which cannot show the method of verification or falsification of its results (be it even in the sense of a process, and not in the form of a single crucial experiment) cannot claim to be scientific. (This is a contribution to the controversy over empiricism, which, in following Althusser's reasoning, we shall discuss in a later section.) The requirement of a *methodical* presentation of the results of an act of cognition as a condition of its being scientific accounts for another problem: the variety of those forms of presentation which deserve being called *methodical.* One factor is common to them all: logic, in the strict and restrictive sense of formal logic. For one can philosophize about human cognition in many ways and call such philosophies logic, in some special sense of that word, but one cannot fail to accept, for instance, the principle of contradiction. A person who can be shown to have accepted contradictory propositions in his reasoning (in the sense valid since Aristotle) is defeated in the field of science, although he can peacefully work, e.g. in the field of mysticism. Now, beyond that principle which is to be accepted universally, various methods may be constructed in various ways and may function in various ways, too, without running the risk of being disqualified as non-scientific. That freedom reflects the variety of fields and aspects of science, and although it makes it more difficult to settle whether a given idea has been presented methodically enough to claim the status of being scientific, it does not abolish the possibility of distinguishing in that way that which is science from that which is not.

When we now revert, after these excursions, to the issue of science and ideology, and in particular to the problem of *scientific ideology*, our position is even stronger than that we held earlier, for we have acquired a criterion of making distinctions between scientific and non-scientific thinking, regardless of whether that thinking performs ideological functions (i.e. whether it is genetically and functionally connected with the interests of a given class, or not). It turns out — *horribile dictu* — that the existence not only of scientific and non-scientific ideologies, but even of ideological sciences, is in agreement with the present-day language of the Marxist theory (and much more broadly, with the present-day language of many schools of social philosophy and the social sciences). We mean here science in the sense of the product of cognition, the disciplines which provide the stuff for the construction of ideologies. These are not only social sciences, which – in the case of economics, sociology, social psychology, etc, – are traditionally ideological in nature in the sense defined above (even though they are, or at least can be, according to the way they are pursued, full-fledged elements of the class of specialized disciplines), but also suspicion-free and respectable experimental and exact sciences, such as biology (not only in the Lysenko version, but also in the form of reliable molecular biology), physics (e.g. quantum mechanics in the controversy over determinism; the principle of indeterminacy; the principle of complementarity as formulated by the Copenhagen school, etc.) and astronomy (cf. the Copernican revolution in the past). Which discipline provides the stuff for the construction of ideologies (or an ideology) – and that becomes evident immediately, since such a discipline is at once involved in the ideological and political controversies of the period – depends on the broader social context, that is, on the development of scientific ideas as seen in the setting of social relations. In such a broader social context, and depending on the motion of the various elements of the structure of a given social system (this kind of reasoning and formulating statements should *ex-professo* suit Althusser and his followers) certain disciplines which were politically neutral and functioned only as exact sciences suddenly become ideological ones. Over the last decades such as the case with physics, chemistry, biology and cybernetics, which proves that no discipline is safe and inviolable in that respect. On the other hand, certain disciplines, which under specified conditions are ideological in nature, change their character following a change in the prevailing conditions and become ideologically neutral (such, for instance, was the case of astronomy). The thesis in systems theory which says that one of the characteristics of a system is that a change in the position of one element results in a change in the position of other elements is fully applicable here. But this thesis, which forms part of the structuralist theory conceived in a reasonable way, abolishes the theory of the essential opposition between science and ideology, a theory so much cherished by 'Marxist structuralists'. One can defend the latter theory only if one uses the words *science* and *ideology* so vaguely and loosely that one, in fact, fails to understand them; this results in one's inability not only to grasp the Marxist opinion and the Marxist terminology on this issue but also to comprehend the intricate interrelationships between science and ideology, which result in the emergence of such apparently hybrid terms as *scientific ideologies* and *ideological sciences*, and which are due not only to 'distortions', but also to the spontaneous evolution of the relations between those two spheres of ideas.

To conclude we shall discuss one more issue in the intricate relationships between science and ideology, namely the relation between science and its past forms, such as between the Copernican and the Ptolemaic theory. It is obvious that all present level of knowledge is, in a given discipline, higher than its past forms, which have been overcome or rejected in some way (with the proviso that all this is not so simple in the case of philosophy). Mankind just knows more about the world, and knowing more means qualitative changes, too, and not only quantitative ones. This gives rise to various problems and queries, of which only two will be discussed here as they bear a direct relation to the issues with which we are concerned.

The first problem is how to evaluate and define the past stages in the development of a scientific theory.

Althusser has a ready answer to that, an answer which he has often repeated in his works: the past of a scientific theory is an ideology.[51] We can list this formulation, which because of the order in which I discuss things has been mentioned only now, as his eleventh definition of the term *ideology*. Thus, according to Althusser, a theory which is considered scientific does not have any past, because the past of that theory is an ideology, and since ideology is an enemy of science ('besieges' it), that past ought to be rejected. Althusser's followers sense a difficulty here. François Châtelet, when opening a discussion on 'Science and ideology', held at the Centre d'Etudes Socialistes, had to grapple with the problem of an evaluation of the Ptolemaic system. He started from the assumption that the now rejected, past forms of science must be distinguished from ideology, and said: 'There can be, for instance, no doubt that Ptolemy's idea was born of ideology ... nevertheless Ptolemy's idea as such cannot be interpreted as directly connected with political, moral, or social interests.'[52]

And that in spite of the fact that Châtelet tends to treat as ideology those views which are genetically conditioned just in that manner. But the problem is not confined to this: the difficulty goes much deeper.

If the past of science is ideology (because of the imperfections of the knowledge represented by that past science) and ought to be rejected, then this is also the future of science as it is now. For there is no doubt that what today is the peak of scientific cognition will likewise be overcome by a future development of science, as was the case of achievements of science in the past. (With the only difference that today science develops much more quickly than it used to in the past, and years, or even months, witness achievements for which people in the past had to wait for decades or even centuries.) We accordingly face a paradoxical situation: the present attainments of science are all results of errors of human cognition in the past; science emerges from ideology, which is its opposite, just in order to be inevitably transformed in ideology, and hence in non-science, again. The whole development of science is thus reduced to a sequence of non-scientific ideologies which culminate at the present moment in ephemeral science, which we know to be not science, but a future ideology. Nevertheless only a madman could deny the real progress of human knowledge and its cumulation. Where does it all come from? From ideology, from non-science? Something obviously is wrong here.

One cannot fail to see a complete analogy between Althusser's view and the positivist theory of absolute truth and the denial of relative truths (which is one more, and by far not the last analogy between Althusserism and positivism). Kazimierz Twardowski,[53] already quoted earlier, was a classical representative of that view: in his opinion, cognition is either an absolute truth or a falsehood. Since human cognition in principle makes use of relative truths (in the sense of partial and accordingly not ever-lasting ones), and not of absolute truths, and since the relative truths were held by him false by definition, we arrive at the paradoxical and untenable conclusion that the progress of human knowledge is just a chain of falsehoods, including the link that stands for the present-day stage of knowledge. And yet we know that human knowledge does develop in the course of history.

This kind of reasoning led the positivists inevitably toward a disaster that befell their theory. In Althusser's case the disaster is analogous, but its inevitability was not logical in nature. It would have sufficed not to renounce the Marxist theory of cognition, a theory in which one of the essential points is the thesis that cognition is an *endless process* of cumulation of partial (and in this sense relative) truths, a process which Engels compared to an asymptote to the hyperbola (cf. *Anti-Dühring* by

F. Engels). If one understands the meaning of that theory of truth viewed as a process, then one cannot propound (at least in one's capacity as a Marxist philosopher) that queer theory of the development of science according to which the past history of science is not any theoretical knowledge (obviously less advanced than the present one), but merely a sum of ideological errors.

One need not be a Marxist to abstain from propounding such a nonsense, untenable in the light of the unquestionable progress of human knowledge. It suffices to know the history of science and to make use of one's common sense. As an example we can refer to Thomas S. Kuhn, the already quoted author of a best-seller on the structure of scientific revolutions. Kuhn writes on the issue now under consideration:

> ... historians confront growing difficulties in distinguishing the 'scientific' component of past observation and belief from what their predecessors had readily labeled 'error' and 'superstition'. The more carefully they study, say, Aristotelian dynamics, phlogistic chemistry, or caloric thermodynamics, the more certain they feel that those once current views on nature were, as a whole, neither less scientific nor more the product of human idiosyncrasy than those current today. If these out-of-date beliefs are to be called myths, then myths can be produced by the same sorts of reasons that now lead to scientific knowledge. If, on the other hand, they are to be called science, then science has included bodies of belief quite incompatible with the ones we hold today. ... Out-of-date theories are not in principle unscientific because they have been discarded.[54]

This is a pertinent answer, to which nothing, not even any comment, need be added.

We now pass to the second problem of those indicated earlier. Is the development of human knowledge cumulative? If we refer to Engels' metaphor: Is that asymptotic curve continuous? Or, to use another metaphor: If we compare the development of human knowledge to making a heap of sand, does the cumulation of sand make that heap higher?

The question about the cumulative nature of human knowledge covers, in fact, two different problems, and hence the answer may have two aspects. According to the aspect chosen, it will be in the affirmative or in the negative.

First, if we begin with the problems discussed by Engels, we may pose the question of whether *human knowledge*, understood as the acquisition by *mankind* of the objective knowledge of the world (with man as part of that all-comprising object of cognition), is cumulative in nature. The empirical data we have about the development of science tell us that mankind knows more and more about the world (we can quote hundreds and thousands of convincing examples which show that we now know something which people did not know 2000 or 120 years ago, and that such an increment of knowledge in each case is something important for mankind, whether from the theoretical or the practical point of view, and this confirms Engels' thesis on truth as an endless process). This is to be interpreted in two senses:

(i) that mankind *cumulates* partial truths; that the said heap of grains of partial, and hence relative, truths is growing; that mankind *cumulates* real knowledge of the world; that the process is *not* what the neo-Kantians have conceived: they claim that human cognition is a process, but one which is always taking place without the past — as if a person were climbing the ladder whose rungs disappear as he leaves them, so that it would be impossible to say that he is going up, because without any reference to his previous position the concepts of 'upwards', 'advance', etc., become meaningless;

(ii) that the said process of cumulating knowledge is *endless* and hence the absolute truth, in the radical sense of the term, should be interpreted as the *limit* of a sequence (in the mathematical sense of the term), i.e. the limit which a sequence constantly approaches without ever reaching it (hence the comparison with any asymptote): that infinite character of the process of cognition (and hence also of truth treated as a process) is connected with the fact that the object of cognition is infinite, too (not only in the sense of an infinite number of elements and the relations among them, but also in the sense of incessant variability of those entities), so that reaching the limit of the absolute truth in one act of cognition would mean — to use Engels's metaphor in *Anti-Dühring* — the miracle of counting an infinite series.

Secondly, when we ask about the cumulative nature of human knowledge we may mean human knowledge in a restricted sense of the term, namely a *specified scientific theory*. Hence, while using the same formulations, we may be asking about something quite different from that which Engels had in mind, i.e. not whether mankind knows more and more by cumulating partial, and hence relative, truths, but whether scientific theories develop in a continuous manner (*evolutionally*, in a strictly defined sense of the word), or whether — to use the language of Hegelian dialectics — quantitative changes turn into qualitative ones, which break the continuity of the development of a given theory (i.e. *revolutionarily*, also in a strictly defined sense of the word). Historians of science, and all reasonable watchers of the development of science, interpreted as specified scientific theories, point to their non-cumulative, and hence non-evolutionary, but revolutionary development. No reasonable person, familiar with the history of science, will deny the Copernican revolution in astronomy and various revolutions in any other disciplines. Such revolutions are not always so important as the Copernican, but they are revolutions none the less.

This is what Thomas S. Kuhn had in mind when he wrote in the continuation of the passage quoted above: 'The same historical research that displays the difficulties in isolating individual inventions and discoveries gives ground for profound doubts about the cumulative process through which these individual contributions to science were thought to have been compounded.'[55]

Thus human knowledge, scientific cognition, science, are both cumulative and non-cumulative (revolutionary). Is this a contradiction? Not at all. Even Aristotle knew that there is a contradiction only if we have to do with an affirmative and a negative statement which both refer to one and the same object and in one and the same respect. In our case, the appearance of a contradiction emerges only if we overlook the fact that — despite analogous formulations — we have to do with two different questions. If we grasp this, we see complementarity, and not contradiction.

To a Marxist the issue is just trivial if he really takes the Marxist standpoint on the theory of cognition. I will take the liberty to note (I have written on that more extensively elsewhere[56]) that 'to be a Marxist' means not only to declare one's membership in Marxism as a school, but also to satisfy at least two additional conditions: to know the doctrine adherence to which one declares, and if one modifies or rejects its theses, to do that openly and by using scientific arguments. Now, for such an interpretation of the statement 'I am a Marxist', a Marxist will see no problem in stating both that human knowledge is cumulative, and that there are revolutions in the development of the various theories, and that in this sense human knowledge is not cumulative. He will accordingly not oppose today's science to its past as an 'ideological' falsehood, and will understand — which is obvious also to Kuhn, a non-Marxist — that scientific convictions which belong to the past are not just myths or 'ideologies', because a Marxist interprets the process of human cognition as an infinite one, which consists of partial truths that accumulate as that process continues.

We have thus concluded our analysis of one issue only, but one which is essential for Althusser's reasoning, namely the relation between science and ideology. We shall now formulate our conclusions briefly.

First, we have found, in Althusser's statements, such conceptual vagueness concerning the fundamental terms *science* and *ideology*, and, as a result, such glaring contradictions in what he says on the subject that discussion becomes pointless. Marginal comments could be made on the issues he raises, but no discussion with him is possible, because his standpoint can be understood only as his emotional response to his political traumas.

Secondly, we have found that Althusser's standpoint is at variance with Marxist theory on many fundamental issues although he passes those obvious discrepancies with silence. He is also unable to realize how the language of Marxist theory is now being used in analyses concerned with science and ideology.

Thirdly, when analysing Althusser's standpoint in relation to the issue under consideration we are not in a position to notice any essential influence on him of the structuralist theory and method. He does use the term *structure*, but without any close connection with the main problems he raises, except for one case in which he tries to define ideology as a structure which is lived, but not via human consciousness. This smacks of idealism, but it certainly does not in any way discredit structuralism, at least in its rational form, associated with the new classical structuralist theory in linguistics.

Fourthly, Althusser's reflections on ideology and science disregard the recent literature of the subject, which makes his comments inadequate.

Anti-empiricism or Idealism?

In the preceding section we subjected Althusser's conception to immanent analysis: our intention was to find out what he meant by the terms *ideology* and *science* and how he handled them. For all the negative results of that analysis the essentials of the problem must be examined. A person may use concepts which lack precision, but he may nevertheless raise real problems and formulate proposals that deserve attention. This is a procedure which, in the case of a philosopher, is neither good nor commendable, but it cannot be dismissed. This is why we have to pass from the analysis of the semantic apparatus used by Althusser to the content analysis of his focal demand which calls for extracting the scientific content of the Marxist theory and for the removal of ideological impurities. What then, is his point?

To answer this question we must, of course, make a selection of the problems raised by Althusser, if only for their number. This inevitably introduces the subjective factor in the form of the assessment of the relative importance of the various problems in Althusser's system. For instance, I leave aside issues in the history of philosophy, except for the problem of the 'break' in Marx's philosophical production, the break which, as Althusser suggests, is to account for the fact that we have in fact to do with two different philosophers, and not with one Marx. My disregarding certain problems may evoke protests, but no one will presumably object to my attaching special importance to the following three issues, which will be discussed as decisive for Althusser's views, and which may be labelled: anti-empiricism, anti-historicism and anti-humanism. These are the focal point on which Althusser attacks the Marxist theory which, in his opinion, has become ideology-dominated; this also explains the negative formulation of those labels, reflected by the prefix *anti-*. Althuser holds that not only does not Marxism stand for empiricism, but that it represents an anti-empirical approach; the same applies, in Althusser's opinion, to the relation which the Marxist theory bears to historicism and humanism. My intention, on the contrary, is to demonstrate that, on each of these points, Althusser's views are erroneous and at variance with the fundamental theses of Marxist philosophy.

We shall begin with the issue of empiricism, because this will take us immediately to the very foundations of philosophy, namely to gnosiology.

What have Althusser and his structuralist followers to say on this point? Their argument is very simple: empiricism is an ideological philosophy, the liberation from which is one of the markers of the said break, the caesura which separates the mature (scientifically minded) Marx from the young (ideologically minded) Marx as the author of his early writings. According to Althusser, the Marxist theory interpreted as a science means anti-empiricism.

It must be said that Althusser's statement on the relation Marxism bears to empiricism must astonish, and even embarrass, a competent reader, both because of its being in contradiction with statements made by the founders of the Marxist theory, and because of what we know about the philosophical meaning of the term *empiricism*. It is accordingly reasonable to suspect that Althusser, who, as we have seen, does not err on the side of excessive concern about the semantic precision of the terms he uses, must have given the word *empiricism* some special meaning, different from that adopted by the classics of Marxist theory and also different from the usage now current in philosophical writings. What then is that meaning he has in mind? I shall try to explain this by analysing those texts by Althusser in which he gives vent to his anti-empiricist opinions, but before doing that I will show why we are astonished by the way Althusser uses the term *empiricism*, and in particular by his claim that Marxism is anti-empiricist in nature.

Let us begin with some quotations from works written by Marx and Engels. Such quotations could be multiplied, but this is not a study in the history of Marxist philosophical terminology, and a few quotations chosen by way of example will suffice to explain our astonishment. One of them is a fragment from Engels' letter to Marx; it is true that, being dated 19 November 1844, it is earlier than the notorious break, so cherished by Althusser, and hence he could argue that the letter still comes from the ideological period in Marx's life, but it must be said plainly that the letter is very symptomatic from the point of view of the problems we are concerned with, and other quotations will help us to decide whether the language of the mature Marx had brought any change in this matter. Engels wrote to Marx about Stirner's work *Der Einzige und sein Eigentum* (The Individual and His Properties) that was about to appear, and in particular about Stirner's discussion with Feuerbach about the interpretation of 'man' by the latter.

> Stirner is right when he rejects Feuerbach's 'man', at least that found in *Das Wesen des Christentums* (The Essence of Christendom); Feuerbach's 'man' originates from God, Feuerbach moved from God to 'man', and this is why, self-evidently, his 'man' is still surrounded by a theological halo of abstraction. The proper way of reaching 'man' is in the reverse direction. *We must start*

from the 'ego', from the empirical individual in his flesh, not in order to stick
in that, as Stirner does, but in order to rise to 'man'. 'Man' always remains
ghostlike as long as he is not based on the empirical man. To put it briefly, if
our ideas, and in particular our 'man', are to be something real, we must start
from empiricism and materialism; what is general must be deduced from what
is particular, and not from itself or from the air in the manner of Hegel. . . .
And besides all that theoretical talking bores me more and more, and I am
angered by every word which is still to be wasted on the subject of 'man', and
by every line which must be written or read against theology and abstraction
and against vulgar materialism. For to be concerned with all those mirages –
for even a man who is not yet a reality is a mirage until he becomes real – and
to be concerned with concrete, living issues, with historical development and
its results are two quite different things.[57]

But let us cross Althusser's barrier: it is 1849 and Marx publishes his
lectures, delivered, it is true, in 1847, but prepared for the press in 1849,
and hence after *The Communist Manifesto*, and entitled *Hired Labour and
Capital*. Marx begins his work thus:

We have been blamed from various quarters for not having presented the
economic relations, which form the material foundation of the class and
national struggles today. We were raising the issue of those relations in the
intended manner in those cases only in which they imposed themselves
directly in political conflicts. It was necessary, above all, to watch the class
struggle in the everyday current of history and to demonstrate *empirically, on
the already existing historical data which were emerging everyday anew*, that
the yoking by the defeat of its adversaries, the bourgeois republicans in
France. . . .[58]

In this case, too, like in that of Engels' letter cited above, we find,
above all, the word *empirical* used in the sense of 'given by experience',
'based on experience', which agrees with the basic meaning of that word as
accepted to this day. Let us, therefore, move further into Marx's maturity
and look into his fundamental work, i.e. *Capital*. I quote a fragment from
the *Afterword to the Second German Edition*, where Marx approvingly
quotes the words of the author of the Russian review of *Capital* (1872)
who, as he put it, 'pictures what he takes to be actually my method, in this
striking and . . . generous way':

Consequently, Marx only troubles himself about one thing, to show, by
rigid scientific investigation, the necessity of successive determinate orders of
social conditions, and *to establish*, as impartially as possible, *the facts that
serve him for fundamental starting-points*. . . . That is to say, that not the idea,
but the material phenomenon alone can serve as its (the criticism of culture)
starting-point. Such an inquiry will confine itself to *the confrontation and the
comparison of a fact, not with ideas, but with another fact*. For this inquiry,
the one thing of moment is, that *both facts be investigated as accurately as*

possible, and that they actually form, each with respect to the other, different moments of an evolution. . . .[59]

This clearly imputes empiricism to Marx, and Marx says to this that the author of the review pictured his method in a generous way!

Finally a quotation from Engels' *Anti-Dühring*, and hence a late work (dated 1878), in which not words but formulations attack the *a priori* approach from the standpoint of genetic empiricism, and which, by accepting a specified theory of abstraction, is in open contradiction with what Althusser says on the subject.

> Like the basic forms of existence, the whole of pure mathematics, too, can be substantiated, as Herr Dühring thinks, in an *a priori* manner, that is, without reference to the empirical data provided by the external worlds, can be deduced from one's mind. . . . Yet it is not true that in the case of pure mathematics human reason is concerned exclusively with its own products and fancies. The concepts of number and (geometric) figure are taken not from nowhere, but from the real world.[60]

Many similar quotations, in which the terms *empiricism* and *empirical* occur in their positive sense, can be found in the works by Marx and Engels. Their content refutes nativism and the *a priori* approach and thus implicitly points to the empiricist standpoint of their authors; they also expand that theory of abstraction which extracts that which is general from that which is particular, the theory which Althusser labels derogatorily as 'ideological empiricist philosophy'. In this connection we had better not mention Lenin, who erred very much in that respect by referring to practice and to incessantly recurring experience — the approach which Althusser ridicules without indicating the addressee, but allowing him to be known perfectly well.

What I shall say now is a school-level lecture on the meanings of the term *empiricism*. My doing so is justified by the extravagance with which Althusser interprets the sense of that word. My intention is to intensify that astonishment which — in view of Althusser's assurances that Marxism is anti-empirical — must have already been evoked by the quotations above. Let us therefore see what it means to take the anti-empiricist standpoint in philosophy, if the term *empiricism* is taken not in a whimsically adopted sense, but in its philosophical meaning.

The problem of empiricism and the opposing trends — nativism in one case and the *a priori* approach in the other — emerges in philosophy in connection with the controversy over the sources of human cognition. The problem takes on the form of two different but interconnected issues, that of the *origin* of cognition, and that of the *paths that lead to true cognition.* In the former case, the controversy is between genetic empiricism and nativism, otherwise termed genetic rationalism; in the latter, the controversy is between methodological empiricism (otherwise termed the *a posteriori* approach) and the *a priori* approach (otherwise called methodological rationalism).

Genetic empiricism claims that human mind shapes cognition in the light of experience in the broad sense of the latter word (that trend, which formed the foundations of gnosiology, has its classical representatives in John Locke and David Hume); in some cases genetic empiricism was associated with sensualism (whose classical representative was Condillac), i.e. with the thesis that all cognition comes through senses in the form of sense data. Genetic empiricism has its opponents (*has*, because this applies not only to the past, but to the present as well) in the advocates of genetic rationalism (nativism), who propound the doctrine of innate ideas, i.e. ideas which are independent of experience and are based on the structure of the human mind (the doctrine has its classical representatives in Plato, Descartes, Leibniz, and, in a more intricate form, in Kant).

Methodological empiricism claims that true cognition is always based on experience, and accordingly only accepts *a posteriori* truths as generalizations of a special kind (which is closely connected with the inductive theory of abstraction); moderate empiricism admits the possibility of cognition based on reasoning alone when it comes to analytic judgements. Genetic rationalism (the *a priori* approach) claims that true cognition dissociated from all experience is possible (Kant's *a priori* approach, Husserl's eidetic cognition); it has a special form in conventionalism, which in its radical form (Duhem, Le Roy, Ajdukiewicz, and — in a different interpretation — Vaihinger and Dingler) claims that all cognition, including what is termed *faits bruts* (bare facts) in science, is a result of convention.

If we now ask on whose side modern materialists, including representatives of Marxist materialism, stand, our reply — quite obvious and confirmed by the history of philosophy — is that they defend both genetic empiricism against nativism and methodological empiricism against the *a priori* approach. This applies *in toto* to the standpoint adopted by the founders of Marxism, who very forcefully criticized the *a priori* approach;

that was due to the then topical issues in gnosiology, connected mainly with the Kantian influence. Their position was thus that of methodological empiricism; Engels in his *Anti-Dühring* and *The Dialectics of Nature*, and Lenin in his *Materialism and Empiriocriticism* many a time unambiguously declared themselves in favour of empiricism. I claim more: in philosophy, the materialistic standpoint cannot be combined with any other position than the empiricist one, unless one imparts to the term *empiricism* some other meaning than that which is current in philosophical terminology. This is why Engels wrote to Marx in his letter already quoted above: 'To put it briefly, if our ideas, and in particular our "man", are to be something real, we must start from empiricism and materialism; what is general must be deduced from what is particular, and not from itself or from the air in the manner of Hegel.' Engels strictly associated the materialistic standpoint with empiricism, and also with a specified theory of abstraction and the theory of reflection.

But what, then, is the meaning ascribed to the term *empiricism* by Althusser and his followers if, while declaring themselves in favour of the Marxist philosophy, and hence accepting the standpoint of materialism, they at the same time consider it possible, and even necessary, to reject empiricism? Are they followers of nativism or the *a priori* approach? No, this is not the case. In accordance with our supposition, formulated at the beginning of this section, they use the word *empiricism* in a different sense, which diverges from that universally adopted, also in the Marxist literature of the subject. In what sense then? Here are some quotations which answer this question.

We begin, of course, with Althusser himself. In his essay 'On the Materialistic Dialectic' he writes:

> Contrary to the ideological illusions — illusions which are not 'naive', not mere 'aberrations', but necessary and well-founded as ideologies — of empiricism or sensualism, a science never works on an existence whose essence is pure immediacy and singularity ('sensations' or 'individuals'). It always works on something 'general', even if this has the form of a 'fact'. . . . It does not 'work' on a purely objective 'given', that of pure and absolute 'facts'. On the contrary, its particular labour consists of *elaborating its own scientific facts* through a critique of the *ideological 'facts'* elaborated by an earlier ideological theoretical practice.[61]

Let us deliberately disregard all side issues, and above all Althusser's fancy philosophical language, and let us try to understand the meaning he ascribes to his rejection of empiricism. Since, according to Althusser, science is incompatible with empiricism, we have to refer to his statements about what science is, and what it is not, to find out how Althusser sees empiricism.

First, according to Althusser, empiricism says that the subject-matter of science is existence, pure immediacy, and singularity.

Secondly, according to him, empiricism claims that science works on a purely objective 'given', on pure and absolute 'facts'; he claims that the contrary is true: scientific work consists in elaborating its own scientific facts through a critique of ideological 'facts'.

For the time being let us leave this statement without comment and let us pass to another statement of his, which contributes new elements to our comprehension of the meaning which Althusser ascribes to the word *empiricism.*

In the same essay, a few pages later, we read in connection with Althusser's analysis of Marx's views at the time when Marx had renounced Feuerbach's philosophy and his vocabulary, that

> he (Marx) had consciously abandoned the empiricist ideology which had allowed him to maintain that a scientific concept is produced exactly as the general concept of fruit 'should be' produced, by an abstraction acting on concrete fruits. When Marx says in the *Introduction* that any process of scientific knowledge begins from the abstract, from a generality, and not from the real concrete, he demonstrates the fact that he has actually broken with ideology and with the mere denunciation of speculative abstraction, that is, with its presuppositions.[62]

Let us record Althusser's two ideas formulated in the passage quoted above.

First, empiricism is an ideology which maintains that scientific concepts are produced by abstraction of the general from that which is singular and concrete.

Secondly (this applies not to empiricism, but to Marxism), Marx renounced the ideology of speculative abstraction (obviously, not only the words, but also the opinion they express, are Althusser's) when he stated in his *Introduction* to *Grundrisse* that all scientific cognition begins from the abstract, from the general, and not from the real concrete.

We still abstain from comments and confine ourselves to reporting on Althusser's ideas on empiricism; as I have introduced a new issue, namely that of the connections between empiricism and Marxism, I must add, in order to avoid misunderstandings, that this issue, as will emerge later, is closely related to the problems we are concerned with, and that there is a point in taking it into consideration here. I anticipate our analysis of that issue, especially when it comes to Althusser's interpretation of the 'Introduction', to say that his interpretation consists in the essential incomprehension of the text he cites; this confirms the assertion that demanding that *Capital* be read does not in itself prove the ability of putting that into effect. *Quod demonstrandum est.*

Althusser's opinions, as quoted above, were clearly proposed by his followers during the above-mentioned discussion held at the Centre d'Etudes Socialistes. Of course, Althusser can disclaim responsibility for that, because the disputants were not his close collaborators. This is true, but their statements were just paraphrases of Althusser's formulations, they go in the same direction, and they enable us to grasp the meaning imparted to Althusser's far-from-clear formulations by those Marxist intellectuals who draw inspiration from his statements.

To anticipate quotations we may say that all those disputants who agreed with Althusser meant anti-empiricism to be the negation of the opinion that science operates in the sphere of *ready* facts, and defended the opinion that science *produces* facts. François Châtelet, who delivered the introductory paper on 'Science Versus Ideology', at the very outset posed the question: 'What is science?' And this is how he answered it: 'In my opinion, science begins at the moment when the mind comes to realize that facts do not exist. Empiricism — both classical and revived — is always based on facts; its followers hold that there are given facts. i.e. events, which impose as having their unambiguous meaning.'[63]

And during the discussion he added a very significant comment: 'If Althusser has his *bête noire*, then that is empiricism, and I, too, in my paper delivered today tried to debunk empiricism, that is facts which speak for themselves, from all points of view.'[64]

F. Châtelet's further statement shows where that anti-empiricism takes him. When coming out against the thesis on the existence of pure data, which are integrated in science into a system of thought that imparts meaning to what exists, he says: 'Marx formulated his theory not by roaming about in factories, but in the course of his polemics with texts written by Feuerbach, German romanticists, and representatives of the historical school of law, etc.'[65]

Poor Marx, who believed, when writing his *Afterword* to *Capital*, that he had just observed facts; poor Marx, who availed himself of the services of a legion of such roamers; who drew one of the first questionnaires in the history of empirical sociology in order to use it in his study of the international worker movement; who fully approved of the pedestrian empirical research conducted by Engels and adopted by the latter as the foundation for his *Condition of the Working Class in England*, etc. But we are concerned here not with Marx, but with the consequences of that anti-empiricism of Althusser and his followers.

What do they mean when they talk about empiricism? In any case not what people who are competent in philosophy have in mind, i.e. neither genetic nor methodological empiricism; and not what Marx and Engels had in mind when using the terms *empiricism* and *empirical* to express approval of the intellectual trends so labelled. As we have seen, Althusser interprets the term *empiricism* otherwise. We shall soon try to grasp his interpretation more clearly. But even at this point we have to express disapproval of the odd habit (the same applies to his use of the words *anti-historicism* and *anti-humanism*) of using words which have their well-established meanings in the history of philosophy in general, and in the history of Marxist philosophy in particular, in different senses without making the provision that they are used in such a special sense. This confuses not only the readers, but also, and even above all, the author himself, who succumbs to the automystification that his polemics and his supposed victories in disputes pertain to opinions to which they are in fact not applicable because the terms used are the same, but the meanings given to them are different from what they are supposed to be.

There are no natural links between the words of a language and the things and events they denote, and this is why we may change the sense of words and give words new meanings, provided, however, that this is done consciously and that the listeners and/or readers are explicitly informed about such changes. Further, the rule is that we should not change the received meanings of words, especially in the case of the language of science, if such changes are not necessary. It is true that when we want to say something new we need not resort to old terms, we may coin new ones. This is just the case of Althusser's *anti-empiricism*: when using this word he means something other than philosophers ordinarily do, but he does not say that explicitly. As a result of this he misleads others, but at the same time he himself falls a victim of mystification, because he begins to believe himself that he means *empiricism* in the current sense of the term. Althusser wants to say something *new* with reference to issues in the Marxist theory, but instead of doing that explicitly, by introducing adequate words, he uses the old term, but he distorts its received meaning.

What do then Althusser and his followers mean when they use the term *empiricism* and when they join the battle for the scientific nature of the Marxist theory under the banner of anti-empiricism? The problem reduces, in accordance with the ideas drawn from Althusser's works and reflected in the quotations given above, to the following points.

First, Althusser claims that empiricism is a doctrine which states that science uses direct and singular data which follow from pure and absolute facts (Châtelet is clear on this point: he says that they follow from ready facts, in the sense that they speak for themselves, impose on us, and have an unambiguous sense).

Secondly, Althusser claims empiricism to be equivalent to such a theory of abstraction which extracts the general from the particular.

Thirdly, he claims that empiricism always starts from the real, the concrete, and denies the fact that science starts from general concepts and that the levels of generality may vary.

On reading this, and on extracting the meaning of these formulations, we may say that, unlike the case of the relation between science and ideology, Althusser now gives precise meaning to the concept he uses: we not only know what he means, but we also understand his concern for a certain philosophical issue. For behind his anti-empiricist harangue we find a real problem of great philosophical importance, which we shall discuss later. The serious difficulty is that Althusser does not speak about empiricism in the accepted sense of the term, but about empiricism in the sense he has given that word himself. Since, however, he neither says that explicitly nor — to make matters worse — notices the fact himself, a general confusion ensues: Althusser thinks he criticizes empiricism in general, while in fact he criticizes what he himself means by empiricism and which do not coincide with what is called empiricism in the sense accepted in philosophy. This is why he loses the sight of other *anti*'s, namely anti-nativism and the anti-*a priori* approach, which by definition are specific to empiricism proper. To be against those *anti*'s would mean to accept nativism and the *a priori* approach, i.e. genetic and methodological rationalism, which cannot be linked with materialism in philosophy and with the acceptance of the standpoint of specialized disciplines on these issues. I do not suspect Althusser and his followers of that: their respect for physics as the model for science in general is even exaggerated. The whole thing is just a misunderstanding, because in that empiricism which Althusser criticizes we have to do with something else: a criticism of the *positivist* idea of constructing science as a mosaic that consists of facts treated as minute pieces of stone or glass (to use Lucien Febvre's simile in his criticism of the positivist concept of *histoire historisante*) Why, then, not call that something by its name, why hide it behind the screen of a cryptonym which conceals the real subject-matter under a name which means something else?

But is not that to which Althusser refers to be entered on the debit side of empiricism, even though the essential characteristics of that trend have been lost by him? No, it is not, for it is not true that empiricism takes ready facts as its starting-point, because empiricism is not identical with positivism. Positivism did accept a version of empiricism, but the converse does not hold. The obstacles encountered by the empiricists were usually to be sought elsewhere, namely in the concept of experience. Nor is it true that the empiricists, when adopting the real concrete as their starting-point, fail to understand that in science we always use some generalizations; the latter thing follows, say, from Marx's 'Introduction', to which Althusser refers; the real concrete, e.g. the category of population, is a generalization.

It is true, however, that the theory of abstraction which Althusser criticizes is characteristic of empiricism. But this does not alter my general objection that Althusser uses the term *empiricism* in a non-legitimate manner as he passes over in silence the main problems connected with that intellectual trend.

Althusser and his followers do not attack empiricism, even if they believe that. What they do attack is a specific form of the theory of reflection, hidden under the cryptonim *empiricism*. That this is so can be seen not only from what they say (cf. their principal argument against what they call empiricism, their veiled mentions of 'reflection' and of the sensualist theory of impressions as the starting-point of cognition), but also from what they do not say. It is unbelievable that such a learned Marxist scholar as Althusser, who certainly did read not only the works of

Engels and Lenin, but also contemporary discussions on the subject, should not know that there are Marxists who maintain that Marxist gnosiology just means the theory of reflection. Of course, Althusser knows all that perfectly well. Why then does he not say anything on the matter; why does he not, when writing about Marxism, even mention the name of that theory? The objection of accepting readily available facts is just aimed at *that* theory, although in its vulgarized, mechanistic version.

Let us revert to the above-mentioned issue of the principal troubles of Althusser and his school, to that which is the real problem hidden behind the tangle of anti-empiricism. Their point is to say plainly that science does not consist in collecting readily available facts, that a scientific fact is always a mental construction in the emergence of which an important role is always played by the scientist, who thereby contributes the subjective factor to the process of cognition. This is a correct idea, and I side with those who *as Marxists* campaign for that truth (to which I have given testimony in my writings[66]). In their campaigning Marxists find an obstacle in the form of the *vulgarized* theory of reflection, which – while it sometimes enigmatically refers to the role of the subjective factor in cognition – blocks the path that leads to the understanding of the role of the scientist in the process of cognition, in the construction of scientific facts. What is the conclusion for a Marxist philosopher who has grasped that truth? He has to refute the vulgarized, mechanistic version of the theory of reflection, which is based on the model of 'ready facts and cognition as the mechanical reflection of these', by formulating a theory of reflection based on a model which takes into account the active role of the cognizing subject in the process of cognition and eliminates ready facts, although it does not eliminate objective reality. The latter point is of immense importance, for one cannot be a Marxist and cannot adopt a Marxism-based materialistic philosophy if one completely rejects the theory of reflection: in such a case the only choice left is the adoption of the idealist standpoint, because the repudiation of the theory of reflection eliminates objective reality, which is then claimed to be created by man, and not just cognized by him.

Althusser has, for some reason, decided to disregard the problem (he must have known it), and has, for some reason, camouflaged it as anti-empiricism, and as a result has lost sight of the necessity of retaining the theory of reflection as an element of gnosiology. All this has taken place in a roundabout way, including mystification of texts. For in order to avoid the reefs of the theory of reflection (although he is prudent enough not to mention it at all), and in order to win over Marx as his ally in his dislike of facts and a supporter of his idea of the active role of the scientist in the process of cognition Althusser reads into Marx's works what is not there and constructs the theory of two objects of cognition, a theory which is of his own invention. Yet we have to make a distinction between two questions: (a) what is really to be found in Marx, to whom Althusser ascribes his own conception, and (b) what that conception represents from the point of view of Marxist philosophy, for although it has been erroneously ascribed to Marx, it does exist as Althusser's conception, from which the latter draws far-reaching conclusions.

We accordingly confront what Althusser ascribed to Marx with the formulation to be found in Marx's text of 1857, to which Althusser refers. The conclusions drawn by Althusser from that text were received by his followers with an outburst of euphoria. I do suspect, however, that they know the text in question, namely the text of the 'Introduction' to *Grundrisse*, from the edition of *Contribution to the Critique of Political Economy*, to which it is appended,[67] without having studied thoroughly the text of *Grundrisse* itself (probably because of the strange fortunes of that work, which was an outline of *Capital*, but was first published only in 1939 and 1941, in two parts; World War II practically prevented the study of the book of over 1000 pages, and the first post-war edition in German appeared in 1953, and its French language version in 1967). If they had studied it they would be far from feeling euphoric about it. I find much satisfaction in vivisecting their pet ideas by making use of *Grundrisse*: for we see the mature Marx, Marx of the period of *Capital*, who raises the problems and uses the language of *Manuscripts* as if he had just read them anew and wanted to incorporate them in his new work; we see Marx of the period of humanistic ideology, with all his alienations, reifications, etc. But for the time being let us stick to the text of 'Introduction' and let us look in it for the theory of two objects of cognition.

Let us first listen to Althusser and see what he has found in the text. He formulates his opinions casually in many places in his works. I have chosen two passages from *Reading Capital*, because — as I see it — they express Althusser's ideas most clearly and forcefully.

The text of the *1857 Introduction* which distinguishes between the real object and the object of knowledge also distinguishes between their processes, and what is crucial, brings out a difference in *order* in the genesis of these two processes. . . . This distinction obviously has great bearing on one of the most disputed questions in *Capital*, the question as to whether there is an identity between the *so-called 'logical' order* (or order of 'deduction' of the categories in *Capital*) and the *real 'historical' order*. . . . I propose to pose this question (this problem) not in the field of an ideological problematic, but in the field of the Marxist theoretical problematic with its distinction between the real object and the object of knowledge. . . .[68]

The second quotation, which contributes a new element, important for the understanding of Althusser's standpoint, is related to Engels' 'Introduction' to Vol. II of *Capital*. By referring to the history of chemistry, namely the dropping of the phlogiston theory following the discovery of oxygen, Engels shows what is Marx's achievement in the theory of surplus value as compared with what had been done by his predecessors, Smith and Ricardo. Althusser, who many a time blamed Engels for his succumbing to empiricism, the empiricist theory of abstraction, etc., in the same spirit criticizes Engels' statements in the 'Introduction'. This brief explanation is necessary for the reconstruction of the context of the next quotation, which I do not want to make too long. From our point of view the important thing is not what Engels did say, nor is there any need to support him; the important thing is what Althusser has to say on the issue, for his theory of two objects of cognition reappears here, although in a somewhat different light.

> We have already noted the ambiguities of his conception on this point of which he was very much aware: they can all be reduced to the empiricist confusion between the object of knowledge and the real object. Engels clearly fears that by risking himself beyond the (imaginary) security of the empiricist thesis he may lose the guarantees he obtains by proclaiming a *real* identity between the object of knowledge and the real object. He has difficulty in imagining what he is saying, although he does say it and the history of science reveals it to him at every step: the fact that the process of production of a knowledge necessarily proceeds by the constant transformation of its (conceptual) object; that it is precisely the effect of this transformation, which is the same thing as the history of knowledge, that it produces a *new* knowledge (a new object of knowledge) which still concerns the *real object*, knowledge of which is deepened precisely by this reorganization of the object of knowledge.[69]

Let us now try to extract the main theses contained in these two quotations.

First, Althusser claims (in the first of these two quotations) that Marx in his 1857 'Introduction' made a clear distinction between the real object and the object of knowledge (the object of cognition) and that this distinction is an element of the set of theoretical problems with which Marx was concerned.

Secondly, Althusser claims (in the second quotation) that the thesis on the real identity of the real object and the object of knowledge is erroneous and originates from the empiricist confusion of these two objects.

Thirdly, Althusser claims (in the second quotation, too) that the production of a new knowledge is the production of a new object of knowledge, whose transformations enable us incessantly to acquire a better knowledge of the real object. (In addition we learn — from a passage that follows the second quotation — that Lenin took the same stand in his *Materialism and Empiriocriticism*.)

On my part I maintain that: first, Marx did *not* make, in his 1857 'Introduction', any distinction between the real object and the object of cognition, and that the whole thing has been invented by Althusser; second, the idea of two objects, as defended by Althusser, is idealistic and marked by all the deficiencies of Kant's distinction between *noumena* and *phenomena*.

The proof will be given in the above order.

The first issue can, and must, be settled on the basis of an analysis of Marx's writings. Before, however, we pass to the proper text, i.e. that of the 'Introduction' to *Grundrisse*, we must refer to another text, without which the problem at issue cannot be understood. It is at least strange that Althusser and his followers, who specialize in reading *Capital*, have overlooked that passage, essential for the comprehension of the method adopted by Marx in *Capital*.

Marx stresses there that the method of exposition of the subject-matter (beginning with such abstract categories as value) *differs* from the method of investigation. This is the counterpart of his statements on what is concrete in the sense of the unity of diversities, and on the moving upwards from the abstract to the concrete, statements to be found in his 'Introduction' to *Grundrisse*, to which Althusser refers.

> *Of course the method of presentation must differ in form from that of inquiry. The latter has to appropriate the material in detail*, to analyse its different forms of development, to trace out their inner connection. Only after this work is done, can the actual movement be adequately described. If

this is done successfully, *if the life of the subject-matter is ideally reflected as in a mirror, then it may appear as if we had before us a mere* a priori *construction.*[70]

Marx here upholds explicitly the *principle of empiricism* in research (and points to the illusion of the *a priori* nature of constructions in science). This explains his approval of the previously cited opinion of his Russian reviewer, who presented the author of *Capital* as an empiricist.

But this passage, taken together with the above-cited formulation on the dialectics of the concrete and the abstract, to be found in the 'Introduction' to *Grundrisse*, sheds additional light upon an important issue: the method of *presentation of results*, as used in *Capital*, is not to be confused with the method of *investigation*, which yielded the results presented in that work. The researcher must follow the tortuous path of the study of facts (in the sense of objective reality, as Marx recalled many a time in the 'Introduction' quoted by Althusser), he has to take the painstaking course of the abstract elements (formulations) which combine to form that concrete,[71] but when he presents the *results* of his investigations he need not take his reader along the same course; on the contrary, he may start from the end, from the results he has obtained. But one cannot – as Marx warns both in the 'Introduction' and in the already cited 'Afterword' to *Capital* – succumb to the illusion that human thought creates reality: it 'reproduces' or 'assimilates' it (the terminology used in 'Introduction') or 'reflects' it (the term used in the 'Afterword').

We now pass to the text to which Althusser refers. The reader is expected to approve a lengthy quotation, for we have to follow Althusser attentively in search of those two objects which he claims to have found in that text. Regardless of whether we find them, the text is of great importance for the comprehension of the problem we are discussing now, and provides data for further reflection. Because of the significance of that passage it is also quoted in a footnote in its original version, because even a best translation is not always sufficient, and in the case of certain subtleties, which are encountered here, even delicate shades of meaning must be taken into consideration (compare the still unended controversy over the translation of *Theses on Feuerbach*). Making the quotation that long is necessary because Althusser himself, despite the far-reaching conclusions he draws from the text in question, does not quote the appropriate passages to support his claims, but simply reports on what he supposes to be their content and, contrary to his customary procedure, limits quotations to those passages which refer to secondary issues.

> When we consider a given country politico-economically, we begin with its population, its distribution among classes; town, country, the coast, the different branches of production, export and import, annual production and consumption, commodity prices, etc.
>
> It seems to be correct to begin with the real and the concrete, with the real precondition, thus to begin, in economics, with e.g. the population, which is the foundation and the subject of the entire social act of production. However, on closer examination this proves false. The population is an abstraction if I leave out, for example, the classes of which it is composed. These classes in turn are an empty phrase if I am not familiar with the elements on which they rest, e.g. wage labour, capital etc. . . . The concrete is concrete because it is the concentration of many determinations, hence unity of the diverse. It appears in the process of thinking, therefore, as a process of concentration, as a result, not as a point of departure, even though it is the point of departure in reality and hence also the point of departure for observation (*Anschauung*) and conception. Along the first path the full conception was evaporated to yield an abstract determination; along the second, the abstract determinations lead towards a reproduction of the concrete by way of thought . . . the method of rising from the abstract to the concrete is only the way in which thought appropriates the concrete, reproduces it as the concrete in the mind. But this is by no means the process by which the concrete itself comes into being. For example, the simplest economic category, say e.g. exchange value, presupposes population, moreover a population producing in specific relations; as well as a certain kind of family, of commune, of state, etc. It can never exist other than as an abstract, one-sided relation within an already given, concrete, living whole. As a category, by contrast, exchange value leads an antediluvian existence. Therefore, to the kind of consciousness . . . the movement of the categories appears as the real act of production . . . whose product is the world; and . . . this is correct in so far as the concrete totality is a totality of thoughts, concrete in thought, in fact a product of thinking and comprehending; but not in any way a product of the concept which thinks and generates itself outside or above observation and conception; a product, rather, of the working-up of observation and conception into concepts. The totality as it appears in the head, as a totality of thoughts, is a product of a thinking head, which appropriates the world in the only way it can, a way different from the artistic, religious, practical and mental appropriation of this world. The real subject retains its autonomous existence outside the head just as before. . . .[72]

Let us now pose the question: what ideas have we found in the passage quoted above, and which have we not found there? Let us answer it by beginning with the second part of the question.

First, in Marx's text there is not the slightest trace of the theory of two objects, whose discovery Althusser ascribes to himself. No words are used there that could be counterparts of the Althusser's French phrase *objet de connaissance* (object of knowledge); Marx uses such formulations as *das Reale* (the real), *das Konkrete* (the concrete), *das Abstrakte* (the abstract) and only once, *in fine* of the passage quoted above, *das reale Subjekt* (the real subject), but *nowhere* does he use the formulation *das Objekt der Erkenntnis* (the object of knowledge). And when it comes to the content of Marx's text, from which we could draw an implicit conclusion about Marx's standpoint on the issue of the theory of two objects, i.e. the real object and the object of knowledge (object of cognition), the passage includes the thesis, which is stressed several times, that there is *only one* concrete, i.e. real, object, which human thought assimilates (*sich aneignet*) and reproduces (*reproduziert*), but does not produce. Marx's statements are a sharp protest – which is understandable – against the idealistic tendency (specifically, the Hegelian idealism) to undermine the thesis that there is only one object, *das Konkrete* (the concrete), and that illusions develop when we fail to grasp that *human thought merely reproduces reality* as the individual perception of reality, and that this process of reproduction in no way means the process of the formation of reality. I think that all this need not be repeated here.

There is no doubt that ascribing to Marx the theory of two objects on the strength of the passages cited above consists in a mystification. But one could say that it is true that we cannot find that theory in Marx's text; it is not contained there either explicitly or implicitly; on the contrary, Marx stands clearly for the materialistic thesis of objective reality, which is *the only* concrete reality, and defends it against objective idealism. He also refers to *Gedankenkonkretum* (mental reality), which is a product of a thinking mind. But then if Althusser speaks about two objects is that not just his *façon de parler*? As a materialist he obviously accepts the category of objective reality and, for instance, in the previously cited passage from *Reading Capital* (cf. note 69) he states explicitly that the formation of new objects of knowledge always pertains to a real object, the knowledge' of which is improved by a transformation (*remaniement*) of the object of knowledge.

I can disregard the obvious inner contradiction of the said statement made by Althusser and its inconsistencies (if there are two objects, the real object and the object of knowledge, then what improved cognition can there be in addition to that object of knowledge, and what does that 'improved knowledge of the real object' mean if it is to take place *through the intermediary* of the object of knowledge, but is to be something other than that object?) and admit willingly that Althusser knows that there is no materialism without the acceptance of the objective existence of reality (it would be ridiculous to impute other opinions to him) and that he would firmly oppose the Hegelian thesis, criticized by Marx, that the real is a *result* of thinking, etc.

Are then these two objects just his *façon de parler*, unnecessary perhaps but rather innocuous, if we understand the intentions which underlie Althusser's statements? Not at all. This is not a *façon de parler*, but a theoretical assertion, incompatible with Marxian materialism, and the fact that Althusser is at the same time a Marxist philosopher and supports materialist theses merely shows that he is inconsistent and that his views are self-contradictory; it does *not* mean that the theory of two objects can be just dismissed as a *façon de parler* intended to be original.

Althusser understands those two objects literally (which is proved by all his statements on the issue, and in particular the last quoted one, in which Althusser blames Engels for maintaining that there is only one object, the real one, and human cognition which assimilates it in the asymptotic process of approaching the objective reality, because he *negates the theory of reflection*, not some form of it, but *the theory of reflection in general*) and hence he deviates from Marxism, which finds its external manifestation in his theory of two objects. Pointing to the fact that he, of course, accepts materialism is of no avail: yes, he does accept it, but at the same time deviates from it, for anyone who negates the existence of the cognitive relation that holds between the subject and the object, in accordance with which the object exists really (objectively), is not formed by the process of cognition, but is reproduced by it, strays away from Marxism and materialism (the terms used are: *reproduced* (Marx), *reflected* (Engels, with the full approval by Marx, who had read all Engels' philosophical works published during his lifetime), *mirrored* (Lenin)).

I have already said that the conception of two objects suffers from all the deficiencies of the Kantian distinction between *noumena* and *phenomena*. Regardless of Althusser's intentions, his is a Kantian idea, for if a person claims that, regardless of the existence of the real object, there is also a separate object of knowledge, which is not just a reflection or reproduction of that real object (with the preservation of all possible active functions of the object in the process of cognition), then he adopts the Kantian conception and the Kantian distinction between two objects. Kant consistently harmonized his theory of cognition with that conception; he accepted a *sui generis a priori* approach and nativism, and explained that the forms *a priori* perception make it possible to *construct* the object of cognition. Althusser, although himself an anti-empiricist, has not reached the precision characteristic of the anti-empiricist Kant: he could not have done so as an adherent of Marxism. But this accounts for the inner contradictions and inconsistencies in his statements.

The anti-empiricism propounded by Althusser makes us think of other paths of thought to be found in the above quotation from Marx's 'Introduction'. This time, however, we shall not speak of what is not there, but of what *is* there.

Thus, secondly, we find there Marx's extremely interesting ideas about the active role of the thinking subject in the process of cognition, ideas which prove clearly that the theory of reflection can, but need not, function as a mechanistic theory according to which reflection is interpreted as something passive, as a relation in which the cognizing mind is something like a mirror. This, as has been said, gives rise to the worries experienced by Althusser and his followers, and makes them protest against the doctrine of ready facts, because as Marxists they are, of course, not alarmed by the withering of the positivist doctrine within bourgeois philosophy; what alarms them is the inner problems of Marxism. As far as such a danger exists — and it does exist — combatting it is both rational and recommended, for the development not only of the modern gnosiology, but, most important, that of specialized disciplines, such as psychology, physiology of the brain, linguistic theory, etc., makes the vulgarized version of the theory of reflection simply inacceptable. Are we, then, to renounce the theory of reflection? I pose this important question again and my answer again is No, because the renunciation of the theory of reflection inevitably results in abandoning the doctrine of materialism, and hence Marxism as well. We simply have to turn to another, unvulgarized version of the theory. We find it in that passage of 'Introduction' with which we are now concerned.

Marx, who clearly adopts the standpoint of the theory of reflection (the term itself is of secondary importance: when Marx speaks about reality being reproduced by the mind, when he speaks about reality being assimilated by the mind, he refers to the theory of reflection), does not see any problem in accepting the active role of the subject in the process of cognition. He even does so in a radical manner: mental reality is a product of thinking, 'the totality as it appears in the head, as a totality of thoughts, is a product of a thinking head. . . .' He thus forcefully emphasizes the active role of thinking in the grasping of reality, in ordering it and organizing it as a whole. But, at the same time, he warns that this is the manner in which the mind assimilates concrete reality, but does not produce it: concrete reality continues to exist independently outside the human mind.

Thirdly, in connection with Althusser's anti-empiricist harangues and his seeking an ally in Marx, it is worthwhile noting that it was Marx who developed the empiricist theory of abstraction for which Althusser blames Engels. After stating that for consciousness the development of categories is like the creation of the world, which is justified as far as a concrete whole is a product of thinking, Marx adds: 'but not in any way a product of the concept which thinks and generates itself outside or above observation and conception; a product, rather of the working-up of observation and conception.' This is aimed directly at Hegel's philosophy, but indirectly at the anti-empiricist theory of abstraction presented by Althusser.

Fourthly, we have to point to the dialectic of the concrete and the abstract, as shown in the passage in question; this must again be done in connection with Althusser's anti-empiricist philippic. We have read several times in Althusser's texts that empiricism consists in starting, in research work, from the individual and the concrete, whereas in science we always start from generalizations and pass to their higher levels. This is why we are astonished to find the following 'unscientific' statement, written by the mature Marx after 'the break' at the very beginning of the 'Introduction': '*Individual* producing in society – hence socially deter-mined, individual production – is, of course, the point of departure.'[73]

In *Grundrisse* we find dozens of such statements, while earlier, in *The German Ideology*, Marx did not hesitate to say that in *research* (although not in the presentation of results) it is individuals who are the point of departure; he adds cautiously that he means individuals who live and act in society, but he nevertheless means *individuals*. He says so because they are concrete reality, and he did not hesitate to accept, as any empiricist would do, the concrete as the point of departure in research.

I have quoted this example only to bring the issue into better relief. Marx knows other real points of departure, to which he refers in his 'Introduction' when discussing the method of political economy: population, classes, etc. Marx considers them to be the real starting-point, and hence the real starting-point of viewing and representation.[74] Marx is not afraid of adopting such realities as his starting-point, he is not afraid of empiricism. He *is* afraid of transforming those concretes into abstractions if their complex nature is not realized, if the methodologically significant truth which states that 'that reality is reality because it is the concentration of many determinations, and hence unity of the diverse', is not realized.[75] And when he says that 'it (the concrete) is . . .', the word *is* functions as copula, i.e. in the sense of 'equals', 'is the same as'. It is not the case that science makes that reality become a unity: the reality *is* unity. Marx says that when he refers to the category 'population', which becomes an abstraction if we do not take into account the fact that population (not the concept *population*) really consists of classes, which in turn really are based on hired labour, etc. Just because concrete reality is really such a unity, the proper method of investigating the concrete is to start from various abstract concepts and to rise toward the concrete. This is, as Marx calls it, the method of reproducing the concrete by thinking, a way of assimilating the concrete mentally, and not the process by which the concrete comes into being. This is why the real and the concrete remain the real starting-point, and the paths of the mental reproduction of the real and the concrete, the paths of the mental assimilation of the whole (the unity) (in the process of thinking which reproduces the concrete as its own product) go upward from the abstract to the concrete. For Marx, the concrete is thus not anything worse than the abstract: its significance is not lesser, but, on the contrary, much greater, both as the real starting-point and as the unity of many definitions, when it comes to the reproduction of the concrete by the process of thinking. Althusser and his followers have failed to grasp the sense of the dialectic of the concrete and the abstract, because in their anti-empiricist euphoria they have shifted their analyses from the sphere of materialism, in which they belong in Marx's works, into the sphere of the idealist conception of two objects of cognition.

We have thus reached the end of our analysis of the meaning of

Althusser's anti-empiricism. In the face of the real *embarras de richesse* of problems which have emerged during that analysis we shall try to sum up its results in three points.

First, it turns out that Althusser's anti-empiricism is not aimed at empiricism as the philosophical trend commonly known by that name, but merely serves as a cryptonym of the criticism of the theory of ready facts, which theory assigns a passive role to cognition. The essence of empiricism is its opposition to rationalism as represented by nativism and the *a priori* approach. These issues are not raised by Althusser at all. The acceptance of the existence of ready facts, which are merely reflected in the process of cognition, is not typical of empiricism, although it can occur in the opinions of philosophers who otherwise claim adherence to empiricism. They are, on the contrary, characteristic of positivism and of the vulgarized, mechanistic variation of the theory of reflection. Althusser as a Marxist protests against the last-named theory, but when doing so he unnecessarily makes use of the cryptonym *empiricism* and does not state explicitly what he really means.

Secondly, Althusser, when opposing the idea of cognition as a passive reflection of facts which exist in a ready-made form, does not negate the vulgarized form of the theory of reflection; he negates that theory in general, and hence becomes involved in a contradiction with one of the fundamental theses of Marxist philosophy. His theory of two objects – the real object and the object of knowledge (cognition) – which clearly savours of Kantian philosophy and is burdened by its shortcomings, is a glaring manifestation of his attitude. Althusser's claim that his theory was first formulated by Marx in his 'Introduction' to *Grundrisse* is just a mystification: Marx did not formulate any theory like that either explicitly or implicitly. On the contrary, by pointing to the fact that the theory of reflection assigns an active role to the process of cognition, Marx firmly defended the view that there is only one real object of cognition.

Thirdly, we must say that the opinions we have analysed reveal no trace of structuralist ideas whatever. The situation is the same as in the case of our analysis of the relation between science and ideology: Althusser from time to time uses such terms as *structure, the field of problems*, etc., but without any further semantic consequences at all. The use of the word *structure* alone does not turn its user into a structuralist. We therefore still have to wait for our contact with Marxist structuralism as we pass to

Althusser's next great *anti*, namely his anti-historicism, which will be the next subject-matter of our discussion.

Anti-historicism or Eleatism?

The problem of historicism should, it can be expected, contribute extremely important factors that would shed light upon the attitude of Althusser and his school towards both Marxism and structuralism. Let us, therefore, take the bull by the horns and ask about Althusser's attitude toward historicism. It is, of course, that of disapproval. He claims that Marxism means anti-historicism and that he, being in his own opinion a Marxist, fully accepts anti-historicism.

Before we quote Althusser's own statements on the subject we have to explain that Althusser is convinced that he understands Marxism better than Marx and Engels did. He accordingly defends Marxism not only against miscomprehension and distortion by third parties, but by its founders as well. It is not only Engels who has deserved scolding by Althusser (for having misunderstood Marx, for differing from Althusser in his attitude towards Hegel, for having sinned by empiricism, for propounding historicism, etc.); the same applies to Marx who, as Althusser claims, failed to work out the proper appraisal of his own texts and did not understand his own ideas. For instance, he writes:

> ... the theoretical incompleteness of Marx's judgement of himself has produced the most serious misunderstandings, and, as before, not only among his opponents, who have an interest in misunderstanding him, but also and above all among his supporters.[76]

> Marx did *produce* in his work the distinction between himself and his predecessors, but – as is the fate of all inventors – he did not think the *concept* of this distinction with all the sharpness that could be desired; he did not think theoretically, or in an adequate and advanced form, either the concept or the theoretical implications of the theoretically revolutionary step he had taken.[77]

> We found that Marx did not really succeed in thinking the concept of the difference between himself and Classical Economics. . . . We can only recognize this emptiness by emptying it of the obviousnesses of the ideological philosophy of which it is full. We can only rigorously define Marx's few and as yet inadequate scientific concepts on the absolute condition that we recognize the ideological nature of the philosophical concepts which have usurped their places. . . .[78]

Fortunately, Althusser will accomplish that which for Marx had proved too great a task. I am openly sarcastic, because Althusser deserves that.

There is no rule that everyone has to agree with Marx and his theory; it may also happen that a Marxist wants to state something which is in agreement with his scholarly conscience, but is at variance with Marx's opinion on the issue. But if one has something like that to say, he should say that openly, to show respect both to the great thinker that Marx was, and to oneself. It makes sore hearing to listen to Althusser's incessant harangues on what Engels failed to comprehend in the Marxist theory, what Marx himself failed to understand, too, and what, on the contrary, is perfectly well grasped by Althusser. All this does not do service to Marxism, but it does not do service to Althusser either. It would be difficult to protest when Raymond Aron blames Althusser for resorting to the well-known theological trick that consists in presenting one's own ideas as the orthodox ones.

> As a member of the (Communist) Party Althusser must, like many generations of Marxists before him, use carefully chosen quotations to ascribe to Marx what he wants to say himself. By making use of this method, invented by theologians, he properly selects the texts and is bold enough to claim that Marx himself did not fully comprehend his own ideas and the importance of the scientific revolution he had initiated.[79]

One regrets to have to quote this, but Aron's criticism is correct. In the case of the previously discussed categories of ideology and empiricism, Althusser could interpret or 'explain' Marx's ideas, but when it comes to historicism such a procedure is no longer possible. Marx's statements on this issue are clear and non-ambiguous enough to discredit the claim that he did not accept historicism as the foundation of his method. Hence there is only one way out for Althusser: to claim that Marx did not know himself what he was speaking about, and that although he openly declared himself in favour of historicism, he was in fact opposed to it.

It is common knowledge that Marx based his criticism of classical economics on the objection that the classical approach in economics was ahistorical, and that he assumed the historical approach to be the foundation of a *scientific* analysis of economics. He formulated that expressly in a number of works, from *Misère de la Philosophie* to *Grundrisse* to *Capital* (which Althusser thinks to be Marx's mature work, not confined to economics alone, in which he is perfectly right). Now Althusser does not deny that Marx did formulate such opinions, since it would be sheer impossibility to deny that; on the contrary, he reports them in a matter-of-fact manner.

> The fundamental criticism Marx makes of the whole of Classical Economics in texts from *The Poverty of Philosophy* to *Capital* is that it had an ahistorical, eternal, fixed and abstract conception of the economic categories of capitalism. Marx says in so many words that these categories must be historicized to reveal and understand their nature, their relativity and transitivity. The Classical Economists, he says, have made the conditions of capitalist production the eternal conditions of all production, without seeing that these categories were historically determined, and hence historical and transitory.[80]

Althusser even quotes Marx in support of his description of Marx's standpoint. But then comes the *clou*: according to Althusser, Marx did say that, but because he did not understand Marxism. This is what Althusser writes on the issue:

> As we shall see, this critique is not the last word of Marx's *real* critique. It seems superficial and ambiguous, whereas his real critique is infinitely more profound. But it is surely no accident that Marx often went only halfway with his real critique in his declared critique, by establishing the only difference between him and the Classical Economists as the non-history of their conception. This judgement has weighed very heavily on the interpretation not only of *Capital* and of the Marxist theory of political economy, but also of Marxist philosophy. This is one of the strategic points in Marx's thought — I shall go so far as to say the number one strategic point — the point at which the theoretical incompleteness of Marx's judgement of himself has produced the most serious misunderstandings, and, as before, not only among his opponents, who have an interest in misunderstanding him, but also and above all among his supporters.
>
> All these misunderstandings can be grouped round one central misunderstanding of the theoretical relationship between Marxism and history, of the so-called radical historicism of Marxism. Let us examine the basis for the different forms taken by this crucial misunderstanding.[81]

Thus it turns out that Marx did speak about historicism and avowed it, but only because he did not understand his own work, which Althusser, of course, does understand and accordingly can explain to Marx what Marxism really is.

Before I describe in detail Althusser's opinion of historicism and the viewpoint adopted in this issue by Marx and Engels, I wish to settle one point first. For the time being I disregard the problem of who is right, Marx or Althusser. I resort to a specific philosophical *epoché* on this point. I ask another question: Who may call himself a Marxist? Now it is trivial to say that many people, including renowned scholars, think that Marx was wrong, that his ideas were wrong in general or on certain issues. Those people do not claim to be Marxists, on the contrary, they often claim to be anti-Marxists, and then their position is clear. But what are we to think of a person who wants to be called a Marxist, but does not agree with Marx, and that not on secondary issues, but on *fundamental* questions, such as the theory of reflection, empiricism, historicism, etc.? We have to say that such a person is wrong in terming himself a Marxist, for one cannot be a Marxist without accepting the main body of Marx's theoretical theses. If one does not accept them because scholarly conscience forbids one to do so, then one may be a brilliant scholar, but not a Marxist, and that cannot be helped. One does not thereby become an anti-Marxist, for that requires intention and an emotional conviction. One just is not a Marxist.

These comments are made in connection with the controversy over historicism in the Marxist theory, because the problem comes out in sharp relief in Althusser's books, but they are of a much broader significance and refer to the whole problem of Marxist structuralism in Althusser's version.

But let us now return to the basic problem now under consideration, namely, that of historicism. Althusser claims that Marx adopted the standpoint of historicism because he failed thoroughly to comprehend his own work. It follows from this that Marx and Engels must have very 'thoroughly' failed to comprehend their own work, since they were so stubbornly sticking to historicism and were so fond of making use of it in their research. I shall now quote some of their statements from the period which even Althusser considers scientific in their evolution.

Let us begin with Marx's signal declaration in *The German Ideology*, the declaration (to be found in a footnote, because in his manuscript he deleted the whole paragraph for considerations of the composition of the text) which semantically fits very well the opinions defended by Marx and Engels both in that book and in their later works: '*We know only one science, the science of history.*'[82]

This statement sets the course of all of Marx's and Engels's further methodological analyses. Here is a passage from Marx's letter to Annenkov, in which Marx criticizes Proudhon for anti-historicism: 'M. Proudhon the more so failed to understand that men who produce social relations according to their mode of material production also produce *ideas, categories*, i.e. the abstract, ideal expression of those social relations. Hence categories are not eternal, like the relations which they express. *They are historical and transitory products.*'[83]

When criticizing Proudhon for his failure to understand that Marx blames him for making capitalism eternal by negating — as bourgeois thinkers do — its historical and transitory nature. Marx continues his criticism and thus gives rise to the idea which becomes the leading motif of all his later criticism of political economy (his *Capital* included), namely his emphasis on the transitory, historical nature of the bourgeois form of production. This is the principle of historicism, and it can be removed from Marx's theoretical achievements only by the rejection of his work. Marx writes: 'None of them understands that the bourgeois form of production is a historical and transitory form just in the same way as the feudal form was.'[84]

The same idea is expressed by Marx in his letter to J. B. Schweitzer.

> For the evaluation of his [Proudhon's — A. S.] thick work of two volumes I must refer you to my polemic study. I have demonstrated there how little Proudhon has penetrated the secrets of scientific dialectic; how, on the other hand, he shares the illusions of speculative philosophy since instead of interpreting *economic categories* as the *theoretical expression of the historical relations of production that correspond to a specified level of the development of material production*, he talks nonsense about them as *eternal ideas* that have existed since the very beginning; in such a roundabout way he comes back to the standpoint taken by bourgeois economists.[85]

Misère de la philosophie has many similar ideas and passages. One of them was quoted by Althusser to demonstrate Marx's theoretical weakness. But it is precisely the idea of historicism as applied to economic problems which is the foundation of the analyses carried out in *Contribution to the Critique of Political Economy*, in *Grundrisse* and in *Capital*. The idea recurs in those works literally hundreds of times. Quotations are therefore not necessary. The case is obvious: those works state the *principle of historicism*, repeated unambiguously and consistently, as applied to the study of economic facts. Let me quote only one passage connected with *Capital*: I mean the review of that work, approvingly cited by Marx and referred to earlier in this book, written by Professor Kaufman of Petersburg University and published in 1872.

> The one thing which is of moment to Marx, is to find the law of the phenomena with whose investigation he is concerned; and not only is that law of moment to him, which governs these phenomena, in so far as they have a definite form and mutual connexion within a given historical period. [Structuralists please note: reference is made here to structural, or coexistential, laws. — A. S.] Of still greater moment to him is the law of their variation, of their development, i.e., of their transition from one form into another,

from one series of connexions into a different one. . . . Marx treats the social movement as a process of natural history, governed not only by laws independent of human will, consciousness and intelligence, but rather, on the contrary, determining that will, consciousness and intelligence. . . . According to him, such abstract laws do not exist. On the contrary, in his opinion every historical period has laws of its own. . . . The scientific value of such an inquiry [of economic life – A. S.] lies in the disclosing of the special laws that regulate the origin, existence, development, death of a given social organism and its replacement by another and higher one. And it is this value that, in point of fact, Marx's book has.[86]

Marx says that the reviewer presented his method in a pertinent way. Today, in the light of the structuralist controversies, we can say that Kaufman also proved to be very penetrating intellectually, because even at that time he grasped that element of the concept of structural laws which now forms the rational component of structuralism, if the latter is interpreted broadly as a method used in the social sciences; he also succeeded in bringing out *the* point of Marx's method, namely its *historicism*, i.e. questions about the laws of development, questions, as Kaufman put it, about 'transition from one form into another'. This is the problem which present-day structuralistically minded inprovers on Marxism fail to comprehend; this is, therefore, the point on which they move away from Marxist theory.

There is, I think, no need to quote Engels in order to support the undisputed statement that the standpoint of the founders of Marxism was that of historicism. Althusser is very subtle on this point: he does not claim in the least that the founders of Marxism adopted an anti-historicist standpoint, he merely says that Marxism, as their product, implies anti-historicism. When it comes to Engels, it suffices to read two of his works, *Anti-Dühring* and *Ludwig Feuerbach*, to see what his position was. I shall confine myself to quoting only one sentence from his review of Marx's *Contribution to the Critique of Political Economy* to conclude the series of quotations with a passage which repeats the formulations with which we have begun the review: that there is only one science, that of history. Engels somewhat modifies this idea by saying that all social sciences are historical, but it is the historical sciences with which we are concerned here.

'The statement that the mode of material production conditions the social, political, and spiritual process of life in general, was a discovery that revolutionized not only economics, but *all historical sciences (and all those disciplines which are not natural science are historical*).'[87]

There can thus be no doubt that the standpoint of Marx and Engels was that of historicism. Moreover, it was not a sin of their youth, but, on the contrary, a mental product of maturity. After all, this is quite understandable if we consider that we have to do with thinkers who deliberately adopted the viewpoint of dialectics, interpreted in the materialistic sense as the science of the most general laws of the development of the world, thinkers who considered the theory of the materialistic interpretation of history to be their principal theoretical achievement (as formulated by Engels in the passage cited above). But how is that historicism of theirs to be interpreted?

It must be admitted that Althusser is consistent in being carefree about using ambiguous concepts: after ideology, science and empiricism, historicism's turn has come. Althusser uses that concept as if it were universally and unambiguously comprehensible, although it suffices to look up any dictionary of the social sciences to see that the concept is even more ambiguous than those analysed before. Not only is the term extremely ambiguous, but in some cases its various meanings even contradict one another. What then is the sense of the term anti-historicism? To which kind of historicism does Althusser's *anti-* apply?

First of all, we must realize what Marx and Engels meant by historicism, in order to be able to answer the question what Althusser intends to negate, and what he in fact negates, when he says that Marxism implies anti-historicism.

Marxian historicism has probably been best defined by Kaufman in his review of *Capital*, approvingly referred to by Marx and cited twice earlier in this text. The following elements, essential for the definition of historicism in the Marxian sense of the term, can be extracted from his formulation.

Historicism is such a theoretical viewpoint (with the resulting methodological consequences) which assumes that:

   (i)   all social phenomena are changing (development is a qualified form of change, namely such in which the change takes place in the form of transition from lower to higher forms; Marx did not in the least claim that development is universal, although he claimed that change is a universal process);

  (ii) those changes are subject to specified regularities, reflected in what are called the dynamic laws of science;

(iii) those laws also cover transition from one system to another (today we would say: one system with a specified structure to another such system); to put it more picturesquely, they cover the birth and the death of such a system, and also its life, i.e. its existence;

(iv) the life, i.e. relatively stable existence, of a system is subject to specific laws which govern it 'in so far as they [phenomena – A. S.] have a definite form and mutual connexion within a given historical period' (today we would say: in so far we have to do with a system with a specified structure).

Historicism interpreted in this manner implies the following theses:

(a) that social facts change;

(b) that their changes are marked by regularities which are reflected in the dynamic laws of science;

(c) that changes result in periodic states of relative rest, which are marked not by the absence of all change, but by a relative stability of forms and mutual connections (today we would put it more precisely: *of the structure of a given system*).

The first thesis cannot be denied in the light of present-day science. The second has been and is disputable, especially in the science of history (cf. the controversy between idiographism and nomothetism), but in the Marxist theory it has been settled in favour of radical nomothetism.

The third thesis proves that structuralist ideas are not so original as it might seem (I, of course, mean the rational component of what today is inexactly termed structuralism). This problem will be discussed later in connection with those of genesis and structure.

And now let us pose the question: Does Althusser apply his *anti-* to that historicism which we have characterized above, i.e. *Marxist historicism*? The question is justified in view of the plurality of historicisms which are to be found in the literature of the subject, but in most cases have little in common with the definition formulated above, and in some cases are in contradiction with it on certain points. The answer to this essential question is plain: No. Althusser's negation does not refer to Marxist historicism, and the whole issue again is a mystification, due to his most irritating habit of using ambiguous, and hence vague, terms. Althusser in fact refers to different things as he uses the term in different meanings. The error may seem rather trivial because of being so obvious, but it is jarring in Althusser's case: he not only commits it very frequently, but — we can feel it that way — resorts to it deliberately if that makes it easier for him to argue for his theses.

What does he mean, then, when he speaks about historicism and proclaims triumphantly that Marxism implies anti-historicism? As I have said, what he means is not historicism in the Marxist sense of the term, but something else. What then?

As I have written earlier, I had considerable and genuine difficulties with understanding the problem, for while I oppose Althusser in my discussions with him I treat him very seriously. In this case, however, it all looked very trivial, which I could not believe. I accordingly assumed, as I remembered how carefree Althusser was on other semantic issues, that he used the term *historicism* in a different sense from that which is current in the Marxist theory. It was Raymond Aron who helped me understand what the meaning of that term was. He immediately grasped the sense of Althusser's anti-historicism, as Sartre also grasped immediately what was the sense of Althusser's anti-humanism (which I had found easier to comprehend). They grasped that without difficulty because they are familiar with the Hegelian language of philosophy, which apparently is the current language of the French philosophical milieu. This is how Raymond Aron understands Althusser's anti-historicism: 'This Theory [of religion — A. S.] would, if we are to believe the adherents of the Althusser school, still be within the sphere of Hegel's problems and would inevitably lead to historicism that results from absolute knowledge or from man's return to himself at the end of the process of becoming.'[88]

I neither joke nor exaggerate. I would have never come upon the idea myself. To be able to write on the methodology of history I have read a lot, including works on historicism. In the course of that reading I had to do with various definitions of historicism. But probably none of those who are interested in the problem, not as a speculative philosopher but as a person who is concerned with the methodology of history, has come upon the idea of going back to Hegel (especially in such a form) in order to proclaim triumphantly that Marxism implies anti-historicism. Where and when did Marx, when proclaiming the theses of historicism, refer to the notorious wandering of the absolute idea, where and when did he advocate, instead of materialistic determinism, such a fanciful teleological conception to be interpreted as historicism? As I have mentioned earlier, one of Althusser's misfortunes is that while he rebels against Hegel he rebels on his bended knees. He is totally submerged in Hegel, his language and his problems which occasionally result in deplorable confusion, when he substitutes Hegelian conceptions for Marxian or, more broadly, for Marxist ones. Raymond Aron is, unfortunately, right: this is how Althusser really understands historicism.[89] And that is the base on which Althusser rests his anti-historicist declaration of faith: 'I should like to suggest that, from the theoretical standpoint, Marxism is no more a historicism than it is a humanism ... and that, *theoretically speaking*, Marxism is, in a single movement and by virtue of the unique epistemological rupture which established it, an anti-humanism and an anti-historicism.'[90]

Well, this sounds fine and provoking, and serves the purpose of causing excitement in the professional milieu. The only point is that the idea is burdened by a small error: Althusser has confused different meanings when claiming that Marxism is anti-historicism. In order to make the impression that he speaks about the Marxist conception of historicism, which in fact he does not mention at all, he presents his own idea. In the last analysis this is simply a mystification.

Were it merely to boil down to this, it would not deserve being discussed. Yet there is another problem which accompanies an ordinary confusion of ideas: a *specific conception* of structuralism is opposed to the conception of Marxist historicism. To put it more plainly: the tendency to replace an analysis of dynamic conditions by an analysis of static conditions; to oppose structure to genesis; to interpret dynamic phenomena by static ones. In a word, a renaissance of Eleatism, to use Henri Lefebvre's pertinent phrase.

Can anything like this happen to a Marxist? Yes, it can. Something analogous, though much more interesting, happened to Bukharin in the 1920s; the case is worth recalling because it helps us better to comprehend the problems we are concerned with and also because Althusser, for reasons that are difficult to understand, does not mention it at all.

As has been said before, the structural analysis of systems (i.e. the analysis of the structural, coexistential laws which govern them) forms part of the Marxist conception of historicism as *complementary* to the analysis of the dynamic aspects of systems (i.e. the analysis of the dynamic laws), with the proviso that, in accordance with the theory of dialectics, the starting-point is that of dynamics and its laws, and the state of a relative rest of the system, to be investigated by the structural laws, is a product of dynamic changes. The analysis of the errors committed by the Eleatic school in the interpretation of the possibility (or impossibility) of motion, and the apories of the arrow, of Achilles and the tortoise, etc., which fascinate philosophers even now, show clearly that these errors reduce to endeavours to explain motion by a lack of motion, a state of rest. The errors of the Eleatic school were later many a time repeated in the history of philosophy, and Bukharin's theory of equilibrium is one of them.

The complementarity of the dynamic and the structural aspect of reality and the resulting complementarity of methods of investigation in terms of the Marxist theory was well understood in the Russian literature of the subject already in the 1880s, as is proved by the quotation of Kaufman's review of *Capital*. A. Bogdanov's work on the general theory of organization, entitled *Tektologia*,[91] was in many respects a pioneer study, although it was for many reasons doomed to the 'biting criticism' of oblivion. It was a pioneer study precisely on the point which today is of interest for structuralism and general systems theory. Bukharin, who was one of Bogdanov's disciples, in his handbook of historical materialism, took up the aspect of structure of systems, an issue which had been neglected in the Marxist theory in the twentieth century. Bukharin's theory of equilibrium may be assessed in various ways, according to how it is interpreted: it may be interpreted as a mechanistic theory if we assume that the equilibrium of a system is, in his interpretation, the starting-point for treating motion as a disturbance of equilibrium, the state of equilibrium being regarded as the natural initial state of systems; but it can also be assessed more favourably, if we assume that for him the equilibrium of a system was not the starting-point, but, on the contrary, a result of the changes of the system, a state of relative equilibrium. Bukharin's work in that respect is neither clear nor formulated with precision, yet it was he who developed a theory of aggregates and systems, a theory of relative external and internal equilibrium (relationships between society and nature in the former case, and between elements of a social system in the latter), and also a theory of transition from one structure to another.

We have so far been considering mainly the *structure* of society, the

> structure of the existing social formation. In what follows we will have to speak above all about transitions from one formation, one structure, into another. At this place we wish to emphasize once more that the law of *unstable* equilibrium not only does not exclude opposites, but, on the contrary, *assumes antagonisms, opposites, unadjustment, clashes, conflicts, and – which is of particular importance – under specified conditions assumes the necessity of catastrophes and revolutions. The Marxist theory is that of revolutions.*[92]

I will disregard here the correctness of such or another interpretation of the theory of equilibrium, since this is not an issue we are particularly interested in at this moment. Suffice it to note that in the history of Marxist ideas the adherents of Marxist structuralism have had a forerunner, even though they do not admit that. More important still, that forerunner of theirs, while he accepted the existence of real aggregates and systems, and analysed their structure, saw the main problem in the transition from one structure to another, because he considered the Marxist theory to be that of revolutions, and in this connection he worked out a theory of disturbances of the equilibrium of systems.

And what is the approach of present-day Marxist structuralists? What does their structuralism consist in? How do they solve the problem of transitions? Does their theory provide for revolutionary changes in a system, changes which they accept in their political opinions? All these issues must be analysed if we are better to understand Althusser's anti-historicism.

Although in his texts he often uses the term *structure*, it is difficult to find there any specific theory of structuralism. His most frequent references are to a *complex structured whole* and a *structure in dominance*, with which he links a theory of *overdetermination* (why does he complicate matters by using psychoanalytic terminology if he just means a protest against an excessively economically minded distortion of Marxist analyses?), but all this does not contribute anything new to our knowledge of structuralism.[92a] We rather have to say that, as compared with Bukharin's analyses (his comments on such concepts as aggregate, system and structure), the theoretical approach of the group termed Marxist structuralists is marked by a lack of semantic precision. They have adopted poor conceptual apparatus from the French structuralists (who usually even cannot make the distinction between system and structure) and handle the term *structure* without any further analyses whatever. The term *complex structured whole* is used by them instead of the term *system*, current in the literature of the subject, which certainly does not mean a novelty.

I am interested in something else: How do the Marxist structuralists solve the problem of transition, i.e. the problem of history? In the last analysis we have to say that regardless of our interpretations the world does change; it would be impossible to deny the history of mankind and, in a specific sense, the history of Nature. The problem seems evident, but it turns out to be a hard nut to crack for those, from the members of the Eleatic school to at least some groups of the structuralists, who take a specific theoretical viewpoint. The adherents of the Eleatic school adopted a very convenient attitude, they denied the objective nature of motion and change and claimed that these are illusions. For the structuralists the problem of transitions is the Achilles' heel (I wish to make it plain that when I refer to structuralists I exclude from their group the representatives of structuralism proper, i.e. the structural linguists). Is it for the Marxist structuralists, too? It turns out that it is, although they have left for themselves a convenient way out in the form of the theory of two objects of cognition, so that their abandoning the theory of reflection has a specific justification.

Of course, Althusser does not deny change, and in this sense he does not deny history; were it otherwise, his opinion would have to be treated as a curiosity, but all discussion of his ideas would not be to the point. The question is different: does Althusser, as a Marxist dialectician, think that change is primary, and that the states of relative rest, structured as systems, are secondary, or does he think that it is the other way round? It turns out that in his opinion it is the other way round. In that respect Althusser has become influenced by a *sui generis* structuralism: it is a structure, a structured whole, which decides which is the starting-point, but on the condition that the system adopted as the starting-point of a given analysis is itself a product of history. But if one does so, then one has to pose the problem of transitions, the problem of dynamic laws, and the problem of change and development. Althusser has just disregarded these problems.

He criticizes the linear and ideological conception of time and history (mainly in 'The Object of *Capital*', which forms Part II of his *Reading Capital*), which is a *pendant* to his interpretation of historicism (as

Hegelian historicism). I shall not engage in a discussion of this as I have deliberately left apart problems of the history of philosophy, in particular Marx's attitude toward Hegel's works. The important point is that, according to Althusser, Marx started from structure and not from history. Althusser concludes this from a passage in *Misère de la Philosophie*, where Marx criticizes Proudhon for not having understood the nature of the structural laws which govern a given system and for his considering elements of that system as succeeding one another whereas they are simultaneous, or, as Marx puts it, 'of the same age'. Marx writes in this connection:

> The production relations of every society form a whole. M. Proudhon considers economic relations as so many social phases, engendering one another, resulting one from the other like the antithesis from the thesis ... In constructing the edifice of an ideological system by means of the categories of political economy, the limbs of the social system are dislocated. The different limbs of society are converted into so many separate societies, following one upon the other. How, indeed, could the single logical formula of movement, of sequence, explain the body of society, in which all relations co-exist simultaneously and support one another?(93)

The analysis of this passage is very interesting and helps us understand the method of mystification and auto-mystification which Althusser uses, not in this case only, when dealing with Marx's texts. For what did Marx really say in the passage cited above and what does really follow from his text? First, that Marx did comprehend that the world has a systemically structural aspect and that he recommended that it be taken into consideration in research (which is important because structuralists today often refer to Marx). Secondly, that Marx criticized Proudhon for using, in his analysis of society, a *single logical formula of movement* which formula was supposed by Proudhon to serve as a panacea in research work. Thus, in the passage cited above, Marx defended the analysis of structural (coexistential) laws in the study of society against Proudhon's unwise endeavour to use, in such a case, the single logical formula of movement, which would be at variance with the objective fact of the coexistence of given social relations within a single whole. On the other hand, however, he did not say a word — for how could he, being a dialectician? — about the repudiation of history or about the priority of structural research before historical research. It is pure imagination which makes Althusser draw from that passage the following structuralist (or, to put it plainly, pseudo-structuralist) conclusions: '. . . we can see that it is essential to reverse the order of reflection and think first the specific structure of the totality in order to understand both the form in which its limbs and constitutive relations *co-exist* and the peculiar structure of history.'[94]

This is not Marx's conception, this is Althusser's mystification and *his* conception; in fact, the anti-historical in the worst version of neo-Eleatic pseudo-structuralism. Of course, Althusser could not have adopted it directly, in its pure form, and hence all that meandering of ideas, which has two aspects, one of them almost mystical, and the other openly brutal. We are here interested mainly in the latter, but the mystic aspect also deserves being revealed, because it testifies to inconsistencies in so-called Marxist structuralism.

Althusser considers the problem of whether there is one historical time, or many times that each depend on the system from which we start. He is in favour of the latter conception and claims the former to be ideological [? — A. S.] and empiricist. I shall not discuss that, but I am interested in Althusser's following statement on the issue:

> In the capitalist mode of production, therefore, the time of economic production has absolutely nothing to do with the obviousness of everyday practice's ideological time: of course, it is rooted in certain determinate sites, in biological time (certain limits in the alteration of labour and rest for human and animal labour power; certain rhythms for agricultural production) but in essence it is not at all identified with the biological time, and in no sense is it a time that can be *read immediately* in the flow of any given process. It is an invisible time, essentially illegible, as invisible and as opaque as the reality of the total capitalist production process itself. This time, as a complex 'intersection' of the different times, rhythms, turnovers, etc., that we have just discussed, is only accessible in *its concept*, which, like every concept is never immediately 'given', never *legible* in visible reality: like every concept this concept must be *produced, constructed.*[95]

This clearly smacks of mysticism; I note this as a matter of record only, for I am interested in the theoretical substantiation of that structuralist anti-historicism. It can be summed up thus: the real object has its history, the object of cognition has none, for the former does change, whereas the latter does not.

Althusser refers to two statements made by Engels (in the *Preface* to the third German edition of *Capital* and in *Anti-Dühring*) on the changing nature of reality, reflected in the changing nature of concepts, statements which he criticizes, and writes thus:

The whole misunderstanding in this reasoning lies in fact in the fallacy which confuses the theoretical development of concepts with the genesis of real history. But Marx carefully distinguished between these two *orders* when in the *1857 Introduction*, he showed that it was impossible to institute any one-to-one correlation between the terms which feature in the order of succession of concepts in the discourse of scientific proof on the one hand, and those which feature in the genetic order of real history on the other. Here Engels postulates precisely such an impossible correlation, unhesitatingly identifying 'logical' development and 'historical' development. And with extraordinary honesty he points out the theoretical precondition for this identification: the affirmation that these two developments are identical in order depends on the fact that the necessary concepts of any theory of history are affected, in their conceptual substance, by the *properties* of the *real* object. . . . In order to be able to identify the development of the concepts and the development of real history, he therefore had to identify the object of knowledge with the real object, and to subject the concepts to the real determination of real history.[96]

Now there are two further mystifications in this passage, by means of which Althusser tries theoretically to substantiate anti-historicism:

(i) As we know from our earlier analyses, Marx, contrary to Althusser's claims, did not formulate any theory of two objects, and yet Althusser refers to such an alleged theory to substantiate his demonstration.

(ii) In the texts cited by Althusser, Engels did not speak about any identity of thought and reality (only an idealist could identify them), but merely referred to the cognitive relation between the subject and the object, which underlies the theory of reflection, a theory which Althusser, as we know, rejects.

These two mystifications make Althusser totally lose sight of the problem of transitions, which Bukharin had found so puzzling (for the sake of justice we have to say that Maurice Godelier, who vigorously supports Althusser's claims that structure is prior to history and that Marx had repudiated all historicism, does notice the problem of transitions and tries to solve it).[97]

This is what J. P. Sartre means when he sees the specific feature of structuralism in the rejection of history,[98] and the specific feature of Marxism, precisely in the understanding of transitions. 'Repudiation of Marxism would mean repudiation of the understanding of transitions. Now I think that we are all the time in a state of transition, that we all the time distribute by producing and produce by distributing . . ., I therefore cannot understand how one can confine oneself to structures; for me, this is a logical scandal.'[99]

Hence his very severe assessment of that structuralist anti-historicism an assessment which some people find shocking, but which is objectively correct:

> The aim, via history, of course is Marxism. The point is to formulate a new ideology, the last barrier which the bourgeoisie is still able to erect against Marx.... It is to be claimed that history as such is intangible and that all theory of history is, by definition, to use Foucault's expression, doxological. By renouncing the explanation of transitions one opposes to history, which is the domain of uncertainty, an analysis of structures and claims that such analysis alone makes true scientific research possible.[100]

This is an assessment which a Marxist must exphazise. This can also be the end of our excursion into the sphere of that anti-historicism which aspires to the label *Marxist*. We accordingly have to make, as usual, a summary of the conclusions drawn in this section of our analyses.

First, Marx and Engels undeniably declare themselves in favour of historicism (which Althusser does not deny either). By historicism they mean the opinion that the world changes and that its changes are governed by specified regularities, reflected in the dynamic laws of science. Interpreted in this way historicism emphasizes the fact that the said changes result in periodic states of relative rest, and the system, with its specified structure, which comes to being in this way is subject to specific regularities, reflected in the structural laws of science (the wording of their ideas has been modernized).

Secondly, when speaking about anti-historicism Althusser means a quite different sense of the term *historicism*, namely that sense which is associated with certain ideas of Hegel. Hence when he says that Marxism implies anti-historicism we have to do with carefree handling of ambiguous concepts, which is typical of him, and moreover with a typical logical slip, because the premises refer to one concept and the conclusion refers to another, although the shape of the words may be the same.

Thirdly, Althusser substantiates his anti-historicism by referring to the theory of two objects, which is in fact the denial of the theory of reflection in gnosiology: it is the real objects which are said to be subject to changes, and not the objects of cognition, which are independent of the former. He ascribes that theory to Marx, which, as we know from the discussion of empiricism, is simply a mystification.

Fourthly, as a result of his anti-historicism Althusser is unable to solve the problem of transitions from one social system to another. This means abandoning Marxism both in theory and in practice.

Anti-humanism or Anti-Marxism?

And thus we have come to the central issue which has induced me to take up this discussion: Does Marxism mean anti-humanism, or is a person who propounds anti-humanism an anti-Marxist?

Althusser is firm in his proclaiming the anti-humanism of Marxism. He does so on many occasions, and it is one of the fundamental theses of his structuralist interpretation of Marxism. Here is the passage which is a very clear formulation of his idea:

> Strictly in respect to theory, therefore, one can and must speak openly of *Marx's theoretical anti-humanism*, and see in this *theoretical anti-humanism* the absolute (negative) precondition of the (positive) knowledge of the human world itself, and of its practical transformation. It is impossible to *know* anything about men except on the absolute precondition that the philosophical (theoretical) myth of man is reduced to ashes. So any thought that appeals to Marx for any kind of restoration of a theoretical anthropology or humanism is no more than ashes, *theoretically.*[101]

This sounds formidable, and — unfortunately — has become for Althusser himself, and his collaborators in particular, the starting-point for the pseudo-Marxist version of Foucault's *bon mot*: *'l'homme est mort'*. I shall revert to this later, and now I shall try to dissipate the dread of anti-humanism by what follows the passage cited above: 'For the corollary of theoretical Marxist anti-humanism is the recognition and knowledge of humanism itself: as an *ideology*. . . . Marx's theoretical anti-humanism . . . recognizes a necessity for humanism as an *ideology*.'[102]

Now this sounds less formidable than it did at first: it is true that, in Althusser's opinion, Marxism as a theory still means anti-humanism, but at the same time Marxism recognizes the necessity of humanism as an ideology. Let us not pretend — even though it would be legitimate to do so — that we do not know what Althusser means by ideology and why the Marxist theory would have to accept the necessity of humanism as an ideology while we have been told by Althusser himself that all ideology is to be eradicated. Let us not be small-minded. But we have to ask what Althusser really means when he refers to humanism. His statements on the subject sound strange and make us suppose that he has something very peculiar in mind, something which differs from the accepted meaning of the term *humanism.* For else how could he claim that in 1845 Marx broke with every *philosophical* anthropology or humanism,[103] this being an obvious untruth, as is proved by *Grundrisse* of 1857? How could he suggest such a nonsense as his claim that production relations are not relations among human beings[104] (which, by the way, is the pet phrase of Althusser and his collaborators), in view of Marx's plain statement in Vol. I of *Capital*, in the chapter on commodity fetishism, that such an opinion is wrong? How could he subscribe to Etienne Balibar's formula-tion 'The concept of "men" thus constitutes a real point where the utterance *slips away* towards the regions of philosophical or commonplace ideology',[105] although Marx would ridicule anyone who would disagree with his, Marx's, opinion that men themselves make their own his-tory?[106] This is why we have to find out in what sense the term *humanism* is used by Althusser. Our previous experience has taught us that we cannot rely on Althusser when he uses a general term so as if he used it in a universally accepted sense.

We certainly cannot rely on him in the case of his use of the term *humanism.* If suffices to look up philosophical dictionaries. Eisler's (1910) refers to humanism only in the sense of F. C. S. Schiller's pragmatism, i.e. in the sense of the Protagorean doctrine, which relates the truths to man by treating them as his work. Lalande, who is culturally closer to Althusser, gives more semantic variations of the term, but does not include that which is current in the Marxist theory. The Russian philosophical encyclopaedia,[106a] on the contrary, has a long and multi-aspectual analysis of the term *humanism*, which begins with a general characteristic of the word, described, in its broad sense, as a progressive trend in social thought, marked by advocacy of human dignity, freedom, many-sided development of human beings, and social relations worthy of humans. Marxist humanism is later described as a higher form of humanism, inspired by the goals of the social struggle of the proletariat. Does Althusser mean that when he negates humanism? Obviously not. But what, then, does he mean? He gives an indirect answer to this question when he writes that 'In 1845, Marx broke radically with every theory that based history and politics on an essence of man.'[107]

Thus, according to Althusser, the term *humanism* is the name of the trend which bases its political and social conclusions on 'an essence of man'. That 'essence of man' covers such elements as freedom, equality, etc., from which the said political conclusions follow. The anti-humanistic protest would have to consist in making socialist demands, in particular the demand for a change in the social formation, result not from a humanistic 'ideology' (i.e. not from any conception of 'essence of man'), but from a purely scientific analysis of social structures.

One thing is beyond dispute: Althusser is not only original, but imaginative as well. His meaning of the word *humanism* is not to be found in any dictionary of philosophical terms; nor is it used in his sense in the literature of the subject by anyone except for the Marxist structuralists. Althusser is, of course, not bothered by the fact that his meaning of the word has nothing to do with that to which we have become accustomed in the Marxist literature, whether classical or contemporary. I have shown earlier, by referring to such terms as *ideology, empiricism* and *historicism*, that Althusser is not disturbed by such a trifle that he uses certain words in very odd meanings while drawing conclusions so as if he used them in the meanings current in the Marxist literature of the subject. Certainly, we may call the table the chair and vice versa, but why should we do so? In any case we cannot do so without informing others about the semantic operation we have performed. One cannot expect one's readers to possess the gift of telepathy. Why, then, does he term that speculative idealistic conception *humanism*? In particular, why does he try to persuade us that the idea was that of Marx and Engels, which is a falsification of history? He needs that to support his thesis about the *coupure*, the (epistemological) break, that is, the thesis about 'two Marxes', which negates the obvious fact, explicitly confirmed by Engels in his *Ludwig Feuerbach*, that before 1845, too, both he and Marx had been adherents of materialistic philosophy, Marx never drew political and social conclusions from the considerations of that 'essence of man' alone, although these considerations, interpreted as moral requirements, did play a role for him not only in his youth, but to the end of his days. But let us leave this problem aside for a while. It suffices now that we have decoded Althusser's interpretation of the term *humanism*, although his anti-humanism includes, next to the humanism interpreted in the sense explained above, a few additions such as the denial of man's role in social changes, and hence also the denial of the validity of a philosophical analysis of his role, an analysis which

Althusser discredits as being an anti-scientific ideology (this applies above all to the problem of alienation).

A much more sensible (less hysterical and less radical, not intended to defend the thesis on the *coupure* at any price) explanation of the rejection of 'humanism' by Marxist structuralists is to be found in M. Godelier. Apart from the still-open issue, why the opinions they oppose should be termed *humanism*, one can agree with the viewpoint presented by Godelier. I sum up his argumentation for the sake of a well-intended criticism which makes it possible to find rational elements even in paradoxical formulations.

Godelier, when replying to Lucien Sève's criticism[108] of his article in *Les Temps Modernes*,[109] explains his position with regard to the criticism of the anti-humanism of Marxist structuralists.[110] Sève says that by opposing process to structure the structural method identifies structure with relations among things, and places relations among human beings in the sphere of ideological consciousness. Godelier indignantly rejects the accusation that the structuralists avow theoretical anti-humanism.[110a] We can only say to this that Sève gave an accurate summary of what Althusser wrote in *For Marx* in the passage cited above. Godelier next dissociates himself, in a sense, from the erroneous theses of his companions, and his explanations help us comprehend what the needlessly emotional thesis on Marxist anti-humanism means.

> What then is left of the accusation of 'theoretical anti-humanism'? We do not in the least conceal the fact that we have many a time opposed all endeavour to adopt humanism, even in its materialistic version, as the basis of the proof of the historical necessity of transition to socialism, and of socialism's superiority over the capitalist mode of production. For when Marx writes that by constantly developing the forces of production capitalism 'unconsciously creates material conditions of a higher mode of production', then the only reason of that necessity and that superiority is the fact that the socialist structure of production relations functionally corresponds to conditions for the emergence of new, gigantic and increasingly socialized forces of production, engendered by capitalism. That correspondence is an 'unintentional' fact, which expresses the 'objective properties' of a certain social structure, and is in its nature totally independent of all *a priori* idea of happiness, 'essence of man', 'true' freedom. . . .
>
> In fact — and this is precisely the stake of the discussion over the works of the young Marx — to become a Marxist Marx will have to base his thesis on the inevitability of the decomposition of capitalism and the birth of socialism upon the scientific analysis of the capitalist mode of production, and not upon philosophical and political ideology, were it even materialistic and 'communistic', as in the case of his *1844 Manuscripts*.[111]

As I have said, Godelier is much less emotional, and hence more sensible: in any case, his text shows clearly that the supposed anti-humanism just opposes the tendency to draw socially valid conclusions exclusively from speculative *a priori* ideas about 'human nature'. The protest is well founded, but it is still unknown why that speculative approach is labelled *humanism.* We could likewise call any person who is a student of ideas an idealist, and a student of the military art a militarist, etc., thus becoming submerged in a whirlpool of terminological confusion which makes all communication impossible. Does this want to say that the alleged structuralist anti-humanism is just one more verbal mystification as it introduces the term *humanism* in a sense which differs from that current in the language of the Marxist theory, so that its *anti-* is aimed at something quite different, at an imaginary idealistic theory which is ascribed to the young Marx contrary to the historical truth?

No, this is not so, because in addition to the mystification referred to above that approach is connected with several real issues that should be discussed in connection with label *anti-humanism.*

First, the point is what are the underlying assumptions of the socialist principles, in particular of the thesis about the inevitability of the replacement of the capitalist economic formation by the socialist one.

Structuralists say that such assumptions follow from a scientific analysis of the structures of production relations and forces of production, and not from an 'ideology'. They also say that for Marxism to become a science it was necessary that Marx carry out that analysis. We can agree with the first part of that statement if, by an analysis of structures, we mean an analysis of the dynamics of structures. In fact, moral principles (linking them with the 'essence of man' is something secondary as they can equally well be deduced from the commandments of God, from the evolution of the absolute idea, etc.) and our indignation at their infringement do not prove that the evolution must be in the direction we postulate. Such a proof can be provided only by an analysis of objective social relations, and hence an analysis which is scientific in nature.

But does a *scientific* analysis really reduce to an analysis of real relations and disregard human beings? Of course it does not — from the Marxist point of view. Such an analysis would not be scientific as it would be quite inadequate, be it alone for the fact that the 'real structures' like the one which in the Marxist theory is termed the *base*, contain, as a component, human beings with all their abilities, attitudes, etc. It is to be borne in mind that the base includes the forces of production and production relations, and human beings are not just the agentive force of production relations, but also an element of the forces of production, which consist of raw materials, instruments of production, and the appropriate abilities to use them (that is, the human beings who have such abilities).

We still have to consider what Marx meant by saying that men themselves make their own history. They make it, as he added, not in an arbitrary way, because they are socially conditioned. But there is no point in engaging in a discussion with a person who denies the fact that human beings act consciously and that both their actions and the consciousness which underlies them are significant for social development. In any case, this must be clear for the Marxists, who in their practical activity are guided by Marx's well-known statement that an idea which has dominated the masses becomes a material force, and who are engaged seriously, and not spuriously, in the ideological campaign whose objective is that the Marxist idea dominate the masses. Here, too, *ideology* intervenes, but not in the vague sense of something which is opposed to science, as has been assumed by the structuralists by definition, but in the sense of a system of opinions and attitudes which indicates the objective of social actions of men and which can be (and is – in the case of the Marxist theory) scientific as far as its genetic conditions are concerned.

He who wants to restrict the socialist theory to an analysis of real structures, to the exclusion of the human beings and ideologies, does not understand the Marxist theory, is not a Marxist but a positivist of the traditional kind. As has been said many a time, it is such tendencies which the Marxist structuralists reveal, because their opinions are traumatic responses to ideologies and a traumatic response to existentialism with its hypertrophy of subjectivism. We can agree with the diagnosis formulated by Domenach, who says that structuralism is a reaction to existentialist mythology (*'donne un bain froid à la mythologie existentialiste'*),[112] but this cannot change our assessment of that trend.

Marxist socialism claims to be scientific, not only when it comes to its treatment of the base, but in its approach to the superstructure, too – Marxist ideology included. He who fails to understand this does not understand Marxism. And the error is not in structuralism, not in the use of the methods of structural analysis, but in an incorrect use of that analysis, in its abuse, to which the terminology which mystifies the problem contributes signally.

Secondly, there is the problem of production relations, which are alleged to be relations among things, and not among human beings. This is an absurdity, which is a result of the elimination, by definition, of the human beings from the world of structures. There is no point in engaging in any comprehensive discussion on an obvious issue. I shall therefore confine myself to quoting a passage from *Capital*, where Marx explains the reasons of such an erroneous opinion. In the section entitled *The Fetishism of Commodities and the Secret Thereof* Marx says:

> A commodity is therefore a mysterious thing, simply because in it the social character of men's labour appears to them as an objective character stamped upon the product of that labour: because the relation of the producers to the sum total of their own labour is presented to them as a social relation, existing not between themselves, but between the products of their labour. . . . There is a definite social relation between men, that assumes, in their eyes, the fantastic form of a relation between things. . . . This I call the Fetishism which attaches itself to the products of labour, so soon as they are produced as commodities, and which is therefore inseparable from the production of commodities.[113]

Now that 'fantastic form of a relation between things', that fetishism, is specific not only to commodities, but to production relations between men in general. For how could one overlook the obvious fact that production relations are relations between producers, and not between things produced, even though, self-evidently, those relations between men are conditioned by the existing structure of the system? How could one overlook Marx's classical formulation in the 'Preface' to *A Contribution to the Critique of Political Economy*, which leaves the least doubt about the fact that Marx interpreted production relations as relations between human beings? 'In the social production of their life men enter into specified relations with one another, relations which are necessary and independent of their will, relations of production which correspond to the specified level of development of their material forces of production.'[114]

In the light of these obvious truths and Marx's unambiguous statement how are we to assess the following formulation (in no way unique) made by Althusser? 'And if by chance anyone proposes to reduce these relations of production to relations between men, i.e. "human relations", he is violating Marx's thought. . . .'[115]

If Althusser wanted to emphasize that all social relations between men are bound by existing objective conditions, by existing structures – which certainly is correct – then he should have stated that explicitly, and not to have fallen into the error of objectivism by avoiding the error of subjectivism. To put it plainly: if one wants to avoid the errors of individualistic voluntarism (which was characteristic of existentialism and which explains Althusser's aversion to existentialist ideas), one should not throw out the baby with the bath-water, i.e. lose the sight of man as the carrier of social action when repudiating subjectivism.

Thirdly, there is the problem of man in the Marxist theory. As has been said earlier, there is no symmetry between Althusser's humanism and his anti-humanism: his concept of humanism is narrow and differs in meaning from that current in the Marxist theory, whereas his concept of anti-humanism covers a much broader range of problems, among them the denial of man's place in the system of Marxist thought. This is why Althusser announces (see the quotation at the beginning of this section) that, should anyone try to construct, within the Marxist theory, a system of theoretical anthropology, his efforts would be reduced to ashes. Balibar, who follows in his master's footsteps, is even more radical: he considers the very concept of man to be a path that makes one stray into the sphere of philosophical ideology, which in his opinion is something utterly unscientific.

In the light of such statements, pathetic and fiery, we can admire one thing only: the psychology of blindness resulting from wishful thinking. For when it comes to facts all that is very simple: if this is referred to Marx's works from all periods of his activity, the statements are just false. In no period of Marx's activity did man 'die'. Lucien Sève took the trouble of putting together the appropriate quotations from the various periods of Marx's activity.[116] They amount to several dozen pages, and there would be no sense in doing the same job again. But I cannot help deriving satisfaction from demonstrating the utter groundlessness of Althusser's claim in the light of Marx's *Grundrisse*, a study which undoubtedly comes from the period of Marx's maturity (it is an outline of *Capital*), and at the same time is very dear to Althusser, who formulates his various hypotheses precisely by referring to the 'Introduction' to that study.

In the polemic passages of Marx's works there are some statements which are worded very radically, and which should be referred to in a given context, because if they are interpreted out of context they give a distorted picture of his opinions. This applies, for instance, to Marx's discussion with Adolf Wagner, so willingly cited by Althusser and his collaborators; Marx says there that his method takes a given period of social development (*Gesellschaftsperiode*) and not man as the starting-point. In the context of that discussion it is quite clear what Marx wanted to say and what he opposed. But there are other statements, which remain clear within any context. If we have a sequence of statements of one and the same kind, for instance, those about the *social role of the individual*, then such a series of statements becomes theoretical in nature. My intention is to present here such a sequence of statements, all of them selected from *Grundrisse*. I hope readers will excuse me the large number of quotations, because, first, they are the best reply to the groundless catchwords of Marxist anti-humanism, and secondly, they are still unknown to broad circles of readers as *Grundrisse* which, for reasons explained earlier, still remains an esoteric work.

'Individuals producing in society — hence socially determined individual production — is, of course, the point of departure.'[117]

Marx, by adopting this point of departure of his analysis, criticizes the illusions of bourgeois economists that individuals are freed from social bonds, that they can engage in production outside society. An individual always is an individual *within society*.

'Whenever we speak of production, then, what is meant is always production at a definite stage of social development — production by social individuals.'[118]

Thus an individual always acts through a specific form of society. Marx took precautionary measures with regard to the problem which Althusser finds so intriguing: he opposes the possibility of a subjective and voluntaristic interpretation of an individual's role in society not by a theoretical abstraction of the individual from his society, but by analysing the individual's involvement in society.

'All production is appropriation of nature on the part of an individual within and through a specific form of society.'[119]

I now pass to the conditions and goals of an individual's development within society, the problem which implicitly defines the nature of Marxian humanism and explains its sense. I would recommend to the adherents of the *coupure* (epistemological break) theory a careful study of the quotations from *Grundrisse*; they are also encouraged to pay special attention to the connection between those passages with Marx's *Manuscripts*. Both the problems discussed in *Grundrisse* and the language used there by Marx show no break whatsoever, but a clearly visible continuation, as if Marx, when writing *Grundrisse*, had read his *Manuscripts* and decided to incorporate in the new text some of the ideas formulated in the earlier one. First of all, he reverted to the problems of alienation (*Entfremdung*) and reification, and used them as a basis for his theory of fetishism in the form in which it was later to be continued and developed in *Capital*. The other problem was that of *humanism* in the sense of the goals and conditions of development of individuals within society.

> The reciprocal and all-sided dependence of individuals who are indifferent to one another forms their social connection. This social bond is expressed in *exchange value. . . .*
> The social character of activity, as well as the social form of the product, and the share of individuals in production here appear as something alien and objective, confronting the individuals, not as their relation to one another, but as their subordination to relations which subsist independently of them and which arise out of collisions between mutually indifferent individuals. The general exchange of activities and products, which has become a vital condition for each individual – their mutual interconnection – here appears as something alien to them, autonomous, as a thing. In exchange value, the social connection between persons is transformed into a social relation between things; personal capacity into objective wealth. . . . Each individual possesses social power in the form of a thing. Rob the thing of this social power and you must give it to persons to exercise over persons. Relations of personal dependence (entirely spontaneous at the outset) are the first social forms, in which human productive capacity develops only to a slight extent and at isolated points. Personal independence founded on *objective* (*sachlicher*) dependence is the second great form, in which a system of general social metabolism, of universal relations, of all-round needs and universal capacities is formed for the first time. Free individuality, based on the universal development of individuals and on their subordination to their communal, social productivity as their social wealth, is the third stage.[120]

Note the critical formulations concerning the social nature of human activity, interpreted 'not as their relation to one another, but as their subordination to relations which subsist independently of them', and compare with this the endeavours of the structuralists who would like to persuade us that Marx wanted to confine all scientific analysis to objective structures. This is untrue, this is a glaring contradiction of what the *mature* Marx really wrote. Let us read his other critical comments on alienation and reification (who was that who claimed that after his 'epistemological break' Marx had repudiated the theory of alienation and humanism?): Marx discusses there the role of money as the reified form of social connections, a form in which men have more confidence than in themselves as individuals.

> (. . . But why do they have faith in the thing? Obviously only because that thing is an *objectified relation* between persons; because it is objectified exchange value, and exchange value is nothing more than a mutual relation between people's productive activities. Every other collateral may serve the holder directly in that function: money serves him only as the 'dead pledge of society',[21] but it serves as such only because of its social (symbolic) property; and it can have a social property only because individuals have alienated their own social relationship from themselves so that it takes the form of a thing.)[121]

In *Grundrisse* Marx not only returned to his conception of alienation and reification as formulated in *Manuscripts*, but maintained explicitly that (i) it is human beings and not any alleged connections (structures) who form social relations; (ii) such relations are products of *history*; (iii) they are subordinated to control by universally developed individuals (which, among other things, is the sense of properly understood Marxian humanism).

> (. . . Equally certain is it that individuals cannot gain mastery over their own social interconnections before they have created them. But it is an insipid notion to conceive of this merely *objective bond* as a spontaneous, natural attribute inherent in individuals and inseparable from their nature (in antithesis to their conscious knowing and willing). This bond is their product. It is a historic product. It belongs to a specific phase of their development. The alien and independent character in which it presently exists *vis-à-vis* individuals proves only that the latter are still engaged in the creation of the conditions of their social life, and that they have not yet begun, on the basis of these conditions, to live it. It is the bond natural to individuals within specific and limited relations of production. Universally developed individuals, whose social relations, as their communal (*gemeinschaftlich*) relations, are hence also subordinated to their own communal control, are no product of nature, but of history. The degree and the universality of the development of wealth where *this* individuality becomes possible supposes production on the basis of exchange values as a prior condition, whose universality produces not only the alienation of the individual from himself and from others, but also the universality and the comprehensiveness of his relations and capacities.)[122]

In connection with the economic problems of commodity exchange, based on the production of objects which satisfy other people's needs, Marx takes up the issue of man, his personality, his freedom, etc.

The fact that this need on the part of one can be satisfied by the product of the other, and vice versa, and that the one is capable of producing the object of the need of the other, and that each confronts the other as owner of the object of the other's need, this proves that each of them reaches beyond his own particular need, etc., as a *human being*, and that they relate to one another as human beings; that their common species-beings (*Gattungswesen*) is acknowledged by all. It does not happen elsewhere – that elephants produce for tigers, or animals for other animals.... In so far as these natural differences among individuals and among their commodities ... form the motive for the integration of these individuals, for their social interrelation as exchangers, in which they are *stipulated* for each other as, and *prove* themselves to be, equals, there enters, in addition to the quality of equality, that of *freedom*. Although individual A feels a need for the commodity of individual B, he does not appropriate it by force, nor vice versa, but rather they recognize one another reciprocally as proprietors, as persons whose will penetrates their commodities. Accordingly, the juridical moment of the Person enters here, as well as that of freedom, in so far as it is contained in the former.... Out of the act of exchange itself, the individual, each of them, is reflected in himself as its exclusive and dominant (determinant) subject. With that, then, the complete freedom of the individual is posited: voluntary transaction; no force on either side....[123]

This represents a lot of worries for Althusser and his adherents: the mature Marx appears here as a typical 'ideological humanist'. He speaks about man and his feeling of being a member of a species common to him and other human beings, about equality, about freedom inherent in the juridical concept of person (not an individual, but precisely a person), Of course, Althusser can always claim that this was Marx's relapse into ideology and try to correct his ideas. He does not do that, because that would amount to admitting that he does not agree with Marx. But then Althusser's standpoint would be correct, for both he and others may formulate opinions they like, but on the condition they ascribe such opinions to themselves and not to Marx, because that would mean falsification.

We shall now pass to extremely important, perhaps fundamental statements made by Marx in *Grundrisse* on the subject of the 'social individual'. The appropriate formulation has been cited before the quotations from *Grundrisse*, and what is to be adduced here substantiates Marx's viewpoint. This is a *sui generis* return, but also a commentary, to the problems raised in *Theses on Feuerbach* (especially Thesis VI) and in *The German Ideology*. The point is important because, as I have said elsewhere, the revolution carried out by Marx in the interpretation of the individual's role in history does not consist in Marx's abandoning the idea of the role of the individual in favour of the role of the class and the masses, as some people claim, nor in favour of objective structures, as others see it; it consists in a deep-reaching transformation of the very idea of individual, in treating the individual as a *social individual*, i.e. an individual conditioned and constituted by society. Thus he did not drop the problems of the individual and his role in history, but, on the contrary, developed it and gave it a more profound interpretation. If humanism is based on the acceptance of the role of a concrete individual, then the mature Marx made his humanism *deeper* as compared with his ideas in his young age. From the brief and metaphorical formulation in Thesis VI on Feuerbach that the human being (and not 'the essence of man', as some people render it erroneously) is in fact the totality of social relations, Marx passed to his expanded interpretation of the social individual as formulated first in *The German Ideology* and later in *Grundrisse*. His statements on the subject made in *Grundrisse* are exemplary.

> In present bourgeois society as a whole, this positing of prices and their circulation, etc., appears as the surface process, beneath which, however, in the depths, entirely different processes go on, in which this apparent individual equality and liberty disappear. It is forgotten, on one side, that the *presupposition* of exchange value, as the objective basis of the whole of the system of production, already in itself implies compulsion over the individual, since his immediate product is not a product for him, but only *becomes* such in the social process, and since it *must* take on this general but nevertheless external form; and that the individual has an existence only as a producer of exchange value, hence that the whole negation of his natural existence is already implied; that he is therefore entirely determined by society; that this further presupposes a division of labour, etc., in which the individual is already posited in relations other than that of mere exchanger, etc. That therefore this presupposition by no means arises either out of the individual's will or out of the immediate nature of the individual, but that it is, rather, *historical*, and posits the individual as already determined by society.[124]

The difference between, or even incompatibility of, the standpoint adopted by the Marxist structuralism of Althusser and others and that taken by Marx is even more clearly marked in the passage to be quoted next, although it takes into consideration the existence of those 'objective structures' with which Althusser is so much concerned.

> When we consider bourgeois society in the long view and as a whole, then the final result of the process of social production always appears as the society itself, i.e. the human being itself in its social relations. Everything that has a fixed form, such as the product, etc., appears as merely a moment, a vanishing moment, in this movement. The direct production process itself here

appears only as a moment. The conditions and objectifications of the process and themselves equally moments of it, and its only subjects are the individuals, but individuals in mutual relationships, which they equally reproduce and produce anew.[125]

I recommend this passage to Althusser's and Balibar's special attention. Perhaps their scholarly conscience will make them feel remorse for what they have written about Marx.

If it is *social individuals*, i.e. individuals in their mutual relations and interconnections (Marx says: 'Society does not consist of individuals, but expresses the sum of interrelations, the relations within which these individuals stand'[125a]), who are the starting-point of the analysis, then this means that their individuality is a social product.

> But human beings become individuals only through the process of history. He appears originally as a *species-being (Gattungswesen), clan being, herd animal* – although in no way whatever as a ζῷον πολῑτικόν[4] in the political sense. Exchange itself is a chief means of this individuation (*Vereinzelung*). It makes the herd-line existence superfluous and dissolves it.

Let us now pass to the final humanistic accents, but not in the sense imparted to that term by Althusser: the accents to be found in the theses based on a scholarly analysis of the economic development of society. The development of the economic base of society conditions, *inter alia*, the development of the human individual as posited by Marxian humanism, which covers conclusions drawn from the empirical observations of facts, and not abstract moral norms and related requirements concerning social life. Incomprehension of this issue determines the utter incomprehension by Althusser of the Marxist theory, his distortion and mystification of Marxism. Here is what Marx wrote:

> All previous forms of society – or, what is the same, of the forces of social production – foundered on the development of wealth. Those thinkers of antiquity who were possessed of consciousness therefore directly denounced wealth as the dissolution of the community. The feudal system, for its part, foundered on urban industry, trade, modern agriculture (even as a result of individual inventions like gunpowder and the printing press). With the development of wealth – and hence also new powers and expanded intercourse on the part of the individuals – the economic conditions on which the community rested were dissolved, along with the political relations of the various constituents of the community which corresponded to those conditions: religion ...; the character, outlook, etc., of individuals. The *development of science alone*, i.e. the most solid form of wealth, both its product and its producer – was sufficient to dissolve these communities. But

the *development of science*, this ideal and at the same time practical wealth, is only one aspect, one form in which the *development of the human productive forces*, i.e. of wealth, appears. ... The result is: the tendentially and potentially general development of the forces of production – of wealth as such – as a basis; likewise, the universality of intercourse, hence the world market as a basis. The basis as the possibility of the universal development of the individual, and the real development of the individuals from this basis as a constant suspension of its *barrier*, which is recognized as a barrier, not taken for a *sacred limit*. Not an ideal or imagined universality of the individual, but the universality of his real and ideal relations.[127]

This is the object lesson of how Marx treated, from the point of view of *materialism*, the problems of the human individual and of humanism, and ideology – for Marxian humanism is an ideology as well – can be constructed as a *scientific* ideology, based on a *scientific* analysis of facts.

Let us now pass to the final humanistic conclusions to be drawn from such an analysis. Marx spoke about the role of labour in the formation of values. What Marx wrote on the progressing development of large industry and large-industry production is astonishingly topical today (especially in what concerns science as a force of production), and sounds almost like a prophecy, if we consider that he wrote that in the middle of the nineteenth century. But I am interested here in Marx's ideas about man, as formulated in that context, and in the fact that Marx constructed his *humanism*.

But to the degree that large industry develops, the creation of real wealth comes to depend less on labour time and on the amount of labour employed than on the power of the agencies set in motion during labour time, whose 'powerful effectiveness' is itself in turn out of all proportion to the direct labour time spent on their production, but depends rather on the general state of science and on the progress of technology, or the application of this science to production. ... In this transformation, it is neither the direct human labour he himself performs, nor the time during which he works, but rather the appropriation of his own general productive power, his understanding of nature and his mastery over it by virtue of his presence as a social body – it is, in a word, the development of the social individual which appears as the great foundation-stone of production and of wealth. ... The free development of individualities, and hence not the reduction of necessary labour time so as to posit surplus labour, but rather the general reduction of the necessary labour of society to a minimum, which then corresponds to the artistic, scientific, etc., development of the individuals in the time set free, and with the means created, for all of them.[128]

This is one more proof, not only of the fact that the mature Marx developed the humanistic ideas, but also of the fact that ideology can be based on scientific foundations.

To conclude this series of quotations I shall cite a passage which is a direct continuation of the preceding one. It is not immediately connected with the subject-matter discussed at this point, but is essential for the understanding of Marx's opinions on science. The truth about the role of science as a force of production, which is being rediscovered today, was forcefully stated by Marx in his *Grundrisse* as early as 1857.

> Nature builds no machines, no locomotives, railways, electric telegraphs, self-acting mules, etc. These are products of human industry; natural material transformed into organs of the human will over nature, or of human participation in nature. They are *organs of the human brain, created by the human hand*; the power of knowledge, objectified. The development of fixed capital indicates to what degree general social knowledge has become a *direct force of production*, and to what degree, hence, the conditions of the process of social life itself have come under the control of the general intellect and been transformed in accordance with it.[129]

This sequence of quotations is intended to demonstrate that Althusser is wrong, that his theses on anti-humanism are not based on factual data. My point was to show, by referring to a work written by the mature Marx, that he, Marx, had not abandoned the problem discussed in his *Manuscripts*, in particular the problems of humanism, alienation, reification, etc.; that he developed a humanistic ideology based on scientific foundations; and that he developed the concept of man as a social individual. The last-named issued, that of the *social individual*, was the most important of all. When piling evidence, and even running the risk of being called a pedant, I had not only Althusser and his Marxist structuralists in view. They have natural allies in the interpretation of that problem: all those who, by referring to imaginary orthodoxy, continue, whether consciously or not, the Stalinist idea of negating the individual in the Marxist theory. Such a negation has little in common with Marxism, as can be seen from the above-cited passages from *Grundrisse*. It is a glaring denial of one of the basic ideas in the Marxist theory.

Let us now sum up our reflections on Althusser's anti-humanism. What are the conclusions?

First, Althusser means by humanism a trend which deduces its thesis on the necessity of social development from the speculative idea of the 'essence of man', and thus imparts to that concept a meaning which differs totally from that accepted in the Marxist theory. This is why his anti-humanism has no connection whatever with Marxist humanism, and suggestions to the contrary are based on a mystification.

Secondly, anti-humanism as interpreted by Althusser is not symmetrical to his specifically understood humanism, and hence is not a simple negation of the thesis that the necessity of social development results from what is *a priori* posited in the 'essence of man': it also claims that production relations as understood by Marx are not relations between human beings, and includes the thesis which negates the role of the human individual, or, even more sweepingly, the role of human beings in general, which is alleged to be an element of the Marxian conception.

Thirdly, the claim that according to Marx production relations are not relations between human beings is evidently false in view of Marx's unambiguous statements on the issue. Such a standpoint was criticized by Marx in *Capital* in his comments on commodity fetishism, comments which are results of his analyses to be found in *Grundrisse*.

Fourthly, the negation of man's role in social development, which is a consequence of the reduction of social mechanisms to objective structures, is erroneous in the light of the Marxist theory of the social individual, as is proved by the data drawn from *Grundrisse*.

One Marx or Two Marxes?

The theory of the 'epistemological break' (*coupure*) is that element which links Althusser's conception into a whole. The theory is that of two Marxes: the young Marx was ideologically minded, the mature Marx's approach was scientific, because he broke with the past, and his works written in the mature period are marked by anti-humanism, anti-historicism, anti-empiricism, etc. That notorious 'epistemological break', which splits Marx's activity into two parts, is supposed to have occurred *ca.* 1845.

In advancing his idea of the break in the evolution of Marx's views Althusser refers to Gaston Bachelard, but it suffices to go through the latter's work to see that Bachelard cannot be held responsible for the use Althusser made of his theory of *rupture épistémologique*. Bachelard's theory is that of revolutions in science, of little interest today. Bachelard in turn refers to the now classical theory formulated by Comte and distinguishes four periods in the development of human knowledge, the fourth period, the contemporary one, being that of a revolutionary transition from everyday knowledge to scientific knowledge.

We are thus of the opinion that contemporary scientific revolutions can be termed, in the manner of Comte's philosophy, the *fourth period*, the first three corresponding, respectively to antiquity, the Middle Ages, and the modern epoch. The fourth period, the contemporary one, witnesses the break, the transition from everyday knowledge to scientific knowledge, from everyday experience to scientific experience.[130]

Bachelard later refers to the *rupture épistémologique*: 'It would certainly be difficult to indicate with precision what tribunal should judge such an epistemological break.'[131]

This theory of revolutions in science, which locates them in the contemporary period only, because this fits the general schema, is oddly speculative. But we will leave it aside as we are concerned with Althusser, and not with Bachelard. Althusser has specifically radicalized that theory: while Bachelard speaks about the development of human knowledge, i.e. about the development of theories which explain facts, Althusser applies the concept of *rupture*, or, to use his term, *coupure*, to the views of a single thinker. Here is one of his numerous comments on that *coupure*:

(1) There is an unequivocal '*epistemological break*' in Marx's work which does in fact occur at the point where Marx himself locates it, in the book, unpublished in his lifetime, which is a critique of his erstwhile philosophical (ideological) conscience: *The German Ideology*. The *Theses on Feuerbach*, which are only a few sentences long, mark out the earlier limit of this break, the point at which the new theoretical consciousness is already beginning to show through in the erstwhile consciousness and the erstwhile language, that is, as *necessarily ambiguous and unbalanced concepts*.

(2) This 'epistemological break' concerns conjointly *two distinct theoretical disciplines*. By founding the theory of history (historical materialism), Marx simultaneously broke with his erstwhile ideological philosophy and established a new philosophy (dialectical materialism).[132]

According to Althusser (and in this case according to Godelier and others as well) that epistemological break consists in the fact that a certain set of problems (Althusser refers to that set of problems as a 'specific unity of theoretical formation'), which were raised in Marx's works up to 1845, were not raised later, and hence such catch-words as *anti-humanism, anti-historicism, anti-empiricism*, etc.

The epistemological break interpreted in this way is just a figment of Althusser's imagination. All those problems which are found in Marx's works written before 1845 are found in his later works, too; the same applies to his specific terminology used in the *Manuscripts*. It suffices to reach for *1857 Grundrisse* to see that Althusser is just imagining things.

Some authors, among them Lucien Sève, whom I have quoted earlier, have extracted from Marx's works hundreds of quotations which give the lie to the claim about any break in the sense given that term by Althusser. It would be pointless to revert to that issue, the more so as I have given *en passant* quite a number of data which repudiate Althusser's thesis.

As for the three *'anti'*s-' listed above, I have shown earlier that Althusser assigns specific meanings to traditional terms, meanings which have nothing in common with Marxism, and whenever he draws conclusions about the Marxist theory on the strength of his interpretation of these terms he in fact engages in mystification.

If anything remains to be done in commenting on the relation between the views of the young Marx and those of the mature Marx, then it is rather a positive interpretation of the development of those views which bear the name of Marxism.

It is beyond doubt that Marx's views were undergoing modifications, which is a rather trivial statement as it is common knowledge that this is the case of every thinker of some significance. It is also beyond doubt that the style of thinking and philosophizing typical of the young Marx differed from that characteristic of the mature Marx (to avoid misunderstandings in connection with this issue I wish to make it plain that I personally do not like the style of the young Marx whereas I find the way Marx thought and expressed his ideas in the 1850s and later very much to my liking). This also has given rise to various predilections; some consider the views of the young Marx to be the true Marxism and reject the views of the old Marx, others, on the contrary, respect the mature Marx only and negate the Marxist nature of the views of the young Marx. Both schools of thought have their advocates; over the last few decades both have been closely connected with specified political views.

Which approach is correct? Neither; in their radical form both are in the wrong, if only for the fact that Marx was one person, and any endeavour to split him into different and separate personalities is a psychological and scientific nonsense. What was propounded by the young Marx was also a nucleus of the ideas held by the mature Marx and stimulated his further development, and what was propounded by the mature Marx, the author of *Capital* and comprehensive historical studies, had its roots in his earlier ideas, which a careful reading of his later works reveals in the form of specific ideas and even his specific language. These statements are trivial in view of being self-evident, but under certain circumstances it is necessary to repeat trivial statements. I may add that certain conceptions, especially those which Althusser would like to reject without any justification, can be found as motifs through all Marx's works, motifs which impart the specific nature to his socialism; they are: humanism together with Marx's concept of man; the theory of alienation and the ways of overcoming alienation; historicism; etc. I stress those points which the Althusser school finds particularly revolting.

I renounce any broader discussion on those historical issues which are connected with the epistemological break theory, and shall take up only one problem, to be discussed in the light of an analysis of only one work dated after the alleged break. The work is *Grundrisse* of 1857, and the problem is that of alienation. I have selected it because it is the category which, as is known, played an enormous role in the philosophical system of the young Marx and is claimed to have disappeared after the epistemological break together with the whole set of anthropological issues, and to have been replaced by the category of commodity fetishism. I do maintain that as far as the problem of alienation is concerned Marx continued both to discuss it and to use the terminology of his youth — after the supposed epistemological break. Let us bear in mind that Marx wrote *Grundrisse* in 1857, that is 12 years after the date which Althusser adopts as the date of the break, and that the work is nothing less than the first outline of *Capital.* Marx shows there his conception of alienation in its full form, and adds very important comments which help us better to comprehend the relations that hold between alienation, on the one hand, and reification and commodity fetishism, on the other.

Let us show the passages relevant to the subject in the order they occur in *Grundrisse*, beginning with two of them already cited earlier in the present book. The first of them is worth repeating now, because Marx refers in it to the concepts of alienation and reification; he does so clearly in the spirit of *Manuscripts*, but at the same time in the light of a new analysis of economic issues (exchange value).

> The social character of activity, as well as the social form of the product, and the share of individuals in production here appears as something alien and objective, confronting the individuals, not as their relation to one another, but as their subordination to relations which subsist independently of them and which arise out of collisions between mutually indifferent individuals. The general exchange of activities and products, which has become a vital condition for each individual — their mutual interconnection — here appears as

> something alien to them, autonomous, as a thing. In exchange value, the social connection between persons is transformed into a social relation between things; personal capacity into objective wealth.[133]

The next passage, also cited earlier, is important here as it not only proves the vitality of the theory of alienation in the works of the mature Marx, but also shows how Marx understood the relation between alienation and reification, namely, that it is alienation which is the basic factor.

> (. . . But why do they have faith in the thing? Obviously only because that thing is an *objectified relation* between persons; because it is objectified exchange value, and exchange value is nothing more than a mutual relation between people's productive activities. Every other collateral may serve the holder directly in that function: money serves him only as the 'dead pledge of society',[21] but it serves as such only because of its social (symbolic) property and it can have a social property only because individuals have alienated their own relationship from themselves so that it takes the form of a thing.)[134]

Let us now pass to another problem, namely that of the relation between labour and capital, interpreted as alienation. Here again we encounter the terminology and the way of thinking typical of *Manuscripts*.

> It is clear, therefore, that the worker cannot become *rich* in this exchange, since, in exchange for his labour capacity as a fixed, available magnitude, he surrenders its *creative power*, . . . Rather, he necessarily impoverishes himself, as we shall see further on, because the creative power of his labour establishes itself as the power of capital, as an *alien power* confronting him. He *divests himself (entäussert sich)* of labour as the force productive of wealth; capital appropriates it, as such.
>
> Therefore, those who demonstrate that the productive force ascribed to capital is a *displacement*, a *transposition of the productive force* of labour,[16] forget precisely that capital itself is essentially this *displacement, this transposition* and that wage labour as such presupposes capital, so that, from its standpoint as well, capital is this *transsubstantiation*; the necessary process of positing its own powers as *alien* to the worker.[135]

The important thing in the above passage is not only the wording and the terminology, but also the reference to the theory of alienation as the scientific explanation of the relation between labour and capital and of the economic function of capital.

The same holds for the quotation that follows.

> (*Wage labour*, here, in the strict economic sense in which we use it here, and no other − and we will later have to distinguish it from other forms of labour for day-wages etc. − is capital-positing, capital-producing labour, i.e. living labour which produces both the objective conditions of its realization as an activity, as well as the objective moments of its being as labour *capacity*,

and produces them as alien powers opposite itself, as *values* for themselves, independent of it.)[136]

In the next quotation, likewise, the main point is not so much the terminology as the application of the theory of alienation in explaining economic facts.

> Production based on exchange value, on whose surface this free and equal exchange of equivalents proceeds, is at its base the exchange of *objectified labour* as exchange value for living labour as use value, or, to express this in another way, the relating of labour to its objective conditions – and hence to the objectivity created by itself – as alien property: *alienation (Entäusserung) of labour.*[137]

Marx's ideas on the alienation of the means of labour and on science in relation to workers are extremely interesting. At this moment we are mainly interested in alienation, especially as it can explain certain social facts, but ideas on automation and the role of science as a means of production are surprisingly novel.

> But, once adopted into the production process of capital the means of labour passes through different metamorphoses, whose culmination is the *machine*, or rather, an *automatic system of machinery* (system of machinery: the *automatic* one is merely its most complete, most adequate form, and alone transforms machinery into a system). . . . The worker's activity, reduced to a mere abstraction of activity, is determined and regulated on all sides by the movement of the machinery, and not the opposite. The science which compels the inanimate limbs of the machinery, by their construction, to act purposefully, as an automaton, does not exist in the worker's consciousness, but rather acts upon him through the machine as an alien power, as the power of the machine itself. . . . The production process has ceased to be a labour process in the sense of a process dominated by labour as its governing unity. Labour appears, rather, merely as a conscious organ, scattered among the individual living workers at numerous points of the mechanical system; subsumed under the total process of the machinery itself, as itself only a link of the system, whose unity exists not in the living workers, but rather in the living (active) machinery, which confronts his individual, insignificant doings as a mighty organism. In machinery, objectified labour confronts living labour within the labour process itself as the power which rules it. . . . In machinery, knowledge appears as alien, external to him; and living labour [as] subsumed under self-activating objectified labour. The worker appears as superfluous to the extent that his action is not determined by [capital's] requirement.[138]

From my point of view, the essential element in the above passage is again not the terminology, but the *manner of explaining*, by reference to the theory of alienation, the strikingly modern, and today particularly topical, issues in the social consequences of automation.

Let me conclude by quoting the passage which is significant not only for the emphasis laid on the advantages of the theory of alienation in explaining socio-economic issues, but in particular for the unequivocal formulation of the problem of the historical nature of alienation; objectivization (*Vergegenständlichung*) is inevitable in every form of social life, and alienation is historically conditioned; it develops under specified social conditions, and vanishes when those conditions cease to exist.

> The fact that in the development of the productive powers of labour the objective conditions of labour, objectified labour, must grow relative to living labour . . . appears from the standpoint of capital not in such a way that one of the moments of social activity – objective labour – becomes the ever more powerful body of the other moment, of subjective, living labour, but rather – and this is important for wage labour – that the objective conditions of labour assume an ever more colossal independence, represented by its very extent, opposite living labour, and that social wealth confronts labour in more powerful portions as an alien and dominant power. The emphasis comes to be placed not on the state of being *objectified* but on the state of being *alienated*, dispossessed, sold (Der Ton wird gelegt nicht auf das *Vergegenständlichtsein*, sondern das *Entfremdet-, Entäussert-, Veräussertsein*); on the condition that the monstrous objective power which social labour itself erected opposite itself as one of its moments belongs not to the worker, but to the personified conditions of production, i.e. to capital. . . . The bourgeois economists are so much cooped up within the notions belonging to a specific historic stage of social development that the necessity of the *objectification* of the powers of social labour appears to them as inseparable from the necessity of their *alienation vis-à-vis* living labour. But with the suspension of the *immediate* character of living labour, as merely *individual*, or as general merely internally or merely externally, with the positing of the activity of individuals as immediately general or *social* activity, the objective moments of production are stripped of this form of alienation; they are thereby posited as property, as the organic social body within which the individuals reproduce themselves as individuals, but as social individuals.[139]

This is a selection, far from exhaustive, of passages from a single work written by Marx in his indisputably mature period. The theory of alienation, chosen by way of example, shows that, (i) the claim concerning the epistemological break, according to which the problems discussed by Marx before 1845, in particular the anthropological ones, vanish in his later works, (ii) the claim concerning the rejection by the mature Marx of the theory of alienation, are just mystifications. In 1857 Marx did not mention the problems raised by him in *Manuscripts* just for the sake of coquetry (as he uses to say about the Hegelian style of some of his statements), but referred to them directly, both semantically and conceptually. Likewise, he often referred to the theory of alienation to explain socio-economic issues.

The theory of the epistemological break can be left to its own fate. It is a product of the imagination of the thinker who takes his wishful thinking for facts.

I shall not go into any further dispute over the history of Marxian thought for, as I have said before, I consider that to be useless. But it is worth while to reflect, by way of marginal comments to that dispute, on the methodological approach to the views of the young Marx. It is obvious that Marx's works from the late period form part of the body of what we call the Marxist theory. But what about his works from the early period? The answer to this question can be found in Marx himself.

Althusser declares himself for anti-historicism and would like to present his standpoint as the Marxist one. This is why he rejects all that which relates to historicism; this applies to his interpretation of Marxism, too. But he thereby deprives himself of the principal method of understanding the development of Marx's ideas. What are we to do with those concepts, ideas and intellectual stimuli which we find in the works of the young Marx? Are we to discard all that simply because Althusser has labelled that period of Marx's activity unscientific as it preceded the alleged epistemological break? That would be wrong. Althusser says himself[139a] that *Manuscripts* include the outline of *Capital*. It suffices to study *Grundrisse* thoroughly to notice in *Manuscripts* many more elements which came to fertilize Marx's later works. And what about the other excellent works written by the young Marx? And what about the development of the Marxian concept of man and the theory of alienation, which consistently led him to conclude that economics is the foundation of social development? If one is not possessed by the anti-ideological phobia, one cannot overlook those elements in the works of the young Marx. The only reasonable thing to do is to view the young Marx from the standpoint of the mature Marx; in other words, the works of his youth should be assessed from the point of view of their role in shaping his ideas in the mature age. As I have said, such an approach is recommended by Marx himself.

In the excellent 'Introduction' to *Grundrisse* we find a methodologically significant passage connected with the problem of historicism.

> Bourgeois society is the most developed and the most complex historic organization of production. The categories which express its relations, the comprehension of its structure, thereby also allows insights into the structure and the relations of production of all the vanished social formations out of

whose ruins and elements it built itself up, whose partly still unconquered remnants are carried along within it, whose mere nuances have developed explicit significance within it, etc. Human anatomy contains a key to the anatomy of the ape. The intimations of higher development among the subordinate animal species, however, can be understood only after the higher development is already known.[140]

I have on one occasion referred to this passage in the 'Introduction' to substantiate my criticism of the views of Leszek Kołakowski, who also supported the thesis on the existence of two Marxes, but with a predilection for the young one. This was in turn criticized by Althusser, who readily discarded the young Marx and ridiculed those who would like to keep the 'whole' Marx.[141] It is characteristic in this connection that Althusser passed over with silence the recommendation made by Marx that the past is to be judged by its effects.

For what does Marx say in the passage cited above?

First, that the significance of past events is revealed only in their consequences ('The intimations of higher development among the subordinate animal species, however, can be understood only after the higher development is already known'). Secondly, that the structure of past events can be understood only if one understands the higher structures which gave full significance to what had existed in a nuclear form.

The two theses are pithily summed up in the formulation that 'human anatomy contains a key to the anatomy of the ape'.

We should not underestimate the assertion that the anatomy of *Capital* and of other works from Marx's mature period is a key to the anatomy of *Manuscripts*. And that not only because that this follows directly from Marx's own statements, but above all because this is what common sense indicates, on the obvious condition that one is not under the pressure of the *ideé fixe* which claims that in 1845 Marx renounced all his intellectual past. This is a self-evident nonsense, refuted by facts.

But in Althusser's case this is no mere coincidence: the circle closes at this point. We have started with his opposing ideology to science. Later all the embarrassing concepts — empiricism, historicism, humanism — are subsumed under the category of ideology. The crowning claim is that concerning the two Marxes, the young and ideologically minded, and the mature and scientifically minded. The schema is clear, and the structure of the whole is consistent. But all that is erroneous from beginning to end.

But what is the relationship between these claims formulated by Althusser and structuralism?

My answer will be seemingly self-contradictory: the relation between the two is weak, and at the same time an essential one. The interpretation depends on the starting-point of the analysis and the criteria to be adopted.

When analysing the issue of science and ideology and that of empiricism in Althusser's work we could not find there any influence of structuralism. It is true that the terms *structure*, a *structured whole, ideological field, field of problems*, occur in them occasionally, but semantically they have no significance whatever, nor any consequences in the solutions adopted by Althusser. The mere fact that a person uses such words as *structure* does not make him a structuralist.

It is otherwise when it comes to historicism and humanism. Here the adoption of objective structures as the point of departure is decisive as it blocks that path to understanding history in the former case and to understanding the role of man in the latter. As a result we are offered a vision of society as a structure, but deprived of history; we are offered a vision of social relations as relations between objective structures, but without man. This is, of course, a simplified picture, but it shows what is essential in Althusser's views.

Is that structuralism? Certainly they are views which are shaped *under the influence* of a version of structuralist theory. In view of the variety of those trends which use the label of structuralism, nothing prevents us from adding one item to the list – of course, with the proviso (which I have made, I hope, sufficiently explicit in the first essay) that the relationships between those various trends are loose, and that their relationships with that school of thought which has introduced the term into science, i.e. with structural linguistics, are rather illusory.

The characteristic feature of the trend represented by Althusser – among the many other structuralist schools, which are today common, especially in France – is its connection with Marxism, both in the sense that the adherents of that trend are advocates of Marxist philosophy, and in the sense that they try to 'modernize' the Marxist theory in the spirit of structuralism. As I have said earlier, if Althusser spoke on his own behalf, it would all be otherwise, but he speaks in the name of Marx and claims to represent the true Marxism. I have no doubts about it that in view of the indisputable incompatibility of Althusser's standpoint with the Marxist theory (and that on fundamental issues) his opinions will be rejected by the Marxist milieu (only the esoteric nature of Althusser's views can account for the fact that this has not occurred so far). But that should not adversely affect structuralism as such. Such an attitude would be wrong and would deprive the Marxist theory of an important theoretical instrument. This is precisely why, in connection with the criticism of Althusser's opinions and of what is termed Marxist structuralism, we should discuss the positive aspects of the relationships between Marxism and structuralism.

First of all, we have to answer the question about relationships between Marxism and what? For the trouble is that when people refer to structuralism they seemingly refer to something specified, whereas in fact, in view of the plurality of structuralist theories, mentioned earlier in this book, it is often not clear to what a given reference is made. Let it be plainly said that I do not mean such and such a school, or such and such a trend, which, more or less legitimately, is using the label of structuralism, but a certain intellectual trend which I tried to describe in the introductory essay. This is all the more important since we have to take into consideration not only those trends which officially term themselves structuralist, but also those which, like organismalism in biology, the *Gestalt* approach in psychology, and above all the general systems analysis, do not use that label, but contribute to the structuralist theory not less, and probably much more, than the official representatives of that trend. The essential issue is the methodological requirement that the world should be investigated as a system which has s specified structure.

There is no question of any opposition to that requirement on the part of the Marxist theory, if that requirement is interpreted not as a recommendation of an exclusively structural analysis of facts, but as a recommendation of a study of structures in connection with a study of changes. Such an approach, the only reasonable one, does not imply any underestimation of structural analysis and ideas related to it.

I have already stressed the fact that structural analysis (the study of structural, or, coexistential, laws) is an element of Marx's historical method. Kaufman said that explicitly in his review of *Capital*, and Marx approved his opinion. Are we, therefore, to claim, by following the present-day fashion, that Marx was a structuralist? Althusser claims that Marx was a structuralist *à l'insue*, that he used to solve problems as a structuralist, and that he gave rise to the problem, even though he did not pose it explicitly.[142] I think that we can go further in that direction. There is no need to label Marx a structuralist, but we have to state it plainly that both Marx and Engels realized perfectly well that genetic and structural analysis are complementary to one another. This is confirmed by Marx's approval of the complementary nature of these two methods, explicitly formulated by Kaufman. This is also confirmed by Engels' comprehensive comments on the relationships between the investigation of 'things as given complexes of constants' and the investigation of processes, with the stress on the importance of the study of complexes of constants as a precondition of the study of processes. ('One has first to know what a given thing is before one can notice the changes which occur in it.'[143] The principle of studying the structure of a system is not only not alien to the Marxist theory, but, on the contrary, is inherent in its methodological assumptions.

Nothing prevents us from developing structural research at the time of indisputable demand for a better knowledge of things as 'complexes of constants'. Nothing prevents us either, from the point of view of the Marxist methodology, from interpreting that 'better' knowledge not only in the sense of the amount of information, but also in the sense of improving the methods that enable us to gather such information.

The structuralist revolution does not mean the discovery of new vistas in research, for these have been known for a long time, and in some periods were clearly dominant in science; it does not mean a change in research *methods*. But this does not apply to the structuralist vogue in general: that vogue covers both novel trends (the structural method in phonology, the general systems analysis) and parasitic ones, which do not contribute anything new to the problem. The scientific fertility of those trends which claim to be structuralist should be assessed by their ability to develop specific structural methods, adapted to the subject-matter of research.

From the Marxist point of view, the appraisal of a given structuralist trend (regardless of whether the term *structuralism* occurs in its name, or not – the latter case being that of organismalism, the general systems analysis, etc.) should be based on two criteria: (i) whether a given trend has in fact developed its own specific structural method, adapted to the subject-matter of research, and (ii) whether it treats that method not as the only way of investigating facts, but as a method which is complementary to the analysis of processes, i.e. the method of investigating changes.

Hence, my conclusions concerning what is called Marxist structuralism are critical not because Althusser and his adherents want to promote structural analysis, but because what they do does not meet the criteria formulated above: they have not developed any structural method specifically adapted to the subject-matter of research, but have merely borrowed existing ideas; nor have they succeeded in developing their method of structural analysis as complementary to the analysis of processes (historical analysis), but, on the contrary — which is glaring in the case of thinkers who avow the Marxist theory and claim to be its spokesmen — have come to treat it as a rival one, and have in fact eliminated the analysis of processes.

Thus, if I discredit Althusser's approach, this is a result of my assessment of his specific endeavour to graft the method of structural analysis on the Marxist theory, which neither implies my rejection of the structural method as such, nor my exclusion of the possibility of the emergence of schools of thought which in given fields would succeed in assimilating the general requirements of the systems analysis, i.e. the study of structural laws detectable in such systems, such studies being treated as complementary to the analysis of processes. It is on that condition only that Marxist structuralism can develop. It would, however, be thereby so much different from those trends which today claim to be structuralist that it would better be termed otherwise; there would be nothing extraordinary in that, be it alone for the fact that the founders of the general systems analysis deliberately refused the burden of the tradition associated with the term *structuralism*. But, of course, it is not the label which is the most important thing. On the factual side, the situation is clear, from which it does not in the least follow that the resulting requirements and recommendations are easy to carry out. But, from the Marxist point of view, nothing prevents us from trying.

NOTES

1. H. Lefebvre, *Au-delà du structuralisme* Paris, 1971, p. 325.
2. M. Dufrenne, 'La philosophie du néo-positivisme', *Esprit*, May 1967, p. 784.
3. 'Dialectique marxiste et pensée structurale', *Les Cahiers du Centre d'Etudes Socialistes*, 1968, Nos. 76–81, p. 88.
4. *Ibid.*, p. 5.
5. J. Conilh, 'Lecture de Marx', *Esprit*, May 1967, p. 883.

6. 'Ce que veulent les gauchistes', *Preuves*, 1970, III, p. 10.
7. 'Jean Paul Sartre répond', *L'Arc*, No. 30, p. 88.
8. J. M. Domenach, 'Le système et la personne', *Esprit*, May 1967, p. 775.
9. H. Lefebvre, *op. cit.*, p. 325.
10. L. Sebag, 'Marxisme et structuralisme', *La Quinzaine Littéraire*, 1967, No. 29, p. 23.
11. L. Althusser, *For Marx*, London, 1969, p. 22.
12. Althusser, *op. cit.*, p. 23.
13. *Ibid.*
14. Althusser, *op. cit.*, p. 26.
15. Althusser, *op. cit.*, pp. 27–28.
16. Althusser, *op. cit.*, p. 29.
17. Althusser, *op. cit.*, p. 30. This statement is not accidental, which is proved by the fact that Althusser repeated the same idea in his *Lénine et la philosophie*, Paris, 1969.
18. *For Marx, ed. cit.*, pp. 30–31.
19. *For Marx, ed. cit.*, p. 164.
20. F. Bacon, *Novum Organon*, quoted after Th. S. Kuhn, *The Structure of Scientific Revolutions*, Chicago, 1964, p. 18.
21. *For Marx, ed. cit.*, p. 69.
22. *For Marx, ed. cit.*, p. 74.
23. *For Marx, ed. cit.*, p. 170.
24. *For Marx, ed. cit.*, p. 191.
25. *For Marx, ed. cit.*, p. 190.
26. *For Marx, ed. cit.*, p. 223.
27. *For Marx, ed. cit.*, p. 231.
28. *Ibid.*
29. *For Marx, ed. cit.*, pp. 232–3. On p. 167 of the same book we find the following statement which is in contradiction with that quoted above: '. . . ideological practice (ideology, whether religious, political, moral, legal or artistic, also transforms its object: men's "consciousness"). . . .'
30. *For Marx, ed. cit.*, pp. 234–5. Althusser explicitly refers to ideology as *ideés fausses* in *Lénine et la philosophie, ed. cit.*, pp. 49–50.
31. *For Marx, ed. cit.*, p. 235.
31a. *For Marx, ed. cit.*, p. 232.
31b. *Ibid.*
31c. *For Marx, ed. cit.*, pp. 235–6.
32. L. Althusser and E. Balibar, *Reading Capital*, London, 1970, p. 103.
33. Althusser and Baliber, *op. cit.*, pp. 145–6.
34. Althusser and Baliber, *op. cit.*, p. 53.
35. Althusser and Baliber, *op. cit.*, p. 141.
36. A. Schmidt, 'Der strukturalische Angriff auf die Geschichte', in: A. Schmidt (ed.), *Beiträge sur marxistischen Erkenntnistheorie*, Frankfurt, 1969.
37. 'Marxisme, Anthropologie et Religion', *Raison Présente*, No. 18, p. 54.
38. 'Dialectique marxiste et sensée structurale', *ed. cit.*, p. 183.
38a. *For Marx, ed. cit.*, pp. 232–3.
39. J. Szacki, 'Marksowskie pojęcie "świadomości fałszywej"' (The Marxian Concept of 'False Consciousness'). *Studia Socjologiczne*, 1966, No. 2.
40. V. I. Lenin, *Letter to the Northern Union* (in Russian), *Lenin's Collected*

142   Structuralism and Marxism

Works (in Russian), 5th ed., Vol. 6, pp. 362–3.

41. V. I. Lenin, *Materialism and Empiriocriticism* (in Russian), *Lenin's Collected Works* (in Russian), 5th ed., Vol. 18, p. 138.

42. A. Naess, *Democracy, Ideology and Objectivity*, Oslo Univ. Press, 1956.

43. J. J. Wiatr, *Czy zmierzch ery ideologii?* (Is the Epoch of Ideologies Declining?), Warszawa, 1966, pp. 71–74.

44. A. Schaff, 'Funkcjonalna definicja ideologii' (A Functional Definition of Ideology), *Kultura i Społeczeństwo*, 1973, No. 2, p. 48.

45. For a very clear exposition of the issue see Walter Hollitscher, *Der Mensch*, Wien, 1969, pp. 348–50.

46. A. Schaff, *History and Truth*, Pergamon Press, 1976, Chap. 3.

47. K. Twardowski, 'O tak zwanych prawdach względnych' (On What are Termed Relative Truths), in *Rozprawy i artykuły filozoficzne* (Philosophical Papers), Lwów, 1927.

48. Several recent works concerned with the definition of the concept of science are listed below by way of example: M. Bunge, *Scientific Research*, Berlin, 1967; N. Campbell, *What is Science?*, New York, 1952 (first published in 1921); J. G. Kemeny, *Philosopher Looks at Science*, Princeton, 1964 (first published in 1959); P. V. Kopnin, *Logical Foundations of Science* (in Russian), Kiev, 1968; Th. S. Kuhn, *The Structure of Scientific Revolutions*, Chicago, 1967 (first published in 1962); S. Kamiński, *The Concept of Science and the Classification of Sciences* (in Polish), Lublin, 1970; H. Reichenbach, *Modern Philosophy of Science*, London, 1959; L. Tondl, J. Nekola and B. Vobornik, *The Science of Science* (in Czech), Praha, 1964.

49. S. Kamiński's book mentioned in note 48, p. 6.

50. Kamiński, *op. cit.*, pp. 26–27.

51. I quote by way of example the following statement by Althusser in *For Marx*, pp. 167–8: 'In its most general form theoretical practice does not only include *scientific* theoretical practice, but also pre-scientific theoretical practice, that is, "ideological" theoretical practice (the forms of "knowledge" that make up the prehistory of science and their "philosophies"). . . . This is not the place to discuss the dialectic in action in the advent of this "break" that is, the labour of specific theoretical transformation which installs in each case, which establishes a science by detaching it from the ideology of its past and by revealing this past as ideological.'

52. *Les Cahiers du Centre d'Etudes Socialistes, ed. cit.*, p. 186.

53. Twardowski, *op. cit.*

54. Kuhn, *op. cit.*, pp. 2–3.

55. Kuhn, *op. cit.*, p. 3.

56. A. Schaff, 'Que signifie "être marxiste"?', in *L'Homme et la société*, 1971, No. 19.

57. Cf. *Marx-Engels-Werke* (hereafter referred to as *MEW*), Vol. 27, p. 12.

58. *MEW* Vol. 6, p. 397.

59. K. Marx, *Capital*, Foreign Languages Publishing House, Moscow, Vol. I, p. 18.

60. *MEW* Vol. 20, p. 35.

61. *For Marx, ed. cit.*, pp. 183–4.

62. *For Marx, ed. cit.*, p. 190.

63. *Les Cahiers du Centre d'Etudes Socialistes, ed. cit.*, p. 183.

64. *Les Cahiers du Centre d'Etudes Socialistes, ed. cit.*, p. 194.

65. *Les Cahiers du Centre d'Etudes Socialistes, ed. cit.*, p. 197. 'Ce n'est pas en se baladant dans les usines que Marx a découvert la science qu'il voulait élaborer, c'est en polémiquant contre les textes de Feuerbach, du romantisme allemand, de l'école historique du droit, etc. . . .'
66. A. Schaff, *History and Truth, ed. cit.*, Chap. 5.
67. In his 'Preface' to *Contribution* Marx mentions the existence of that 'Introduction', written in 1857, which he decided not to include in the book. This was why the editors of the German text appended it in 1947 to the text of the book, but, characteristically enough, failed to mention the existence of the text of *Grundrisse*, which was published, together with the 'Introduction', as early as 1939.
68. *Reading Capital, ed. cit.*, pp. 46–47.
69. *Reading Capital, ed. cit.*, pp. 155–6.
70. *Capital, ed. cit.*, Vol. I, p. 19 (italics – A. S.).
71. The reproduction, or assimilation, by human thought of the concrete through the knowledge of its elements, and the rising from the abstract to the concrete, are not to be confused with actual research, which, as Marx put it in his 'Preface' to *Contribution*, must 'climb up from the particular to the general'.
72. In view of the importance of this passage, its original German-language version is given, too, after *MEW*, Vol. 13, pp. 631–3. 'Wenn wir ein gegebenes Land politisch-ökonomisch betrachten, so beginnen wir mit seiner Bevölkerung, ihrer Verteilung in Klassen, Stadt, Land, See, den verschiednen Produktionszweigen, Aus- und Einfuhr, jährlicher Produktion and Konsumtion, Warenpreisen, etc. Es scheint das Richtige zu sein mit dem Realen und Konreten, der wirklichen Voraussetzung zu beginnen, also z.B. in der Ökonomie mit der Bevölkerung, die die Grundlage und das Subjekt des ganzen gesellschaftlichen Prokutionsakts ist. Indes teigt sich dies bei näherer Betrachtung als falsch. Die Bevölkerung ist eine Abstraktion, wenn ich z.B. die Klassen, aus denen sie besteht, weglasse. Diese Klassen sind wieder ein leeres Wort, wenn ich die Elemente nicht kenne, auf denen sie beruhn. Z. B. Lohnarbeit, Kapital, etc. . . . Das Konkrete ist konkret, weil es die Zusammenfassung vieler Bestimmungen ist, also Einheit des Mannigfaltigen. Im Denken erscheint es daher als Prozess der Zusammenfassung, als Resultat, nicht als Ausgangspunkt, obgleich es der wirkliche Ausgangspunkt und daher auch der Ausgangspunkt der Anschauung und Vorstellung ist. Im ersten Weg wurde die volle Vorstellung zu abstrakter Bestimmung verfluchtigt; im zweiten führen die abstrakten Bestimmungen zur Reproduktion des Konkreten im Weg des Denkens. . . . die Methode vom Abstrakten zum Konkreten aufzusteigen . . . die Art für das Denken ist, sich das Konkrete anzueignen, es als ein geistig Konkretes zu reproduzieren. Zum Beispiel die einfachste ökonomische Kategorie, sage z.B. Tauschwert, unterstellt Bevölkerung, Bevölkerung produzierend in bestimmtem Verhältnissen; auch gewisse Sorte von Familien – oder Gemeinde – oder Staatswesen, etc. Er kann nie existieren ausser als abstrakte, einseitige Beziehung eines schon gegebnen konkreten, lebendigen Ganzen. Als Kategorie fürt dagegen der Tauschwert ein antediluvianisches Dasein. Für das Bewusstsein . . . erscheint daher die Bewegung der Kategorien als der wirkliche Produktionsakt . . . dessen Resultat die Welt ist; und dies ist . . . soweit richtig, als die konkrete Totalität als Gedankentotalität als ein

Gedankenkonkretum, in fact ein Produkt des Denkens, des Begreifens ist; keineswegs aber des ausser oder über der Anschauung und Vorstellung dekenden und sich selbst gebärenden Begriffs, sodern der Verarbeitung von Anschauung und Vorstellung in Begriffe. Das Ganze, wie es im Kopfe als Gedankenganzes erscheint, ist ein Produkt des denkenden Kopfes, der sich die Welt in der ihm einzig möglichen Weise aneignet, einer Weise, die verschieden ist von der küstlerischen, religiösen. praktisch-geistigen Aneignung dieser Welt. Das reale Subjekt bleibt nach wie vor ausserhalb des Kopfes in seiner Selbständigkeit bestehn. . . .' The English-language version is from *Grundrisse, ed. cit.*, pp. 100–1.

73. *Grundrisse, ed. cit.*, p. 83.
74. *Grundrisse, ed. cit.*, p. 101.
75. *Ibid.*
76. *Reading Capital, ed. cit.*, p. 92.
77. *Reading Capital, ed. cit.*, pp. 120–1.
78. *Reading Capital, ed. cit.*, pp. 145–6.
79. R. Aron, *D'une Sainte Famille à l'autre*, Paris, 1969, pp. 85–86.
80. *Reading Capital, ed. cit.*, pp. 91–92.
81. *Reading Capital, ed. cit.*, p. 92.
82. *MEW*, Vol. 3, p. 18.
83. *MEW*, Vol. 27, p. 459.
84. *MEW*, Vol. 27, p. 460.
85. *MEW*, Vol. 16, p. 31.
86. *Capital, ed. cit.*, Vol. I, pp. 17–19.
87. *MEW*, Vol. 13, p. 470.
88. R. Aron, *D'une Sainte Famille à l'autre*, pp. 224–5.
89. *Reading Capital*, Chap. 4, mainly pp. 91 ff.
90. *Reading Capital, ed. cit.*, p. 119.
91. Bogdanov, *op. cit.*
92. N. Boukharine, *La Théorie du matérialisme historique*, Paris, Ed. Anthropos, 1967, p. 258.
92a. For the terms here under consideration see the index and the glossary in *For Marx, ed. cit.*
93. Quoted after *Reading Capital, ed. cit.*, pp. 97–98.
94. *Reading Capital, ed. cit.*, p. 98.
95. *Reading Capital, ed. cit.*, p. 101.
96. *Reading Capital, ed. cit.*, p. 114.
97. Cf. M. Godelier, 'Système, structure et contradiction dans "Le Capital" ', *Les Temps Modernes*, 1969, No. 246, pp. 838–9; see also L. Séve's excellent reply, 'Méthode structurale et méthode dialectique', *La Pensée*, 1967, No. 135.
98. 'Jean Paul Sartre repond', *L'Arc*, No. 30, p. 87
99. *Ibid.*, p. 95.
100. *Ibid,*, p. 88.
101. *For Marx, ed. cit.*, pp. 229–30.
102. *For Marx, ed. cit.*, pp. 230–1.
103. *For Marx, ed. cit.*, pp. 227.
104. *Reading Capital, ed. cit.*, p. 180.
105. *Reading Capital, ed. cit.*, p. 208.

106. *MEW*, Vol. 8, p. 115.
106a. *Filosofskaya Entsiklopediya*, Vol. I, Moscow, 1960.
107. *For Marx*, p. 227.
108. See note 97 above.
109. See note 98 above.
110. M. Godelier, 'Logique dialectique et analyse des structures', *La Pensée*, 1970, No. 149.
110a. Godelier, *op. cit.*, pp. 20 ff.
111. Godelier, *op. cit.*, pp. 22–23.
112. J. M. Domenach, 'Le système et la personne', *L'Esprit*, 1967, No. 5, pp. 778.
113. *Capital, ed. cit.*, Vol. I, p. 72.
114. *MEW*, Vol. 13, p. 8.
115. *Reading Capital, ed. cit.*, p. 180.
116. L. Séve, *Marxisme et la théorie de personalité*, Paris, 1969.
117. *Grundrisse, ed. cit.*, p. 83.
118. *Grundrisse, ed. cit.*, p. 85.
119. *Grundrisse, ed. cit.*, p. 87.
120. *Grundrisse, ed. cit.*, pp. 156–8.
121. *Grundrisse, ed. cit.*, p. 160 (footnote 21 in the original omitted – *Trans.*).
122. *Grundrisse, ed. cit.*, pp. 161–2.
123. *Grundrisse, ed. cit.*, pp. 243–4.
124. *Grundrisse, ed. cit.*, pp. 247–8.
125. *Grundrisse, ed. cit.*, p. 712.
125a. *Grundrisse, ed. cit.*, p. 265.
126. *Grundrisse, ed. cit.*, p. 496 (footnote 4 in the original omitted – *Trans.*).
127. *Grundrisse, ed. cit.*, pp. 540–2.
128. *Grundrisse, ed. cit.*, pp. 704–6.
129. *Grundrisse, ed. cit.*, p. 706.
130. G. Bachelard, *Le Rationalisme appliqué*, Paris, 1949, p. 102.
131. Bachelard, *op. cit.*, p. 104.
132. *For Marx, ed. cit.*, p. 33.
133. *Grundrisse, ed. cit.*, p. 157.
134. *Grundrisse, ed. cit.*, p. 160 (footnote 21 in the original omitted – *Trans.*).
135. *Grundrisse, ed. cit.*, pp. 307–8 (footnote 16 in the original omitted – *Trans.*).
136. *Grundrisse, ed. cit.*, p. 463.
137. *Grundrisse, ed. cit.*, pp. 514–15.
138. *Grundrisse, ed. cit.*, pp. 692–5.
139. *Grundrisse, ed. cit.*, pp. 831–2.
139a. *For Marx, ed. cit.*, p. 158.
140. *Grundrisse, ed. cit.*, p. 105.
141. *For Marx*, pp. 54–55.
142. *Reading Capital, ed. cit.*, p. 187.
143. *MEW*, Vol. 21, p. 294.

Chomsky's Generative Grammar
and the Concept of Innate Ideas

The present essay is intended to give tentative answers to the following questions:

What is the place of the concept of innate ideas in the system of generative grammar?

How is the adoption of that concept as one of the basic assumptions in that system being substantiated?

What critical comments suggest themselves in connection with that assumption?

When reverting to the discussion of the problem of innate ideas in the system of generative grammar, I must begin with an explanation, if only for the fact that discussions on this issue have been both numerous and comprehensive;[1] that both the advocates and the adversaries of the hypothesis stating that certain grammatical structures are innate to *all* specimens of the species *Homo sapiens* and are in this sense universal have formulated their principal pros and cons, thus formulating their stand-points with sufficient precision; that the controversy can be settled neither by philosophers nor by philosophizing linguists, but by natural scientists and representatives of related disciplines who, at the present-day level of their knowledge of the genetic code and the related inherited mechanisms and man's innate structures of thinking and acting, can at most declare their predilections for certain hypotheses (as has been done by such prominent scientists as Jacques Monod and François Jacob[2]), but cannot yet provide decisive arguments. It seems, accordingly, that we have to wait patiently for further advances in natural science, and especially for further results in molecular biology. Philosophical considerations, including metatheoretical reflections on linguistics, inevitably run the risk of becoming, in this situation, a purely verbal controversy. But one exception may be raised here: such reflections may help the controversy to become clearer by bringing out the latent premises referred to and the related courses of reasoning, and/or by stimulating specialized researches by way of posing new questions and thus indicating new paths of research. It seems that the problems raised below satisfy these conditions at least in part. This may be an illusion, but this subjective conviction at least justifies my late contribution to earlier discussions.

In the controversy over the underlying assumptions of generative grammar I will be interested – in the sense of the field in which I may intervene – in general theoretical, or rather philosophical, aspects of that trend in linguistic reflections. These cannot, of course, be separated from specialized linguistic analyses, in which the linguists solely are competent. But certain philosophical issues situated in the border area of linguistics and logic, make it possible for a philosopher to interfere without exposing himself *a priori* to an objection of incompetence; the more so as certain elements of the theory are clearly philosophical in nature (for instance, the claim that specified grammatical structures have the status of innate ideas).

The School of Generative Grammar and Structuralism in Linguistics

Transformational generative grammar, associated mainly with the name of Chomsky, has its origin in American structural linguistics, namely the school of descriptive linguistics, and is, as is commonly known, an important variation of structuralism in linguistics. But if we compare the principles of generative grammar with those of the Prague school of phonology, which marked the emergence of structural linguistics as the dominant trend in modern linguistic research then it is difficult to understand why these two schools bear the common name of 'structural linguistics'. This astonishment, in the past supposed to give rise to philosophical issues, is proper not only to philosophers who engage in metatheoretical reflections. When it comes to the alleged homogeneity of linguistic structuralism similar scepticism was voiced long ago by A. Martinet, who thinks that the term *structuralism* has become a label of almost any non-traditional trend in linguistics.[3] And when such scholars as E. Benveniste,[4] A. Martinet,[5] and N. M. Gukhman[6] strive to find out what is common to the various trends of structural linguistics, then it turns out that differences dominate, and the common points are mainly negative in nature; they consist in the rejection of the concepts of the neo-grammarians.

The same applies to the school of transformational generative grammar, which stands so far apart even if compared with American descriptive linguistics, from which it has developed, that it deserves a separate treatment and a separate name. The opinion of Paul M. Postal is very characteristic in that respect:

> It must be said that, within the tradition of modern structural linguistics which developed the ideas of immediate constituent grammar, little attention has been directed toward the task of precisely characterizing phrase structure as a generative theory. Rather, in line with the highly methodological and procedural orientation of modern linguistics, most effort has been directed toward the goal of formulating procedures of segmentation, classification, and substitution which could be used to discover the grammatical analyses of arbitrary sentences in arbitrary languages. This naturally led to the focusing of much attention on the notion of structural description, but almost none on the finite devices or linguistic rules which the speaker must learn and which can *assign* grammatical analyses to infinite sets of sentences. There was before Chomsky's work, thus, little interest in the goal of specifying exactly the character of the notions *linguistic rule, grammar,* and so forth. . . . There are also dozens of articles in modern linguistics attempting to describe abstractly the nature of such elements as *phoneme, morpheme, word, constituent,* and other elements of structural descriptions. But for the most part one looks in vain prior to 1956 for works specifying the abstract character of linguistic rules.[7]

This statement is interesting for two reasons: first, it contributes an additional element to the problem of the meanings which underlie the ambiguous term *structuralism;* and, secondly, it introduces us to the main issue, namely an answer to the question about the problems which are focal for, and characteristic of, the school of generative grammar.

The difference between the set of concepts used in transformational generative grammar and those current in other schools of linguistic structuralism are linked with the differences in the subject-matter of study and the research methods applied.

All schools of linguistic structuralism may be said to study language understood as a system; all of them, too, strive for one and the same goal, i.e. finding out the structure of that system. Closer inspection reveals, however, that this statement is so vague a generalization that it obscures the most interesting and the most essential features of each of those schools, namely the differences in the interpretation of the statement that language is a system, and hence the differences in establishing the structure of what they are supposed to investigate.

The phonological school, which was the most precise of all in defining the subject-matter and the method of research, intends to offer a structural description of the phonic aspect of language by starting from phonemes, i.e. the smallest phonic units. The descriptivists strive to describe structurally the various linguistic phenomena by way of segmentating and classifying morphemes as the smallest meaning-carrying units of language. Both schools, differing from one another as they do, start from the requirements formulated by de Saussure, who in fact confined the methods of linguistic analysis to segmentation and classification, and believed the construction of sentences to be independent of the system of language (*langue*) and to be in the sphere of the mechanism of speech (*parole*).[8] Now in this respect the school of transformational generative grammar consciously opposes traditional structuralism by concentrating on sentences and the grammatical rules of sentence formation.[9]

Chomsky and his school point emphatically to the differences between the two types of structuralism; they see a demarcation line between the taxonomic model of grammar, associated with modern structural linguistics, and the transformational model which, according to Chomsky, comes closer to traditional grammar, or, as Chomsky sometimes says pointedly, to philosophical grammar.[10] Chomsky's point is not to give a correct description of an utterance by making an orderly list of its elements (he does not disclaim this task, nor does he reject a phonological analysis, but he does not want to confine linguistic theory, i.e. grammar, to this task only), but to find out how people who communicate with one another by means of language and have a limited repertory of linguistic means at their disposal, can construct and understand an infinite set of grammatically correct sentences. When striving to answer this question he does not find inspiration in modern structuralism, because that school has never been interested in *this* issue; he does find it in philosophical tradition, for even if that problem there was often being formulated in an obscure and ambiguous manner (compare W. von Humboldt's concept of 'Form der Sprache', which Chomsky interprets as a 'generative process'),[11] it was treated as an important one. As Chomsky's sally into the history of philosophy, made in his *Cartesian Linguistics*,[12] has shown, the development of the philosophy of language from Descartes to Wilhelm von Humboldt was in many respects a forerunner of transformational generative grammar.

The stressing of the opposition of the two types of structuralism, and his dissociation from the trend which he terms 'modern structuralism', found a vigorous manifestation in *Current Issues,* which is an expanded version of Chomsky's paper read at the 9th International Congress of Linguists in 1962, the paper which carried Chomsky's *sui generis* declaration of faith. The passage in question deserves quoting not only because of its importance for the development of the school of transformational generative grammar, but before all because it clearly defines Chomsky's point of departure, with all its consequences for the logical construction of the conceptual apparatus of his theory.

> *Modern linguistics is much more under the influence of Saussure's conception of langue as an inventory of elements* (Saussure, 1916, p. 154 and elsewhere, frequently) *and his pre-occupation with systems of elements rather than the system of rules which were the focus of attention in traditional grammar and in the general linguistics of Humboldt.* In general modern descriptive statements pay little attention to the 'creative' aspect of language; they do not face the problem of presenting the system of generative rules that assign structural descriptions to arbitrary utterances and thus embody the speaker's competence in and knowledge of his language. Furthermore, this narrowing of the range of interest, as compared with traditional grammar, apparently has the effect of making it impossible to select an inventory of elements correctly, since *it seems no inventory (not even that of phonemes) can be determined without reference to the principles by which sentences are constructed in the language. To the extent that this is true, 'structural linguistics' will have suffered from a failure to appreciate the extent and depth of interconnections among various parts of a language system.* By a rather arbitrary limitation of scope, modern linguistics may well have become engaged in an intensive study of mere artifacts.[13]

This is not only a criticism of structuralism which, if only because of the time of its birth, we might term traditional, but also a definition of Chomsky's own standpoint even if that definition be by negation only. Before we try, by reference to the above formulations, to reconstruct the inner logic of the idea of transformational generative grammar (which is necessary if we are correctly to understand the place and the role, in that grammar, of the theory of innate ideas, which is the main goal of this analysis), it seems to the point to make one more comment on the method used by the generative grammar school, which will help us better to answer not only the 'what?' question, but also the 'how?' question concerning the subject-matter of the researches carried out by that school.

As mentioned above, Chomsky explicitly stresses the links between his own ideas, on the one hand, and traditional grammar and the issues of the philosophy of language (which, because of its origin, he has termed Cartesian), on the other. He is certainly right in doing so, but this does not suffice if we are to comprehend those filiations of ideas which are essential for the comprehension of the meaning and the methods of transformational generative grammar. What is meant here are above all that grammar's links with modern mathematical logic, in particular with the school of the logical analysis of language in its British and Continental forms (in the latter case, mainly the Vienna Circle and the Lwów—Warsaw school of logic).

The comprehension of these filiations of ideas and the impact of those ideas upon that trend in language analysis which has been taken up by Chomsky is a *sine qua non* of the comprehension and appreciation of the difference between generative grammar and linguistic structuralism in its form to date: while the method used in traditional structuralism, especially in American descriptivism, was inductive, that used in transformational generative grammar is deductive.[14] The latter method consists in the construction of models applicable to the interpretation of infinite sets of elements (those elements in this case being sentences); the procedure resembles the axiomatic method: certain *assumptions* are adopted as axioms on which the whole structure is based. In other words (and from a somewhat different point of view), transformational generative grammar strives not only to describe sentence structure, in the sense of describing the relationships between its elements (morphemes or phonemes), but also to answer the question how a given sentence can be derived from other sentences and from which other sentences it is derivable (which refers to the structure of relations between sentences). Hence the stress on syntax and the criticism of traditional linguistic structuralism as a trend which neglected, or failed to pay due attention to, the problems of syntax.[15] But there have been trends which specialized in those problems exactly and which must have affected Chomsky's ideas: they were those trends in the philosophy and the logic of language which in a certain period (prior to the demonstration by Alfred Tarski that the problems of truth can be introduced into deductive science without the risk of contradictions, which paved the way for the inclusion by logical positivists of semantic issues in their analyses of the language of science) were *solely* confined to an analysis of the logical syntax of language. Two names come to the fore if we consider the forerunners of transformational generative grammar from the point of view of the modern logic and the philosophy of language: those of Rudolf Carnap and Kazimierz

Ajdukiewicz. Without taking into consideration *Die logische Syntax der Sprache,* Carnap's fundamental work, and the works published by Ajdukiewisz in *Erkanntnis* in 1930s[16] we could not, I think, understand the mental work done by Chomsky in his formulation of his concept of transformational generative grammar.

Since this analysis of filiations of ideas in Chomsky's conceptions (apart from those to which he himself points in the sphere of the philosophy of language) is to be continued below, a reservation must be made concerning a certain basic issue. The originality of a given system is not refuted by the demonstration that certain elements of that system used to occur in some form earlier in the history of human thought. The concepts and ideas which come here in question as a rule did not (and could not) occur in the past in the same form, and *a fortiori* could not play the same role in the structure of the whole system, as in the case of the modern theory which is the subject-matter of this analysis. Further, which is the most important of all, the originality and the scientific significance of a theory is not a function of the novelty of its elements (at least, it is not only a function of the ingenuity of the ideas into which that theory can be broken up), but in most cases it is a function of the novel and creative system. This is why it is not paradoxical to state that in the case of many theoretical systems whose role in the history of science was novel and creative, most, or perhaps even all, basic ideas of those systems had been earlier formulated in some way, and hence were not original — in the radical sense of the word. This fact is emphasized here because, in my opinion, the basic concepts and ideas in Chomsky's theory (as stated above, his technique of the description and analysis of language are not assessed here) are — in this radical sense of the word — neither new nor original, while his theory as a whole is held by me to be both novel and valuable.

Let us begin with the distinction between *competence* and *performance,* a distinction which is fundamental in the system of generative grammar. Its forerunners are the theory of *langue* and *parole* in de Saussure's *Cours,*[17] and the distinction between *code* and *message* in communication theory. Another concept which is of fundamental importance for transformational generative grammar is the distinction between *deep structure* and *surface structure,* which in turn has its forerunner in the theory of *double articulation,* as developed in French linguistics.[18] The theory of language rules (rules of sense, also termed meaning postulates, and rules of syntax), non-existent, as Chomsky points out, in traditional linguistic structuralism and so important in the set of concepts used in generative grammar, was being developed in detail by logical positivists, the works of Kazimierz Ajdukiewicz being of special significance in that field. The concept of universal grammar is to be found in the works by representatives of what Chomsky calls 'Cartesian linguistics'; of course, beginning with Descartes is quite arbitrary, because the principle of *nihil novi sub sole*, applicable to all philosophical doctrines, holds for Descartes, too, which in this case is confirmed by Raymond Lull's idea of *calculus universalis.* Likewise, the concept of innate linguistic structures has its roots in the theory of innate ideas of genetic rationalists, which Chomsky himself emphasizes. Other items could be added to this list. This is mentioned here to absolve me of the duty to make excursions into history, when I come to discuss issues which in my opinion are essential for the comprehension of the set of concepts used in transformational generative grammar.

Here is an attempt to reconstruct that set of concepts.

The starting-point is the definition of language as a set (finite or not) of *sentences*, which are constructed from elements whose set is finite.[19] The grammar of a given language is a device which serves to produce sentences that have a specified structure and are in this sense grammatical.[20] Thus the task is not so much to describe the structures of statements actually made, but to simulate and to explain the behaviour of a language user who in the light of his limited experience with a given language can produce and understand infinitely many new sentences in that language. This idea is fundamental for the definition of generative grammar as distinct from traditional grammar. Only a grammar so conceived can explain linguistic creativity, understood as the ability to produce infinitely many sentences from a finite set of elements. The point is, obviously, to produce grammatical sentences, i.e. such which comply with the rules of a given grammar. Hence grammar may be defined as a set of rules (identical with the concept of *device*) which makes it possible to produce in a *given language* an infinite set of grammatical sentences and to describe their structures.[21] Generative grammar, when internalized by a person who has the command of the language, coincides with what de Saussure termed *langue.*[22]

This brings us to the distinction between *competence* and *performance* (with its analogues: *langue* versus *parole* and *code* versus *message*), which is fundamental in the sytem of generative grammar. The person who has internalized the system of rules of a given language, which define both the phonetic form of a given sentence and its semantic content (i.e. the rules which assign specified meanings to specified sequences of sounds),[23] has thereby acquired linguistic *competence*. This breeds a new look at grammar. 'The grammar of a language, as a model of idealized competence, establishes a certain relation between sound and meaning — between phonetic and semantic representations.'[24]

The linguistic study of a given language is intended to discover that grammar which is a specific theory of that language, by formulating the rules of that grammar,[25] whereas the general theory of linguistic structures is a specific theory of grammars and is intended to find out those general conditions which each such grammar must satisfy. Out of the three possibilities (ordered here by the strength of the requirements posed to linguistic theory concerning its relation to the various grammars): providing a method of discovering grammars, i.e. their structures, on the basis of respective sets of utterances (*discovery procedure*); providing a method of deciding which of the possible grammars is the best (*decision procedure*); providing a method of evaluating which of given grammars is better (*evaluation procedure*). Chomsky is in favour of the third possibility, which is the weakest of the three as far as research tasks are concerned, but is realistic and scientifically important.[26]

The above definitions of 'grammar' and 'competence' in transformational generative grammar result in the distinction, in that grammar, of surface structures and deep structures. Grammar is supposed to offer a description of those sentences which are specified by it as acceptable in the light of the rules of a given language, i.e. those sentences which are grammatically correct. But to make such a description it does not suffice to confine oneself to the phonetic form of a given sentence, which is determined by its surface structure, since the latter does not suffice to find out certain, semantically important, grammatical relations within that sentence (these relations are termed the 'deep structure' of that sentence). This distinction, which strikingly resembles the concept of the double articulation of a sentence, namely the phonetic and the semantic one, is the foundation of transformational grammar. That grammar consists of three component parts: (1) the syntactic element (SD — *syntactic description,* which has a surface structure and a deep structure); (2) the semantic element, which, like Ajdukiewicz's rules of sense (meaning postulates), assigns a semantic interpretation to a deep structure; (3) the phonological element, which assigns a phonetic interpretation to a surface structure.[27] When analysing the history of 'Cartesian linguistics', and especially the principles of the Port-Royal *Grammar,* Chomsky illustrates this distinction by referring to the history of what he terms philosophical grammar.[28]

Another important concept, already mentioned above when linguistic theory as distinct from grammar was described, is that of the *universal nature of grammar.* As has been said above, linguistic theory is to find out those general conditions which *every* grammar must satisfy. Now, following the rationalist principles of 'Cartesian linguistics', Chomsky accepts not only the claim that such a *grammatica universalis* does exist, but also the claim that deep structures are common to *all* language.[29] In another formulation of his theory Chomsky also postulated universal phonetics and universal semantics as parts of universal grammar.[30] But the syntactic element, especially the claim about the universal nature of deep structures (surface structures being by definition that element which differentiates between the various natural languages) remain the focal factor, which is also the most interesting one from the point of view with which are we here concerned. 'Universal grammar might be defined as the study of the conditions that must be met by the grammars of all human languages ... so defined, universal grammar is nothing other than the theory of language structure.'[31]

And now comes the last (in the sense of the logical order of elements of his theory) component of the set of concepts in generative grammar, the component which, in view of the goal of this analysis, must be of special interest here: AD, i.e. the *acquisition device* (the machanism of assimilating a language), and AM, i.e. the *acquisition model* (the model of assimilation of a language). The *model* is a formalized representation of what actually takes place when a person assimilates a language by means of the *acquisition device.* In order clearly to visualize the problem and Chomsky's standpoint on this important issue let us quote his words from one of his later, synthesizing works:

> The process of abstraction can be carried one step further. Consider an
> acquisition model AM that uses linguistic data to discover the grammar of the

language to which this data pertains.

$$\text{Linguistic data} \longrightarrow \boxed{\text{AM}} \longrightarrow \text{Grammar}$$

Just how the device AM selects a grammar will be determined by its internal structure, by the methods of analysis available to it, and the initial constraints that it imposes on any possible grammar. If we are given information about the pairing of linguistic data and grammars, we may try to determine the nature of the device AM. Although these are not the terms that have been used, linguistics has always been concerned with this question. *Thus modern structural linguistics has attempted to develop methods of analysis of a general nature, independent of any particular language, and an older and now largely forgotten tradition attempted to develop a system of universal constraints that any grammar must meet. We might describe both these attempts as concerned with the internal structure of the device AM, with the innate conception 'human language' that makes language acquisition possible.*[32]

At the end of the same paragraph Chomsky refers the reader to a footnote which in view of its significance also deserves being quoted. 'The existence of innate mental structure is, obviously, not a matter of controversy. What we may question is just what it is and to what extent it is specific to language.'[33]

We have thus come to face the main subject-matter of our analysis: the problem of innate ideas, or innate structure, on which the hypothetical deductive system of generative grammar is based. Before proceeding critically to analyse the claims of the founders and supporters of transformational generative grammar we shall try to reconstruct them with possible precision and to make clear what place they hold in the ideas of representatives of generative grammar.

Generative Grammar and Neonativism

What has been termed above an analysis of the set of concepts used in generative grammar is, in fact, a tentative reconstruction of the inner logic of that theory. Of course, this has been done with a definite purpose, which is determined by the system of reference of the concepts under consideration and their logical ordering. Chomsky proceeds in a similar manner by analysing the inner logic of the concepts used in generative grammar when the problem of linguistic competence is adopted as the starting-point.[34]

It is important to realize that in the conceptual system of generative grammar the idea of *innate structures,* inherent in the *acquisition device* of a given language, i.e. that 'device' or 'black box' which at the input has acts of speech and at the output, the generative grammar of that language, is not accidental, but *necessary*. Without that idea it would not be possible to substantiate the statement on the universal nature of grammar, and further, if we go in the reverse direction as compared with the analysis made previously, the universal nature of deep structures, the specific interpretation of linguistic competence, and finally, the specific concept of grammar and that of linguistic theory. As has been said, generative grammar is constructed as a hypothetical deductive model, and its structure resembles constructs in mathematical logic rather than traditional linguistic models. In the deductive systems of mathematics and mathematical logic a given calculus is based on the adopted axioms and transformation rules. An axiom is an assumption which is one of the starting-points of a given calculus. The statement on innate linguistic structures whose nature is that of innate ideas, is an *assumption* and functions as an axiom. Such at least is the logical structure of the system. The belief held by the founders of generative grammar that this is not an assumption, but a theorem which they try to prove, and the actual role of that statement in the logical structure of the system are two different things.

It must be emphasized here that the claim that *linguistic universals* exist is a necessary component of generative grammar in the same way as the claim that *linguistic differentials* exist is a necessary component of the Sapir—Whorf hypothesis, i.e., the school of linguistic relativism.

In view of the importance of this statement in the system of generative grammar and because of our interest in that statement it is imperative first precisely to reconstruct the opinions of the founders of generative grammar on the issue. This is the more so important as Chomsky in his successive works reverts to the basic concepts of his theory. We shall accordingly begin with what, in my opinion, are Chomsky's basic formulations on the subject of innate ideas; in doing so we shall follow the chronological order of the publication of his works.

We begin with his review of B. F. Skinner's work, *Verbal Behaviour*,[35] published in 1957. In his review Chomsky sharply criticized Skinner's attempt behaviouristically to interpret verbal behaviour, and in particular the process of learning a language, and in this connection he advanced his idea of LD (learning device), which he later came to term AD (acquisition device).

In discussing Skinner's method of analysis, Chomsky is alarmed not only by Skinner's confinement to the observation of input and output data, but above all by the fact that analysis is restricted to external factors, without consideration of the inner structure of human organism and the way in which that organism processes the information received. 'These characteristics of the organism are in general a complicated product of inborn structure, the genetically determined course of maturation and past experience.'[36]

Chomsky is still very cautious when advancing his concept of innate structures. He does not reject the statements on imitation, on the reinforcement of certain characteristics by repetition, etc., in the process of learning in animals and in children, but he adds that there are indications that observable responses to sign stimuli 'are genetically determined and mature without learning'; that in the case of a child which begins to speak we cannot exclude the possibility that his ability to select, from among the sounds he has heard, those which are phonologically important 'may develop largely independently of reinforcement, through genetically determined maturation'; that it cannot be excluded that the development of the brain accounts for the fact that at a certain age a child produces the rules of the grammar of a given language from the sentences he has heard in that language.[37]

Finally, in opposing the theory that a person understands new sentences by comparing them with previously acquired patterns, Chomsky advances his concept of generative grammar. But in this, too, he is still extremely cautious. In order to formulate meaningful sentences and in order to understand them one has to internalize the grammar of the language in question. How this is done, and especially, how this is done by a child, which in a short time achieves what in the case of a theorist requires much work, and that independently of that child's intelligence, is still not yet known. But he concludes;

> The fact that all normal children acquire essentially comparable grammars of great complexity with remarkable rapidity suggests that human beings are somehow specially designed to do this .... The study of linguistic structure may ultimately lead to some significant insights into this matter. At the moment the question cannot be seriously posed, but in principle it may be possible to study the problem of determining what the built-in structure of an information-processing (hypothesis-forming) system must be to enable it to arrive at the grammar of a language from the available data in the available time.[38]

Thus so far we see cautious hypotheses and no less cautious postulation of a programme of research. The situation then changes rapidly, and that not on the strength of any new results obtained in the course of the postulated research, but rather in the sphere of philosophical reflection which, through the assimilation of rationalist principles, provides a convenient basis for the construction of a model of generative grammar as the universal grammar. But Chomsky's successive works not only show his growing conviction that the concept of innate structures is good for the interpretation of linguistic facts, but also reveal ever stronger reliance on inspiration drawn from philosophical sources.

In his paper 'Explanatory Models in Linguistics' (1960)[39] we find, next to developed and more vigorously formulated opinions on grammar as linguistic theory, a more radical opinion on the *learning device* which, it is now assumed, must include a theory of linguistic structure. 'A general theory of linguistic structure of the sort just outlined would, in this way, provide an account of a hypothetical language-learning device and could thus be regarded as a theoretical model of the intellectual abilities that the child brings to language learning.'[40]

Since the statement that the child contributes his intellectual abilities to the process of language learning is vague and might be interpreted in various ways, another explanation follows, which contains *in nuce* the formulation of the concept of innate structures.

> It seems to me that the relative suddenness, uniformity and universality of language learning, the bewildering complexity of the resulting skills, and the subtlety and finesse with which they are exercised, *all point to the conclusion that a primary and essential factor is the contribution of an organism with highly intricate and specific initial structure.*[41]

This is a brief formulation not only of the concept which will often return in Chomsky's later works, but also the indication of those facts which induced Chomsky to accept it.

In his paper, read at the 9th International Congress of Linguists,[42] Chomsky presented a more radical version of that concept and referred, this time in an expanded form, to W. von Humboldt's philosophy of language, in particular to von Humboldt's well-known idea that a language cannot be taught, but that it is merely possible to incite a person's mind spontaneously to develop his language, and also to von Humboldt's opinion that mankind has only one language.[43] Chomsky's standpoint on the *learning device* is already precisely formulated.

The learning model B is a device which constructs a theory G (i.e. a generative grammar G of a certain *langue*) as its output, on the basis of primary linguistic data (e.g. specimens of *parole*), as input. *To perform this task, it utilizes its given faculté de langage, its innate specification of certain heuristic procedures and certain built-in constraints on the character of the task to be performed.* We can think of general linguistic theory as an attempt to specify the character of the device B. [44]

In the paper under consideration, which was clearly conceived as a programme of research, Chomsky formulated his opinion that the limited nature of the taxonomic model is linked with a narrowed concept of the nature of cognitive processes in man, and that the return to traditional views, made more precise by methods used in modern linguistics, would broaden our views on learning processes in man.[44a] This programme has been carried out in his *Cartesian Linguistics.*

I disregard here the historical data quoted in *Cartesian Linguistics:* it is obvious that in the works of rationalists we can find support for rationalist ideas (even though Chomsky has found in their works, especially in the Port Royal *Grammar,* ideas that came to be forerunners of certain technical aspects of the methods used in generative grammar). What is more important and more valuable for us is the use made by Chomsky of those historical data, the way he generalizes them to use them as evidence for his statements.

In Chomsky's opinion, the focal doctrine of Cartesian linguistics is that which says that general characteristics of grammatical structures are common to *all* languages. Thus, there are certain grammatical universals, which restrict the variety of natural languages, and the study of these universals is what is termed *grammaire générale.* These universals cannot be learned. 'By attributing such principles to the mind, as an innate property, it becomes possible to account for the quite obvious fact that the speaker of a language knows a great deal that he has not learned.'[45]

Likewise, an analysis of the views held by Leibniz, Schlegel and von Humboldt is an opportunity not only for stating that according to them language capacity is innate in man, but also for formulating the opinion, for instance, of von Humboldt so that it can be incorporated, lock, stock and barrel, in the system of generative grammar. 'In short, language acquisition is a matter of growth and maturation of relatively fixed capacities, under appropriate external conditions.'[46]

What is at stake here is not so much the opinions of past thinkers, but what is being read into them and what is the context in which quotations from their works are located. That this is so can best be seen in the case of von Humboldt, in whose works one can find, as it turns out, what one looks for. It is common knowledge that the school of linguistic relativism, which is antipodally opposite to the universalism of generative grammar, has been drawing inspiration, and rightly so, precisely from von Humboldt's works, and is even commonly known as Neo-Humboldtianism.

These excursions into the history of philosophy prove beyond doubt that ideas born in speculative philosophy can work as mental stimuli in the development of science as they have a heuristic value in that respect. To state this is certainly pleasing to a philosopher who in spite of himself may feel frustrated under the impact of positivist trends in modern science. It is also an excellent illustration of the migration of ideas in time: theories and ideas which at one time were *en vogue* and were later abandoned, apparently for good, come back to the arena of science when new discoveries place them in a new intellectual context and bring out such aspects of these ideas which were either unnoticed or eclipsed by other factors. This applies to nativism, which explains our interest in the issue.

Cartesian Linguistics was published in 1966, and the paper on *The Formal Nature of Language* (included as an appendix to a book by Eric Lenneberg [47]) appeared one year later. This paper sums up succinctly the theory of generative grammar and the results obtained until then by the application of that method.

The problem of *learning device* recurs inevitably, this time approached from a different viewpoint as AM (*acquisition model*). Chomsky states that the trend, common in modern structural linguistics, to develop methods of linguistic analysis that are general enough to be independent of any single natural language find support in a much older tradition, and concludes: 'We might describe both these attempts as concerned with the internal structure of the device AM, with the innate conception of 'human language' that makes language acquisition possible.'[48]

When referring later (especially in his phonological considerations) to the issue of that device which makes it possible to acquire a language by means of innate structures, Chomsky formulated an idea which is worth quoting, since it contains an attempt to substantiate the concept of innate ideas, the concept to which we shall have to revert later.

In describing the phonological component of a universal grammar

Chomsky says that the assumption made concerning a universal grammar restricts the class of possible human languages to a very special sub-class of conceivable 'languages', and goes on as follows.

> The evidence available to us suggests that these assumptions pertain to the language acquisition device AM ... that is, that they form one part of the schematism that the child brings to the problem of language learning. *That this schematism must be quite elaborate and highly restrictive seems fairly obvious. If it were not, language acquisition, within the empirically known limits of time, access and variability, would be an impenetrable mystery.* Considerations of the sort mentioned in the foregoing discussion are directly relevant to the problem of determining the nature of these innate mechanisms, and, therefore, deserve extremely careful study and attention.[49]

The standpoint has thus been described with full clarity, but we still can have doubts as to how these 'innate mechanisms', 'innate schematisms' and 'innate structures' are to be interpreted, the more so as in all the cases quoted above the statements in question are marginal to more or less specific issues of generative grammar, which are the main subject of the papers quoted. Another difficulty is that in his works, marked by precision of formulations that comes close to mathematical logic, Chomsky leaves a wide margin of obscurity and ambiguity when it comes to such expressions as 'acquisition device' and all expressions in which the term 'innate' occurs (i.e. innate structures, mechanisms, schematisms, etc.). Assistance in this field is offered by that book by Chomsky which carries his somewhat popular lectures; this rather popular approach makes Chomsky formulate his intentions with precision, also when it comes to marginal or vague concepts and ideas introduced in his other works, especially those ideas which are clearly philosophical in nature. The book in question is *Language and Mind*,[50] published in 1968 and thus chronologically later than the works quoted here previously.

I do not mean in this connection his historical comments on philosophical grammar and its rationalist standpoint, an issue known from his earlier works. The most important thing is the exposition by Chomsky of his own standpoint, which includes a commentary to his earlier argumentation. The most significant and illuminating in this respect is Lecture Three, in which the generative grammar approach is explicitly defined as a specific return to rationalism: ' ... because to a significant extent it is the traditional rationalist approach, now amplified and sharpened and made far more explicit in terms of the tentative conclusions that have been reached in the recent study of linguistic competence.' [51]

Here I am only concerned with a possibly exact reconstruction of Chomsky's opinion on innate ideas, in order to avoid criticism of their misrepresentation. From this point of view it is inessential what Locke and Descartes really thought on the subject; this problem can be left to historians of philosophy. The important issue is what Chomsky thinks on the issue. In this connection his declaration in favour of genetic rationalism is significant, the more so since – as a lawyer would say – we have to do with an authentic interpretation of earlier statements, which were not at all clear.

It is only in the light of this declaration in favour of rationalism that the formulation of the problem, in which the existence of innate structures is adopted as an *assumption* becomes comprehensible. 'Insofar as we have a tentative first approximation to a generative grammar for some language, we can for the first time formulate in a useful way the problem of origin of knowledge. In other words, we can ask the question, *What initial structure must be attributed to the mind that enables it to construct such a grammar from the data of sense?'* [52]

Now it is important, for the further analysis of the problem, to establish that the very fact of the existence of such structures (which, as we have seen above, are very intricate, as they contain grammar in the sense of linguistic theory) is beyond dispute, since it is adopted as an *assumption.* According to Chomsky, it is the limits and the properties of those structures which are disputable and require empirical criteria. But, for all the explicit assurances that these are empirically decidable problems,[52a] this is not always clear. This is so because we are told that:

(i) Such an innate structure is a generic characteristic and is independent of individual intelligence, since those grammars which are in fact constructed by the speakers of a language do not differ much from one another. [52b]

(ii) The claim that these structures are universal applies also to the dialects of one and the same language, and even to different languages which do not reveal any affinity. [52c]

(iii) 'We must postulate an innate structure that is rich enough to account for the disparity between experience and knowledge, one that can account for the construction of the empirically justified generative grammars within the given limitations of time and access to data.' [52d]

(iv) Such a postulated structure should be neither too comprehensive nor too restrictive, in order not to exclude any language: 'There is, in other words, an upper bound and a lower bound on the degree and exact character of the complexity that can be postulated as innate mental structure.'[52e]

We shall still revert to these issues. At this moment it is to be noted merely that when reference is made to 'empirical conditions', what is meant in fact are certain findings or postulates about that 'innate structure', but not its existence, which has been assumed (obviously in the light of certain premises) and is not subject to dispute. The fact that the concept of innate structure has been adopted as an *assumption* of the system is due to the conviction that the rationalist conception is *the only* acceptable one when it comes to the analysis of the problem of language acquisition.[52f] Such being the case, empirical research can pertain only to the *properties* of that structure (for instance, the psychologists are assigned the task 'to discover the innate scheme that characterizes the class of potential languages – that defines the 'essence' of human language.'[52g]

This tour of Chomsky's works has enabled us to establish beyond dispute what he means by his access to genetic rationalists and what role is played, in the system of generative grammar, by the concept of 'innate structure'. We have traced the history of the concept of innate ideas as related to generative grammar, first, in order to show that it is an element in the system of that grammar; secondly, to avoid a possible objection of being inexact in reporting on the opinions which will be the subject-matter of a dispute; thirdly, because this aspect of the issue seems to have been insufficiently treated in the literature of the subject.

For the same reasons, reference will here be made to two works more, one of which has been written by a member of the school of generative grammar, so that his opinion on the concept of innate ideas may be treated as representative for that school;[53] the other comes from an author who is closely linked with that way of thinking and who follows a similar path of reasoning in the study of the biological foundations of language.[54]

Jerrold J. Katz has written, as the title of his book shows, a study in the philosophy of language, based on the concept of generative grammar. As for the latter aspect of the issue he does not contribute anything new, and the originality of his book consists in taking up certain classical philosophical problems and their tentative solution in the light of linguistic analysis conceived in a specific manner. But this is of less interest here, and hence we shall confine ourselves to that aspect of his work which is concerned with the issue of innate ideas.

Katz is right in linking this problem with the old controversy between the empiricists and the rationalists, being of the opinion that in this case the key issue is the role of innate ideas in the process of language acquisition; he thinks that the existing body of knowledge in linguistic theory makes it possible to settle the dispute between the empiricists and the rationalists.

The fundamental problem, as Katz claims in accordance with guiding principles of the system of generative grammar, is the birth of linguistic competence as the child develops from infancy to the moment when he begins fluently to speak a given language (i.e. when under the impact of utterances he has heard in a given language he internalizes the rules of constructing, using, and understanding sentences in that language). The criterion for settling the dispute between the two rival hypotheses would refer to the effectiveness of either hypothesis in solving the problem of the origin of that competence: 'Whichever hypothesis thus provides the most fruitful model of the internal structure of the language acquisition device will be accepted as the best hypothesis'.[55]

The answer is as follows: the empiricist hyphothesis is based, in principle, on an inductive generalization, whereas the rationalist one states that 'the language acquisition device contains a stock of innate ideas that jointly specify the necessary form of language (realized in any actual natural language) and thus the necessary form of a speaker's internal representation of the rules of languages'.[56] But since no rationalist has ever explicitly formulated the concept of innate ideas it would be difficult to speak about any specified rationalist hypothesis on this issue.

This has been done by the theory which underlies the foundations of generative grammar. The necessarily strong hypothesis states that 'the language acquisition device contains as innate structure, each of the principles stated within the theory of language'.[57] The list of these principles is imposing: language universals which determine the form of linguistic description; the form of the components (phonological, syntactic, and semantic) of that description; the formal nature of the laws which govern each of those components; the set of universal constructs which underlie the laws of the various descriptions; the methodology of the choice of optimum linguistic descriptions. But it turns out that this is not enough, that we have to do with an open hypothesis in the sense 'that it asserts that anything which, for good empirical reasons, is found to be part of the theory of language is *eo ipso facto* part of the language acquisition device, and hence part of the child's native language-apparatus, his innate ideas about language'.[58] To put it briefly, all that which is connected with learning, using, and understanding language is innate. This is not an exaggeration: Katz really thinks so and adds that innate ideas are part of the system which organizes experience, a system whose existence 'has been hypothetically inferred from the linguistic performance of speakers in their acquisition and use of language'.[59] Now it simply remains to state that the rationalist hypothesis enables us to explain why every natural language has the properties ascribed to it by the laws of the theory of language (this could not be otherwise, since this has been an assumption); and even more, why not only those languages which have been studied so far, but also those which will be studied in the future (*sic!*[59a]) comply with those laws of the theory of language.

I now proceed to report on the final, synthetic, conclusions to be drawn from this reasoning. As compared with Chomsky's statements quoted above they are more pointed: they state more fully and more clearly the consequences of the ideas to be found in Chomsky's works in an abbreviated form. But this is just the value of these conclusions, since their nature will help us later to reflect on Chomsky's claims. The objection that this is a radicalization typical of philosophical discussions, whereas Chomsky is concerned with constructing a linguistic theory, even if it be based on certain philosophical premises, can be warded off by the explanation that we have to do with the work of one of Chomsky's collaborators which thus has its origin in the same intellectual circle and has never met with any reservation, as to the formulation of the issues under consideration here, on the part of other representatives of the school of generative grammar.

Katz's final reasoning on the issue of innate ideas in the sphere of language is as follows. It cannot be assumed that the occurrence of certain properties in all languages, i.e. the universal nature of those properties, is just accidental. This universality must be explained by the indication of its cause. Since we have to do with specifically linguistic laws we have to disregard, in the explanation, such invariants which are connected with the purely biological community of the species *Homo sapiens* (e.g. the fact that all human beings live on the surface of the earth, that they breathe, etc.). We also have to exclude the geographical, psychological, cultural and sociological factors, since these are variable, and as such cannot explain the occurrence of invariant characteristics of language. What then? And here we find the passage which offers Katz's answer to this question and which is so significant for further discussion that is to be quoted *in extenso* to forestall any possible objections that Katz's views are described inaccurately, or perhaps even contrary to his intentions. We have here to do with a statement which with exceptional clarity, and dotting all the *i*'s, expounds the viewpoint of the school of generative grammar on the problem under consideration.

> Hence, by this process of elimination, the only thing left that can provide the invariant condition that we want to connect with the universal features of language as their causal antecedent is the common innate endowment of human language learners, i.e. some component of their specifically human nature . . . it is also the differentia between language at the human level and its absence at the lower levels of the animal kingdom. . . .
>
> Now, if we bring in the rationalist hypothesis, we can obtain an explanation of this regularity. This hypothesis says that part of the genetic endowment of a human being is the full set of linguistic universals (I)–(V) and that these universals constitute the internal structure of the device which the nonverbal infant utilizes to become a fluent speaker on exposure to a sample of the utterances of a language. Since the innately given language acquisition device incorporates the linguistic universals, we can explain why the linguistic universals are necessary features of any language that is spoken by a human being. Namely, the linguistic universals are found in each and every language because, internalization of the rules of his language by the device that accomplishes its acquisition. The very mechanism which the child uses to acquire fluency in a natural language introduces them as the framework in which his linguistic experience is organized in the form of linguistic rules.[60]

This passage is the quintessence of the issue under consideration as seen by the school of generative grammar. We shall revert to it later, when it comes to a criticism of the standpoint described here with such clarity. On that later occasion the continuation of this passage, in which Katz opposes the expected objection that this explanation is a *petitio principii,* will be quoted, too. That continuation is no less interesting for the problem being analysed than what has been quoted above, but since, for the time being, I confine myself to a presentation of views, I merely mention its existence.

To conclude the review of the opinions of the representatives of the school of generative grammar let us have a closer look at Eric Lenneberg's book which has been mentioned above. Its title, *Biological Foundations of Language,* reflects well the goal and the approach of its author. Lenneberg is much more cautious in his formulations than are the above-mentioned promoters of generative grammar, but he comes close to their reasoning. It was not accidental that Chomsky joined his synthetic exposition of the doctrine of generative grammar (cf. *The Formal Nature of Language* referred to above) as an appendix to Lenneberg's book. He apparently thought, and rightly so, that the book represented a trend which was at least convergent with his own. This is why, to make the picture complete, the book must be analysed here.

Lenneberg in fact says the same as Chomsky and Katz on the issue under consideration, but he does not say it in the same manner. Chomsky constructs a deductive model which, among other things, is to explain what he terms language acquisition; in his model the assumption that the rules of generative grammar are innate in man contributes to a mathematical elegance in the solution of the problem, and also substantiates the claim that the transformational grammar which is based on those rules is truly universal. Lenneberg approaches the issue at a different angle, which changes his viewpoint and also affects his specific *façon de parler*: he speaks as a biologist. But the basic question is the same: why is language ability a generic trait of *Homo sapiens?* And the answer is the same: this is so because it is an innate ability. What is more, Lenneberg refers to the biological community of the human race and says that deep structures (which he terms *latent structures*) are universal in nature and that linguistic structures, in fact identical with generative grammar, are innate.

Let us begin with the conclusions to be found on the last two pages of Lenneberg's book, which are pertinent to our issue.

At one time, he says in the last section, entitled 'Innate Mechanisms', the concept of innateness was banned and believed to be unscientific. This is now over. Biology now is doing nothing else than investigating the innate nature of various forms. 'The discovery and description of innate mechanisms is a thoroughly empirical procedure and is an integral part of modern scientific inquiry.'[61]

This applies to language, too. It is only owing to the rules which underlie syntax that we obtain results in agreement with logic, because we have at our disposal sentences as the initial data of mental operations. This proves, in Lenneberg's eyes, that these rules are an innate property of human mind. 'When we say rules must have been built into the grammatical analyzer, we impute the existence of an apparatus with specific structural properties or, in other words, a specific internal organization.'(62)

I have started from these conclusions — which show a striking resemblance to Chomsky's views — for the following reasons: (i) they reveal a new aspect of the problem, different from that discussed so far, which is important for later analysis; (ii) it is easier to reconstruct Lenneberg's views on the issue under consideration by basing them on these final conclusions. This will make it easier to bring out both what is common to the two approaches and what is specific to Lenneberg's standpoint.

When investigating the problems of language and speech Lenneberg takes up the biological aspect of the issue and consequently, which is self-evident, is interested mainly in the role of human organism in the development of speech. This is not only admissible but necessary if that intricate process is to be studied. Lenneberg can also refer to the fact thay he pays due attention to the role of the social factor in the development of speech (which he does mainly in Chap. IX). Thus when he emphasizes the importance of the process of maturation and the fact that certain functions of human organism are genetically conditioned, this is substantiated by results of biological research and is subject only to experimental verification or refutation when it comes to particular statements.

Let us bring out a comment made by Lenneberg in connection with what he says on the role of maturation of human organism in the development of its specified functions, a comment which sheds bright light on the substantiation of his statements on innate language structures. He strongly emphasizes the difference between the *potentiality* of certain behaviour in the process of the maturation of human organism, and a given *act* of such behaviour.

> The aim of these comments is to direct attention to *potentialities* of behaviour — the underlying matrix of behaving — instead of to a specific *act*.

> If we find that emergence of a certain behaviour may be partially or wholly attributed to changes within the organism rather than to causative changes in the environment, *we must at once endeavour to discover what organic changes there are. Unless we can demonstrate a somatic basis, all our speculations are useless.*[63]

In my opinion this statement and this requirement can only be applauded if we refer to a biological interpretation of language. They will be below tentatively applied to those statements in the theory of generative grammar which explicitly refer to such a biological interpretation (especially when it comes to the acquisition device).

Unfortunately, Lenneberg himself fails to comply with his postulate. When in Chap. V, 'Neurological Aspects of Speech and Language', he takes up the issue of innate mechanisms, he thereby paves the way for the radical formulations to be found in Chap. IX. Animals, he says, function like machines, and their internal structure is not a matter of chance; 'the internal structure is programmed into the ontogenetic process'.[64] If this internal structure is termed *innate mechanism,* and if the ways of functioning determined by those mechanisms are termed *innate behaviour,* then there is nothing more trivial, from the scientific viewpoint, than the statement that they are there.

No objection can be raised against this reasoning as long as it remains in the sphere of general considerations and as long as we bear in mind the above-quoted requirement concerning the scientific meaningfulness of such hypotheses. But now we pass from the sphere of general considerations to a very specific issue, namely that of language. 'There is, then, nothing unscientific about the claim that a species' specific behaviour patterns, such as language, may well be determined by innate mechanisms.'[65]

By *what* innate mechanisms? This question suggests itself on the basis of Lenneberg's own requirements; he has such venerable predecessors as Peirce and the logical positivists who claimed (and the claim is substantiated if given an appropriate framework) that the meaning of a given statement equals the method of its verification, and that it is accordingly meaningful only on the condition of being verifiable.

But here the answer is that 'it would be presumptuous to try to explain the nature of the innate events that control the operation of language'.[66] Lenneberg mentions some neurological mechanisms which may participate in language processes, but he concludes that 'how these phenomena interact to elaborate language remains a mystery'.[67] His further statement that known facts make us assume that 'there is just one peculiar mode of neural activity for aural—oral communication in man' refers to a different sphere of problems and can be readily accepted in such a general formulation. But this does not refer to the problem of 'innate mechanisms', concerning which we can only, according to Lenneberg's own words, form general hypotheses which, however, cannot be treated as verified since the problem remains a 'mystery'. And what is said next on this matter?

Reference to molecular biology does not yield any spectacular results:

> Considerations of this type show that it is possible to talk about language in connection with genetics without having to make shaky assumptions about 'genes of language'. It is true that we do not know what the direct relationships are between man's complement of genes and his mode of communication; we merely wish to outline the theoretical possibilities for relating the two.[68]

What are the final conclusions after these cautious reservations? In Chapter IX, which is a summing up, we find the statement that the process of maturation results in a stage of language-readiness, which, under the impact of the environment that provides the raw material in the form of the language used by adults, develops into actuality, i.e. the command of the language. But the conclusion is surprising.

> The presence of the raw material seems to function like a releaser for the developmental language synthesizing process. The course of language-unfolding is quite strictly prescribed through the unique maturational path traversed by cognition, and thus we may say that language-readiness is a state of *latent language structure*. The unfolding of language is a process of *actualization* in which latent structure is transformed into *realized structure*. The actualization of latent structure to realized structure is to give the underlying cognitively determined type a concrete form.[69]

And the footnote to this statement disperses all doubts as to the meaning of these formulations.

> This formulation might be regarded as the biological counterpart to what grammarians have for centuries called *universal* and *particular* grammar. Latent structure is responsible for the general type of all features of universal grammar; realized structure is responsible both for the particularities of any given statement as well as these aspects that are unique to the grammar of a given natural language.[70]

Not only does Lenneberg declare himself to be in solidarity with that type of reasoning which is characteristic of the school of generative grammar, but he also subscribes, starting from biological assumptions, to the programme of universal grammar. Here again he must be quoted in full: this is done to disperse possible doubts that his views are distorted, the more so as, to my knowledge, Lenneberg disclaims that interpretation of his statements which, in my opinion, follows from his writings quoted above.

> The language potential and the *latent structure* may be assumed to be replicated in every healthy human being because they are a consequence of human-specific cognitive processes and human-specific course of maturation. *In other words, universal grammar is of a unique type, common to all men, and it is entirely the by-product of peculiar modes of cognition based upon the biological constitution of the individual. . . Because latent structure is replicated in every child and because all languages must have an inner form of identical type . . . every child may learn any language with equal ease.*[71]

Hence language behaviour differs from other fields of culture: it is not transmitted by tradition, but all the time formed anew by autonomous individuals. Social contacts activate that process, but 'The individual is seen as functioning by virtue of his own power supply, so to speak; he constructs language by himself (provided he has the raw material to do it with), and the natural history of his development provides for mechanisms by which he will harmonize his function with that of the other equally autonomously functioning individuals around him. . . .'[72]

This explains the final conclusions with which we started to relate Lenneberg's views on innate mechanisms and linguistic structures.

This also concludes the review of the opinions of generative grammarians on innate ideas. The review was somewhat pedantic, but — as has been mentioned above — indispensable as well, since the views which are known mostly in a summary form has to be explained in full, and since it was imperative to do everything to avoid a distortion of those views and the intentions behind them.

I now have to analyse the discussions on the issue under consideration and to formulate my own views on this matter.

Discussions on Neonativism in Connection with Generative Grammar

As has been said earlier, the concept of innate ideas in the generative grammar version has become the subject-matter of numerous discussions, with two types of participants: philosophers and theoretical linguists, who in principle reject Chomsky's conception of innate language structures, and biologists, who are less hostile to it.

Let us begin with the latter group, not only because they contribute new arguments to Chomsky's theory, but above all because the controversy under consideration can be settled by natural scientists only. What is decisive is not whether a given theory of natural phenomena does, or does not, find a place within the framework of one's philosophical views, but how things are in fact. And the issue in question is not only *par excellence* in the field of natural science, but it is also empirical, if decidable at all. Note Lenneberg's words quoted above that if we refer, when explaining human behaviour (hence language behaviour as well), to changes taking place in human organism itself (which is to cover the properties of that organism), we have to state with what changes (and/or properties) we are concerned, since otherwise what we engage in is mere speculation. It is obvious that this requirement is intended to ensure the empirical nature of appropriate statements, and consequently to describe an appropriate crucial experiment. Chomsky, Katz and Lenneberg frequently emphasize in their works that their claims are empirical in nature.

If we ask at the outset the question whether natural science, and molecular biology in particular, can at its present stage settle the dispute under consideration, then the answer must be in the negative.[73] But the problem itself is empirical, since the fact that it cannot be decided at its given stage merely means that the development of science is still insufficient, and not that the problem is empirically undecidable.

If biology cannot decide the controversy now, then this cannot be done by present-day science. Hence the various statements can only have the status of hypotheses, and this is how generative grammarians understand them. But the opinion of biologists, even if it cannot be decisive for the time being, is nevertheless of a special importance in view of the significance of biology as the science which can be expected to solve the problem in the future.

Reference has been made earlier to the standpoint taken on the issue by such eminent biologists as François Jacob and Jacques Monod. These two names have been selected not only because of their scientific status, but also because both of them, and Monod in particular, have made explicit statements on the problem under consideration. But, to be more specific, we have to say that their statements are differentiated: Jacob is very restrained and practically does not express his own opinion, although he mentions the issue, whereas Monod is clearly in solidarity with the hypothesis on the existence of innate language structures. This differentiated attitude of two close collaborators, manifested in their works which have appeared almost simultaneously, is characteristic, too.

Jacob's statements are cautious, to say the least. In his opinion the development of the nervous system in animals is accompanied by a weakening of the rigorous nature of heredity.[74] The genetic programme which underlies the development of every organism has two parts, the closed one, which is strictly defined, and the open one, which leaves to the individual some freedom of response. The closed part of the programme strictly determines certain structures, functions and properties; the open part determines possibilities only. The closed part imposes something, the open one makes a choice possible. The trend of evolution increases the importance of the open part. In the case of man the latter plays such a significant role that we might speak about 'free will'.

> Mais la souplesse n'est jamais sans limites. Même lorsque le programme ne donne à l'organisme qu'une capacité, celle d'apprendre par example, il impose des restriction sur ce qui peut être appris, sur le moment ou doit avoir lieu l'apprentissage et dans quelles conditions. Le programme génétique de l'homme lui confère l'aptitude au langage. Il lui donne le pouvoir d'apprendre, de comprendre, de parler n'importe quelle langue. Encore l'homme doit-it, à une certaine étape de sa croissance, se trouver dans un milieu favorable pour que se réalise cette potentialité. Passé un certain âge, trop longtemps privé de discours, de soins, d'affection maternelle, l'enfant ne parlera pas. Mêmes restrictions pour la mémoire . . . . Mais cette frontière entre la rigidité et la souplesse du programme, on ne l'a encore guere explorée.[75]

On reading this passage, which is a coherent part of his reasoning, we cannot draw conclusions about any leanings towards the idea of innate language structures. On the contrary, we have rather to link that issue with the open part of the genetic programme, to use Jacob's terminology. Jacob declares himself firmly in favour of the claim that *aptitude au langage* (*faculté de langage* in de Saussure's terminology) as a potentiality of learning and understanding any language is genetically conditioned. No one can reasonably deny this, as no one can reasonably deny that a healthy child has an innate faculty of manual operations, which makes it possible for him, for example, to play tennis. But although all analogies are risky and the differences between these two examples are considerable, the gap between the statement on an innate *aptitude au langage* and that on man's innate generative grammar is similar, though not so big, to the gap between the statement on man's innate manual abilities and that on man's innate structures of playing tennis.

Jacob goes on to analyse the binding force of the genetic code in the case of human behaviour. As living beings liberate themselves from the rigid nature of the programme imposed by the genetic code Jacob sees the role of symbols — when living beings begin to use signs — as filters between the organism and its surroundings. This leads to situations in which integration on the level of a single organism and on that of relations between organisms is based not on an interaction of molecules, but on the exchange of coded information. According to Jacob, culture is the second genetic system, which rises above heredity, and this is why the code of these new integrating units transcends the limits of schemata of biological explanation. Hence the study of man and society is not reducible to biology, even though it cannot do without it.[76] At this point Jacob reverts to the issue we are concerned with.

> De tous les organismes, c'est l'homme qui possède le programme génétique le plus ouvert, le plus souple. Mais ou s'arrête la souplesse? Quelle est la part du comportement prescrite par les gènes? A quelles contraintes de l'hérédité l'esprit humain est-il soumis? De toute évidence, de telles contraintes existaient à certains niveaux. Mais où tracer la limite? *Pour la linguistique moderne, il y a une grammaire de base, commune à toutes les langages: cette uniformité refléterait un cadre imposé par l'heredité à l'organisation du cerveau* ... Mais alors, quelle est la rigidité de ce cadre? Quelles sont les restrictions imposées à la plasticité de l'ésprit humain par la programme génétique?[77]

Here again the formulations are very cautious, they are rather questions which imply that they cannot be answered than standpoints that could be interpreted as answers. Let us not be misled by the declarative form of the statement on modern linguistics (which clearly alludes to the school of generative grammar). Jacob merely quotes opinions of linguists, as he later quotes neurophysiologists who think that dreams are an innate feature, or anthropologists who think that aggressiveness is such a feature. Jacob does not take any standpoint on those issues, except for the question with which he concludes his analysis and which reflects his conviction that for the time being science cannot provide any answer.

It is otherwise in the case of Jacques Monod. His book *Le Hasard et la necessité* is in the border area of biology and philosophy, and if we are to judge from his manner of writing and his readiness to risk generalizations, it is rather a philosophical work. This is certainly one of the most philosophically stimulating books which I have read for years. Now Monod does not share Jacob's cautious formulations and firmly backs Chomsky's idea of innate structure. But, while being so firm, he always adds a formula like 'in my opinion' or an equivalent one, which shows clearly that what he has in mind is not a theoretical statement established in modern biology, but a hypothesis toward which he inclines, of course, on the basis of biological data. The difference is obvious and remarkable, even if we fully respect Monod's intuition in that field.

To begin with the fundamental issue, namely the acceptance of Chomsky's claim, let us see whether, and how far, Monod is in its favour.

> On sait que, selon Chomsky et son école, sous l'extrême diversité des langues humaines, l'analyse linguistique en profondeur révèle une 'forme' commune à toutes les langues. Cette forme doit donc, d'après Chomsky, être considérée comme *innée* et caracteristique de l'espèce. Cette conception a scandalisé certains philosophes ou anthropologistes qui y voient un retour à la métaphysique cartésienne. *A condition d'en accenter le contenu biologique implicite, cette conception ne me choque nullement. Elle ma paraît naturelle au contraire, dés lors qu'on admet que l'évolution des structures corticales de l'homme n's pu manquer d'être influencée, pour une part importante, par une capacité linguistique très tôt acquise à l'état le plus fruste.* Ce qui revient à admettre que la langage articulé, lors de son apparition dans la lignée humaine, n'a pas seulement permis l'evolution de la culture, mais a contribué de façon décisive à l'évolution *physique* de l'homme. S'il on a bien été ainsi, *la capacité linguistique qui se révèle au cours du développement épigénétique du cervau fait aujourd'hui partie de la 'nature humaine' elle même définie au sein du génome dans la langage radicalement different du code génétique.* [78]

On another occasion Monod makes a still stronger statement on the same subject.

> Les découvertes modernes [reference is made here to the role of sensory analysers in spatial perception – A. S.] donnent donc raison, en un sens nouveau, à Descartes et à Kant, contre l'empirisme radical qui cependant n's guère cessé de regner dans la science depuis deux cent ans, jetant la suspicion sur toute hypothèse supposant l'"innéité' des cadres de la connaissance. De nos jours encore certains théologistes paraissent attachés à l'idée que les éléments du comportement, chez l'animal, sont ou bien innés ou bien appris chacun de ces deux modes excluant absolument l'autre. Cette conception est entiérement erronée comme Lorenz l'a vigouresement démontré. *Lorsque le comportement implique des éléments acquis par l'experience, ils le sont selon un programme qui, jui, est inné, c'est-à-dire génétiquement determiné. La structure du programme appelle et guide l'apprentissage qui s'inscrira donc dans une certaine 'forme' préétablie, definie dans la patrimoine génétique de l'espèce. C'est sans doute ainsi qu'il faut interpréter le processue d'apprentissage primaire du langage chez l'enfant.* [79]

As a biologist – the point to be emphasized if the picture is to be complete – Monod dissociates himself from genetic rationalism by stressing that genetically *all* that which is to be found in living beings, including innate mechanisms (from instinctive behaviour of the bee to the innate structures of human cognition) originates from phylogenetic, and not ontogenetic, experience.[79a] Even with this reservation in favour of empiricism, Monod's statements fully support Chomsky's claim, with the provision, however, as above, that this is merely his agreement to accept Chomsky's hypothesis, but in no way a statement that we have to do with a scientifically verified thesis. Moreover, which is not insignificant, Monod refers to an unspecified 'form' (which is a Humboldtian term rather than that of contemporary generative grammarians) without taking stand on the issue of 'linguistic universals', which are said to be part of the 'acquisition device' innate in man.

This problem has been taken up by Roman Jakobson, who in his synthetic study *Linguistics*[80] also tackles the issue of the relationship between linguistics and biology. Even though he firmly dissociates himself from the biological trend in the interpretation of language phenomena, he advances, which may seem paradoxical, what are, in my opinion, the strongest arguments in favour of the genetic endowment of man as far as language is concerned.

Jakobson says that over the recent decades various universals have been discovered in phonology and grammatical patterns; it has also been found that the child has innate disposition to learn any language; but that it would be pure speculation to infer from these dispositions that any innate linguistic universals exist. To explain those universals which are known, it suffices to refer to the inner logic of linguistic structures and there is no need to argue about 'genetic instructions'. This is also denied by the existence of syntactic structures which are unknown in certain languages the existence of *argots* and individual poetic languages, etc.[80a]

Jakobson firmly emphasizes the societal aspect of language learning in the child, opposes the claim that the language of adults is just only the 'raw material' for the child, and says that all available data refute the statement that there is no need to teach the child a given language. He then proceeds to discuss the problem of man's genetic endowment when it comes to the foundations of language and, while being himself an opponent of biologism in the study of language, he raises issues which are not philosophical speculations, but refer to facts that make us analyse in depth the correlation between the 'language' of the genetic code and human language.

It turns out that the 'language' of the genetic code (genetic information is transmitted in the four-element language of nucleic acid molecules) is analogical in its structure to human language. The chemical information which determines heredity is recorded along the chromosomes in an alphabet which resembles Morse's alphabet. Since the letters of an alphabet merely are substitutes for phonemes, and Morse's alphabet is secondary with respect to the letters of the ordinary alphabet, the elements of the genetic code may be compared to phonemes. This results in the significant generalization. 'We may state that among all information-carrying systems, the genetic code and the verbal code are the only ones based upon the use of discrete components which, by themselves, are devoid of inherent meaning but serve to constitute the minimal senseful units, i.e. entities endowed with their own, intrinsic meaning in the given code.'[81]

The second striking similarity between the two information systems is that they use binary oppositions between their basic elements (phonemes in one case and the four elements of the nucleic code in the other).

Thirdly, in both cases we have to do with a hierarchical design as the principle of integration of both verbal and genetic information.

Fourthly, there is a strict colinearity in the temporal sequence of the encoding and the decoding of both languages.

And here is Jakobson's conclusion:

> How should one interpret all these salient homologies between the genetic code which 'appears to be essentially the same in all organisms' and the architectonic model underlying the verbal codes of all human languages and, *nota bene,* shared by no semiotic systems other than natural language or its substitutes? The question of these isomorphic features becomes particularly instructive when we realize that they find no analogue in any system of animal communication . . . .
>
> Now, since 'heredity itself, is fundamentally a form of communication', and since the universal architectonic design of the verbal code is undoubtedly a molecular endowment of every *Homo sapiens,* one could venture the legitimate question whether the isomorphism exhibited by these two different codes, genetic and verbal, results from a mere convergence induced by similar needs, or whether, *perhaps, the foundations of the overt linguistic patterns superimposed upon molecular communication have been modeled directly upon its structural principles?* [82]

This is a question of great importance, which shows that we can move far along the path of speculation concerning man's genetic endowment in the sphere of linguistic structures. Here, too, the question has merely been posed, but its underlying evidence makes us reflect on a more general hypothesis.

What are the results of those considerations on which the school of generative grammar could and should have counted most? To put it briefly, it has been shown that the claim concerning the existence of innate linguistic structures remains a hypothesis, and that for the time being there are neither possibilities nor grounds for admitting that hypothesis as an accepted theory. Hence the important conclusion for the generative grammarians that their *hypothesis* has not been disproved, and hence cannot be just dismissed from further considerations; but hence the no less important conclusion that this is a hypothesis which, for the time being, cannot be verified empirically from the biological point of view (and no one has so far taken the trouble to verify it in other ways, to be mentioned below). This gives rise to some polemic remarks in connection with Katz's statement quoted above, and to some general comments, which are marginal to the main issue under consideration, but are worth making in view of their philosophical significance.

Katz's statement, quoted above in full, sums up – in the radical version – considerations on innate linguistic structures. Concerning the problem of how a child assimilates a given language, why he can assimilate any language, Katz declares himself for genetic rationalism, and his answer is: he does so by means of an innate acquisition device, which contains linguistic universals that occur in all languages. Now the weak point of his alleged proof is in the fact that what has to be *proved* (this is the only way of settling the controversy between the rationalists and the empiricists, as Katz suggests in his book) has been here adopted as an *assumption*. In fact, the rationalist hypothesis offers a simple solution of an intricate problem: all languages have a common stock of linguistic universals (quite comprehensive at that, as it covers all rules of generative grammar), and this is due to the fact that human beings, who assimilate those languages, have these universals as their innate features. This is why one can assimilate any language, since it includes the stock of linguistic universals that is common to all languages, and these universals occur in those languages because they are innate features of human beings who assimilate those languages. Apart from the fact that what had to be proved is being assumed, the reasoning arouses doubts as to its logical correctness. Katz seems to realize this clearly and adds the passage which has been announced earlier.

> This explanation, it should be noted, is neither vacuous nor a *petitio principii*. To say that the language spoken by any human has the universal feature of the natural languages because the rules that define his linguistic competence are modeled on inborn archetypical representation of these features would be vacuous if there were no independently arrived at formal statement of these archetypical representations. But there is such a statement. Thus, the explanation is not vacuous because it is formulated in terms of the independently arrived at specification of the linguistic universals given in the theory of language. On the other hand, this explanation is not circular because the justification of the theory of language nowhere presupposes it. Note also that, although no account of the origin of such innate ideas is given, there is no question to be begged because there is no account of the origin of the principles of associative learning which the empiricist takes as inborn.[83]

Piling argument upon argument does not strengthen Katz's position, but rather testifies to his embarrassment, for — in my opinion — none of his arguments holds.

(1) It is not true that the statement of the existence of innate linguistic structures (Katz this time refers to 'inborn archetypical representations', but this difference in terminology does not change the essence of the issue) has been arrived at 'independently'. Independently of what? Should this 'independence' consist in the fact that, as Katz suggests, the listing of the linguistic universals has been made 'independently' *within* the theory of language, then the proof would be as scientific as the various proofs of the existence of God. 'Independence' in this case is to the point if the existence of appropriate innate structure be established *independently* of the theory of language, i.e. within the framework of *another* theory, in this case a *biological theory* being the only possible. Now, as we have seen, this is not so, and hence the theory of generative grammar, when defending the concept of innate linguistic structures (which it must defend if it is to survive in its present form), has found itself in the position of Baron Münchhausen, who saved himself from sinking in a bog by pulling himself out of that bog by his own bob-wig.

(2) The reasoning is vitiated not only by a *petitio principii*, but also by a *circulus vitiosus*, since the linguistic theory (i.e. the meta-theory of generative grammar which Katz defends) does assume — contrary to what

he claims – reference to the concept of innate structures, because, as we have seen earlier, the claim as to the existence of a universal grammar cannot be defended without this assumption.

(3) If the supporters of the associative theory of learning in fact refer to some innate features and do not give any proof of their claim (especially as far as the origin of those innate features is concerned), then this demonstrates the weakness of their theory, but does not exclude the possibility of criticizing the weak points in the theory advanced by their opponents. Note that in the case of generative grammar the point is not to *account for the origin* of innate ideas, to which generative grammarians refer, but to *prove their existence,* which can be expected of natural science only.

The impossibility of settling the issue at the present level of development of natural science, and molecular biology in particular, is thus decisive for the assessment of the concept of innate linguistic structures, with all the consequences of this fact for the models constructed in generative grammar. The hypothesis cannot be rejected, and it keeps its heuristic value by being a stimulus to appropriate research. But neither may we deny the right to disagree to such thinkers as Roman Jakobson, who treats the issue as an 'utterly speculative and sterile question'.[83a]

As mentioned previously, some comments of a broader significance suggest themselves in connection with the biological aspect of the issue.

First of all, why did the founders of generative grammar resort to the nativist hypothesis in order to develop their ideas? The recurrent argument that no other theory explains the fact that the child learns any language in a very short time and even under unfavourable conditions and that otherwise belief in miracles would be the only satisfactory explanation is not convincing, especially if we consider the otherwise well-known logical precision in reasoning on the part of those who advance the nativist hypothesis. The simplest way out would be to abstain from statements which they were in no way bound to make while constructing the specified structural model of language and developing the transformation calculus based on that model. Now if they decided to adopt a biological interpretation (their declaration of access to rationalists' tradition merely means couching their views in philosophical terms), they did so because the neonativist ideas, in connection with recent advances in molecular biology, in a way comply with the spirit of our times. A general interpretation of the problem has been offered by François Jacob, who has based his history of biology, interpreted as *la logique du vivant* (which is the title of his book), precisely on this methodological conception. His idea is as follows: theory is always ahead of research practice, especially in experimental disciplines. In the case under consideration this idea is significant also because of the theoretical implications of the specific rebirth of nativism, especially in connection with research in molecular biology, for the genetic code. The importance of Jacob's comments justifies quoting him in full:

> Pour qu'un object soit accessible à l'analyse, il ne suffit pas de l'apercevoir. Il faut encore qu'une théorie soit preête à l'accueillir. Dans l'échange entre la théorie et l'experience, c'est toujours la première qui engage le dialogue. C'est elle qui détermine la forme de la question, donc les limites de la réponse. 'le hasard ne favorise que les esprits preparés,' disait Pasteur. Le hasard, ici, cela signifie que l'observation a été faite par accident et non afin de vérifier la théorie. Mais la théorie était déjà là, qui permet d'interpréter l'accident.[84]

This is to be interpreted so that what we perceive in the world around us and what questions we ask about it depends on the theory we have at our disposal (which theory, in turn, is a product of our knowledge at a given stage). Indirectly, this helps us understand the biological trend in the interpretation of certain linguistic facts, among other things, the interpretation advanced by generative grammarians.

The advances in molecular biology, with the striking discovery of the genetic code, make us revert both to the issue of heredity and that of genetic endowment with which every man is born, and consequently, the problem of the relationship between what is innate and what is acquired societally. At any rate, the comforting conviction that nativism is dead, that, 'as even Locke said', man is born as a *tabula rasa,* belongs to the past. The problem has been revived and will have to be internalized anew by philosophers, which may give rise to many troubles that will have to be taken into account.

All this evokes two comments.

First, on the fortunes of the various ideas and theories which seemed to be dead and which, under new conditions, start living again. Early in this century, Ludwik Krzywicki, the prominent Polish Marxist scholar, wrote a very fine book on migrations of ideas, which unfortunately is little known abroad because of the language barrier. He analysed there, on the example of social ideas, the migrations of ideas in time and in space, and showed that under new conditions old ideas acquire new aspects and sometimes breed novel concepts. This obviously applies to Chomsky's reference to the history of what he termed Cartesian linguistics. It turns out that the evolution of ideas, especially in science, does not follow a straight line to break off at a certain point: it rather follows a spiral, which makes returns possible, but then at a higher level of general development, and development of human knowledge in particular.

Secondly, the fact under consideration is not only to be stated, but also predicted in a scientific manner. In some cases, especially if such 'returns' have societal implications, be it only indirect ones, they must be not only predicted, but met properly. This undoubtedly holds for neonativism, i.e. the rebirth of interpretations of various facts in the light of the nativist theory. The idea of innate linguistic structures is only an example: we have the well-known facts that children learn languages almost casually, we have the new structure of science, connected with advances in molecular biology, and the result is the concept of innate linguistic structures, because *this* theory now lends itself well to the integration of problems connected with the functioning of the human organism. We may, and we ought to, ponder over this theory, even though it may seem shocking, but we also have to realize that we have here to do with a very 'mild' case as far as its societal implications are concerned: reference is made in it to a *universal* genetic endowment of mankind, i.e. to what *unites* human beings, if only because of the common biological fortunes of the species *Homo sapiens.* But the genetic code, or the plasma language of heredity, may, perhaps, record also factors by which human beings *differ* among themselves, only for the climatic, geographical, social, etc., differences in their history. Could then there not be a genetic substantiation of some forms of racialism? This could not be excluded. At any rate the fact now observed, although quite different in nature, make us take into philosophical consideration that aspect of the issue, too.

As mentioned above, biological reflections form only one aspect of the discussion of the concept of innate ideas within the framework of generative grammar. This aspect of the discussion is, as we have seen, an important one, but it has been pushed into the peripheries, since the discussions reflected in a number of publications (two principal ones were mentioned in the introduction to this paper) have been mainly concerned with philosophical issues.

Before these discussions are summed up here, my intention is to eliminate one aspect, which, as mentioned earlier in this paper, I think irrelevant to the problem under consideration: that of the history of philosophy. Who correctly interprets the works of Locke and Descartes, and what these and other prominent thinkers had to say on the subject of innate ideas has very little, if any, bearing on the settling of the controversy which is connected with the present-day state of science. These are matters of interest to a historian of culture, but they can well be disregarded here and left to historians of philosophy in general, and philosophy of language in particular.[85]

Not all arguments and counter-arguments will be quoted here either. They have been published and are widely accessible; this holds both for criticism and for Chomsky's two papers[86] which are at least partly his reply to such criticism (they have not been mentioned here because, apart from offering somewhat more radical formulations, they do not contribute anything new to his statements, and some replies to criticism can be understood only against the background of the discussion as a whole). While raising here my own objections and making my own suggestions, I will quote, out of the arguments formulated in the discussion, only those two which I consider to be the most important: the one advanced by Nelson Goodman that the lack of an alternative hypothesis does not prove that the hypothesis which is the object of a controversy is in any way substantiated, and the one formulated by Sidney Hook and Thomas Nagel that there is little precision in the distinction between 'knowledge' and 'capacity' when Chomsky speaks about innate linguistic structures which convey to the child, who is endowed with the appropriate acquisition device or learning device, the knowledge of the rules of generative grammar.

Let us begin with those arguments which have been stated by others and with which I am in agreement.

Goodman's argument is a reply to the following type of statements which recur in the writings of Chomsky and his collaborators: we now face the difficult problem of explaining how the child learns a language and we have no hypothesis alternative to ours, hence our hypothesis is true. Of course, this has never been worded *just so*, since that would be too naive, but *this* was the idea implied by many statements. This, of course, is erroneous, and has to be eliminated at the outset when we proceed critically to analyse Chomsky's views. This has been well done by Goodman, and hence it suffices to quote his words: 'Let us now assume that for certain remarkable facts I have no alternative explanation. Of course, that alone does not dictate acceptance of whatever theory may be offered; for that theory might be worse than none. Inability to explain a fact does not condemn us to accept an intrinsically repugnant and incomprehensible theory.'[87]

In his reply, Chomsky[88] concerns himself only with the objection that we have to do with a repugnant (an emotional label which does not contribute anything to the discussion) and incomprehensible theory (since it follows from Goodman's later words that he comprehends Chomsky's theory even though he criticizes it for the lack of precision in certain formulations). I think that Chomsky is right in rejecting these two objections. But he has not taken up the *principal* objection and has not replied to it. The conclusion to be drawn from that objection is in a way trivial, but it is not in the least trivial when it comes to the assessment of Chomsky's views: they just include a hypothesis that requires empirical verification but cannot be accepted merely on the ground of there being no other theory that would explain the same problem in a satisfactory manner. All arguments other than that concerned with empirical verifi-cation are, so to say, auxiliary, but they do not settle the controversy. Since Chomsky's many statements seem to indicate that he agrees with this, the point is to indicate the way of an empirical verification of his theory, a specific crucial experiment conceived for the case under consideration. Of course, the burden of the proof could be passed to the opponents who would then have to adduce facts which *disprove* the theory (this would be in line with the procedure used in penal cases, and Chomsky seems to favour it on certain occasions[89]), but from the scientific point of view such an evasion cannot replace verification, without which opinions remain hypotheses.

Sidney Hook[90] raises another issue and his argument is quite pertinent: if it is said that the child 'is born with knowledge', then we have to state precisely what is meant by 'knowledge'. If this is neither a skill nor biological processes inherited together with cellular plasma, then Platonic anamnesis is the only idea left to explain Chomsky's conception. The same path of argument is followed by Thomas Nagel[91] who makes a distinction between 'innate capacity' and 'knowledge' to demonstrate that Chomsky, despite his misleading terminology, does not in fact go beyond 'innate capacity'.

Let us agree that this lack of precision contributes to a theoretical confusion, but if we are convinced that we have to do with a research hypothesis, we should not reject it even while we pin down some inaccuracies in formulations. But such a hypothesis ought to be subjected to a critical analysis.

With what are we to begin such a critical analysis when it comes to the concept of innate ideas as advanced within the framework of generative grammar?

I think that we ought to begin with the statement that, in the light of the present-day state of science, biology in particular, the hypothesis is legitimate. Hence it may not be rejected merely because of the opinions of one or another philosophical school. But, on the other hand, it is legitimate to demand that this hypothesis be verified empirically, or that, at least, an approach to such a verification be indicated.[92] In this respect, a philosopher may prove useful by posing appropriate questions and, as far as possible, suggesting experiments, research methods, etc.

In my opinion, the neglect of the empirical aspect of the issue on the part of generative grammarians (for all their oft-repeated claims that their theory is empirical in nature) may be interpreted as a consequence of the inclination to construct a hypothetical deductive model. It might be replied that generative grammarians by making use of their transformation model can answer questions in face of which taxonomical descriptivists stand helpless.[93] This is certainly true, and this is certainly an empirical argument. But this does not prove the existence of a *universal* grammar nor, *a fortiori*, is it an empirical verification of the statement that there are innate linguistic structures which coincide with the system of the rules of generative grammar. Is such a verification procedure at all possible? Yes, and in two ways at that.

First of all, and above all, we mean the verification of this hypothesis by molecular biology. The point, as E. Lenneberg rightly says in his *Biological Foundations of Language,* is not to find the gene of language. The problem is much more subtle and much more intricate, but if it is true that not only the *faculté du langage,* but also the whole of generative grammar, being *universal,* is innate and belongs to the genetic endowment of every human being, then, if we are to follow Lenneberg, it must be a verifiable feature in the sense that it should be possible to indicate its somatic background. Hereditary features are recorded in the language of the genetic code, i.e. in the form of specific combinations of the four elements – nucleic acids – along the chromosomes. Molecular biologists have succeeded, by using elaborate research methods, in decoding a number of records in the said code, thus solving various puzzles of the human organism. It may happen that in the future they will also be able to answer the question we are concerned with, either in favour of the generative grammarians by verifying their hypothesis, or against them, by disproving it. In such a case Rome would speak and the controversy would be settled. For the time being they are unable to provide such an answer, and hence the issue must remain pending.

Secondly, there is a chance of verifying the hypothesis in the field where generative grammarians and their opponents are active, i.e. within the sphere of linguistics. I have to admit that I fail to grasp why this self-evident test has never been made (nor, by the way, can I comprehend why, after the original euphoria over Sapir–Whorf's hypothesis concerning linguistic universals, the interest in that hypothesis has vanished in American linguistic circles, even though the hypothesis has never been disproved, and, to make matters worse, no *serious* attempt to disprove it has ever been made).[93a] It seems that it is easier to formulate general linguistic hypotheses that are philosophical in nature, than to try to verify them empirically by sophisticated methods. This is certainly so when it comes to interest manifested in linguistic circles, although their members might be expected to have a different approach to the issue.

The empirical verification which is suggested here is very simple in its general idea, but presumably much less so when it comes to putting it into effect.

Now if it is true that deep structures are *universal* and that surface structures are derived from the former by appropriate transformation rules which are explicitly formulated in transformational generative grammar, then it would be enough to know these rules concerning the three language components: phonetics, semantics and syntax, to be able, following an appropriate descriptive analysis of a given language, freely to move from deep to surface structures, and vice versa. At any rate, nothing would prevent an appropriately programmed computer of adequate power, in view of its great operational speed and its vast memory, from moving between the deep and the surface level.

Assume now that an adequate computer is programmed to move so between deep and surface structures and vice versa not in one language, but in two, or three, or four languages. In the first stage of the experiment we could confine ourselves to one family of languages (e.g. the Indo-European) and − to avoid other complications − to languages at a similar level of development as far as linguistic history, the socio-economic and cultural levels of the users of these languages, etc., are concerned. If the hypothesis stating that deep structures are universal is true, then in this case this fact can be most easily verified. The computer which can move between the two levels of linguistic structures is given the following task: it is to analyse a given text, e.g. in French, to pass from its surface structures to its deep structures, and then to move in the other direction, but, for example, in the field of the English language, thus *translating* the French text into English. In plain terms, this would just be a *translation* from one natural language to another natural language (both covered by the programme of a given computer), with the only provision that the intermediate stage would be that of deep structures, which would have to be, if not identical, then at least *of the same type,* for all the languages involved. The universal grammar hypothesis would be tenable only if this experiment proved successful.

The result of this simple experiment, consisting in translation through the intermediary of deep structures, would be the first empirical test for the hypothesis in question. My opinion is that such an experiment would succeed. Even in this simplest case there would be difficulties, especially with the semantic component (the rules of sense, which assign meanings to sequences of sounds), mainly in the cases of polysemy, but this is just the issue at stake, and recourse to deep structures is expected to solve such problems. The problem of the semantic component has not so far been solved in generative grammar, but this must be done in the near future, if generative grammar is to be considered seriously as a hypothesis. Thus, even if the suggested experiment cannot be carried out at once, then it must be taken into account as a programme for the future. This will stress the empirical nature of the generative grammar hypothesis and point clearly to what the crucial experiment is to be.

But, as mentioned above, this would be merely the first, and the easier, part of the experiment. Part two would consist in a similar translation test that makes recourse to the intermediary of deep structures, but this time it would involve languages which are in different language groups that are remote from one another both genetically and culturally. For instance, translation could be made from English into Chinese, into Hopi, into one of the Eskimo languages, into a language of Australian aborigines, etc. The task would be immense, even if we consider the preparatory stage of describing such languages structurally and working out appropriate computer programmes. Even if we disregard the rather trivial issue that in most cases the languages concerned would be lexically (and hence conceptually) poor, the point would be to describe their respective structures so to say from the inside. This metaphor is intended to convey something which is both very simple and extremely important. When we face the structure of a language, especially a culturally remote one, we may be inclined to make that description comply with an otherwise known model of the structure of another language. As is demonstrated by the well-known examples provided by Malinowski,[94] this procedure may easily yield nonsensical results, but it may also suggest that a given theory, applied in such a way, works well. We can, and we ought to, approach the issue at a different angle, by making an autonomous analysis of the semantic and syntactic components of a given language to serve as a basis of its structural description which would cover phonetics, syntax and semantics. Now, *such* work being done, the proof would be completed if a translation through the intermediary of deep structures (which would have to be the same, or at least greatly similar) really succeeds: the proof would mean both the verification of the hypothesis assuming the existence of a universal grammar and the disproval of the hypothesis assuming linguistic relativism. For the time being we can only have various, often incompatible, beliefs as to the results of such an experiment, but the controversy can be settled only with reference to its outcome, if and when such an experiment is carried out. But even this would not yet prove the existence of innate linguistic structures (since that can be done only in the sphere of natural science, and molecular biology in particular), but it would prove that something like a *universal* generative grammar does exist. Such a proof would make the hypothesis on innate linguistic structures much more probable, and at any rate it would be a big step toward testing that hypothesis empirically.

So much for the preliminary statement that we have to do with a hypothesis which is legitimate, but requires empirical verification if it is to be treated not just as a deductive model based on speculative assumptions. This requirement also suggests the programme for empirical tests. But what can be said about the present shape and meaning of the hypothesis in question?

First of all, we shall quote Nelson Goodman's arguments and those of Sidney Hook, which open the list of questions and objections with reference to the present form of the hypothesis on innate linguistic structures, i.e. before its verification or disproval following appropriate experimental tests.

Hence, first, the fact that we have no alternative theory that would be satisfactory from the scientific point of view cannot be taken as the confirmation of the hypothesis under consideration, which does not comply with all the requirements that a legitimate *theory* ought to satisfy.

Secondly, if, following Chomsky's reasoning, we say that the child's innate acquisition device (i.e. a kind of a black box which for a given input has a given output — in this case the knowledge of a given language) endows him with the knowledge of a given language, then this may be understood in two ways:

(a) In the sense that this mysterious acquisition device is identical with de Saussure's *faculté du langage,* i.e. that the child has an innate capacity to *learn* a language (without explaining how this occurs, i.e. taking this learning mechanism to be unknown). This would rank this aquisition device at par with other innate capacities (from instinctive actions to such which require *learning,* e.g. on the basis of innate manual abilities), thus making the hypothesis something trivial and thereby destroying the intricate concept of generative grammar.

(b) In the sense that the statement on the existence of such an acquisition device is equivalent to the statement that every child has an innate *knowledge* of a set of linguistic rules which make up generative grammar. In this case we would have to do not with a *capacity* to learn a language, but with its ready-made *knowledge.*

This issue has not been formulated by Chomsky and his followers with sufficient precision. On the one hand, it would seem that they mean interpretation (b), without which, as has been said above, the entire hypothesis would become trivial and of little interest, but, on the other hand, the course of their reasoning does not justify going beyond interpretation (a) (for instance, in his paper in *Synthèse* Chomsky protested against being ascribed the intention to defend the theory of instinctive actions), which makes the whole discussion questionable.

I would also add some criticisms of my own.

Thirdly, it must be emphasized that when the advocates of the generative grammar theory use the term *universal grammar* they in fact resort to a fiction. By using the term *fiction* I want to dot the '*i*' in order to resist the psychological pressure of a hypostasis: the fact that there is a term *universal grammar* does not imply in the least that something like a universal grammar — i.e. valid in *all* languages in the form of deep structures — does in fact exist. As long as its existence is not proved we must treat the concept of 'universal grammar' as a fiction, not only because the relevant hypothesis has not been verified, but also because there is a rival hypothesis, namely that of linguistic relativism, which has never been disproved and which is supported by a much more comprehensive body of data than is the generative grammar hypothesis. It may even be said that, in view of the hypothetical deductive nature of the model of generative grammar, its authors are specifically nonchalant on the issue. This was manifest in Chomsky's reply to Hiż (at a symposium organized by Sidney Hook) when the latter objected that Chomsky's constructions are not based on an additional analysis of various languages. Chomsky rejected this argument as groundless by claiming that, for instance, Matthews's study of the Hidatsa language is worth more than a thousand superficial papers on various languages. Now while the assessment of the value of such papers is to be left to experts, let it be noted that no one suggests that superficial papers be written. What is needed is good studies in depth, but it certainly is not true that we may rest satisfied with a single study, be it even perfect. In this respect W. von Humboldt, to whose theory of 'language form' Chomsky so willingly refers, was of a quite different opinion, and rightly so. And when, in Chomsky's reply to Hiż's objection, we read: 'If someone feels that the base of data is too narrow, what he should do is to show that some of the material omitted refutes the principles that have been formulated',[95] then we must disapprove of such a standpoint. As has been mentioned on one occasion earlier, this holds for a penal case, in which all guilt has to be proved, but in science it is otherwise: the fact that a hypothesis has not been refuted does not mean that it has been verified. Anyone who advances a hypothesis must verify it if he wants it to become an accepted scientific theory.

But all these reservations against a hypostasis are merely an introduction to the main argument to be presented here. The point is that should we even prove the existence of a universal grammar (e.g. by means of the experiment suggested above, or in any other way), it would not follow therefrom, as has already been said earlier, that such a grammar be a specific product of certain innate linguistic structures. Such a fact could well be a result of some other causes. The existence of innate structure can be proved only in the sphere of natural science, biology in particular.

But should biologists or other natural scientists prove the existence of innate linguistic structures that would correspond to Chomsky's acquisition device, we still could not conclude that a *universal* grammar exists, unless it be proved additionally that those innate linguistic structures are *the same* in all (healthy) human beings. For as far as the specific records in the genetic code are concerned we know that such records differ, which accounts for various differences not only between individuals, but between fairly stabilized groups (compare such anthropological features as the pigmentation of the skin, etc.). Hence, to verify Chomsky's claim we would have to prove not only that an innate acquisition device in the sphere of language exists as a feature of the human species, but also that this device is *the same* in all humans.

Fourthly, the concept of innate linguistic structures, and consequently the whole concept of generative grammar, is burdened with a lack of clarity when it comes to the relationship between language and thinking. We face here one of the age-old problems in the philosophy of language, without solving which, however, we are not in a position to solve any general problems in the theory of language, which Chomsky's hypothesis claims to be.

According to the concept of generative grammar, deep structures are universal, the same in all languages, which is to substantiate the claim that a *universal* grammar exists. But the semantic component of language cannot be separated from deep structures. The question arises, what it means to say that deep structures are innate (are given by the language acquisition device, which is innate in all humans). This can be interpreted in two ways:

(a) deep structures are innate *together with* the semantic component;

(b) deep structures are innate as purely linguistic entities, to which, in the process of genetic development, the semantic component (i.e. the specific rules of sense or meaning postulates) is somehow adjusted.

In the former case we have to do with the statement which *identifies* language and thinking. The situation is then clear from the point of view of the hypothesis that assumes innate ideas: language as a phonetic-and-semantic whole is *innate* and we are accordingly relieved of all troubles of *explaining* the relevant facts; what we have to do is merely to *describe* them. This is a convenient situation (of course, on the trifling condition that the hypothesis has been verified) − one would even say too convenient − as it relieves us of many difficult problems, which are then accounted for by the innate nature of the relevant facts, but on the other hand requires acceptance of the hypothesis that assumes the *identity* of language and thinking, a hypothesis which is not acceptable even to the staunchest supporters of the idea of their inseparable *unity* (W. von Humboldt, so cherished by Chomsky, defended the statement that we think the way we speak, but we do not speak the way we think; he would accordingly most emphatically disclaim the statement that language is the same as thinking), not to speak of all those who either approach the problem from the genetic point of view and indicate certain forms of thinking (in the sense of problem-solving) at the pre-verbal stage of development of the animal kingdom, or even plainly claim that there are forms of non-verbal thinking (mathematical, musical, etc., thinking). Now it follows from certain statements made by Chomsky (and especially by Lenneberg) that he rejects the hypothesis on the *identity* of language and thinking.

This leaves the second interpretation: only linguistic structures are innate. But what does this mean, and what are its consequences for the issues we are concerned with? If the semantic component is not innate, then are both the phonetic and the syntactic component innate, or is only the phonetic component innate? We could hardly imagine syntax *without* the semantic aspect of language. But should only the phonetic component be innate (suppose we have proved that), then this leaves us in the absurd situation in which language sounds are dissociated from meanings;

moreover, this assumption does not solve the problems we are interested in. In order to arrive at the generative grammar postulated by Chomsky we must have at our disposal its *all three* components; and if that generative grammar is given to every human through the intermediary of *innate linguistic structures*, then we must assume that it is in them that the *identity* of language and thinking is manifested, the conclusion which we wanted to avoid.

We thus face a considerable difficulty resulting from the hypothesis suggested to us. This difficulty requires that the authors of the hypothesis at least make their standpoint more precise; it also requires some answers to the questions which arise when the problem is formulated with sufficient precision.

Fifthly, there is the problem of the social conditioning of language.

That language is a social phenomenon is a trivial statement to make in the light of modern linguistics in general, and not only such of its specialized branches as sociolinguistics. So is also the more general statement that man is a product not of nature only, but of society as well (this statement was first advanced by Marx in his criticism of Feuerbach's anthropology, but it has since become so widely accepted in science that the memory of its Marxian origin has been lost). Chomsky, and especially Lenneberg, emphasize that although the language acquisition device is innate, nevertheless we do not have to do with a purely biological process, since an appropriate input in the form of acts of speech which a child hears in his milieu (i.e. the impact of the social factor) is required to trigger the acquisition device. This is why the supporters of generative grammar say that they accept the role of the social factor, and hence the objection that they stand for biologism (cf. the criticism formulated by R. Jakobson in his article in *Linguistics,* quoted above) is groundless. Yet the problem is much more complicated, and the objection that they disregard the role of the social factor when analysing language seems to be justified when it comes to the concept of innate linguistic structures.

Let us first see to what the role of the social factor, which generative grammarians interpret somewhat specifically, is reduced in their theory. Now they reduce it to a specific input which, in the form of the stimulus provided by the acts of speech of the child's milieu, sets the language acquisition device in motion. Present-day supporters of the theory, stating that language is based on innate ideas, thus differ from their predecessors in the eighteenth century, who believed that a child *totally* isolated from all influence of a human milieu would start speaking spontaneously as a result of the maturation processes; their controversies were confined only to the issue which language such a 'savage' child would speak (they were mostly inclined to think that it would be Hebrew, which as the language of the Bible was believed to be the original language of mankind). Today we know quite well that a child *totally* isolated from appropriate influence of all human milieu would not develop his language capacity, but would, on crossing a certain age limit, remain a *homo alala* for ever. This is also confirmed by the cases of 'savage' children, recorded in greater or lesser detail; facts show that 'wolf' children do not behave like Mowgli of *The Jungle Book*, who knew the languages of all animals, but just become imbeciles, and incurably so, once they have crossed a certain physiological age barrier. No serious researcher, even if he accepts the claims of genetic rationalism concerning language and thinking, will now repeat the eighteenth-century error about a supposed spontaneous emergence of speech in the child merely as a result of maturation processes. But does the statement that an appropriate input in the form of acts of speech heard in the child's human milieu, as the issue is now being formulated by generative grammarians, change *qualitatively* their standpoint as compared with the naïve eighteenth-century beliefs? No, it does not.

For what is being claimed in that respect by generative grammarians? It follows clearly from many statements by Chomsky and Lenneberg (including those quoted above) that they mean only a stimulus, which is analogous to stimulation in chemical processes. We find in those statements that the acquisition device works if excited by external stimuli, regardless of differences between the levels of intelligence of the various persons and regardless of the type of input (i.e. the child develops the correct generative grammar of a given language regardless of *how* his milieu speaks). Thus what is meant is clearly just the stimulation of innate mechanisms, with the provision that such stimulation works toward a *specified* language (following the stimulus of the acts of speech heard by the child), and not in general. But we have to say that the difference between this and the corresponding eighteenth-century beliefs is not so great: in fact it reduces to the requirement of a stimulus, about which no mention was made in the eighteenth century. But otherwise the opinions are identical: the language mechanism develops like innate physiological mechanisms, and we even find the statement that a human being does not learn a language, as he does not learn digestive processes: his language simply develops. This may be an elegant explanation (in the mathematical sense of 'elegance') because of its economy, but it is unfortunately erroneous. It is not true that the quality of the input (the acts of speech heard by the child) does not affect the output (the language of the individual in question): if a person is brought up in a milieu which speaks a given language ungrammatically (by the way, how does this happen if the result is supposed to be always the same, i.e. in the form of a correct generative grammar, independent of the quality of the input?), then he will speak that language ungrammatically himself. Usually this is a life sentence, which refutes the claim that every child develops a generative grammar which is *universal* as it is imbedded in innate linguistic structures. Such defects in linguistic upbringing can be eliminated in the adult age only with greatest difficulty, and not even that in all cases (compare G. B. Shaw's *Pygmalion*).

But even if we disregard the naivety of the standpoint analysed here we still have to discuss the vast sphere of problems connected with the social factor in the field of language. We have to say plainly that when we refer, in analysing the development of the language faculty in man, to the social factor we do not mean only the speech sounds heard by the child (since then a loudspeaker from which the child would hear sounds of even grammatically incorrect speech, as the generative grammarians claim, would suffice), but human speech as related to man's *social actions*. The theory of generative grammar, and especially the hypothesis which assumes the existence of innate linguistic structures, unduly simplifies the issue of the social factor, if it notices it at all. By doing so it eliminates from its field of vision (i) all problems of language in the context of social actions (i.e. the field of study of sociolinguistics), (ii) the problems of the relationship between language and thinking, which also requires the context of social actions.

Now that we revert to the starting-point of this analysis, where it has been said that the hypothesis if innate linguistic structures is legitimate from the point of view of present-day science, but remains an empty structure without an empirical verification, we may add that it also requires at least more precision in certain formulations before its verification can be undertaken.

To conclude, the present writer wants to say that he is convinced of the usefulness of transformational generative grammar for the description of linguistic structures, even if the claim of universality is shattered together with the hypothesis of innate linguistic structures. Making the foundations of generative grammar less comprehensive will probably not please its founders, who are much more ambitious when it comes to the theory of language, but this does not belittle the importance of what they have really achieved.

NOTES

1. See (i) Sidney Hook (ed.), *Language and Philosophy,* New York University Press, 1969; (ii) 'Symposium on Innate Ideas' (Noam Chomsky, Hilary Putnam and Nelson Goodman), *Synthèse,* Vol. 17 (1967).
2. Jacques Monod, *Le Hasard et la nécéssité,* Paris, 1970, pp. 144 ff.; François Jacob, *La Logique du vivant,* Paris, 1970, p. 343.
3. A. Martinet, *Economie des changements phonétiques,* Berne, 1955, Chap. III.
4. In his paper ' "Structure" en linguistique', in: *Sens et usages du terme 'structure' dans les sciences humaines et sociales,* 's-Gravenhage, 1962.
5. A. Martinet, *Eléments de linguistique générale,* Paris, 1960.
6. N. M. Gukhman, *Istoricheskiye i metodologicheskiye osnovy strukturalizma,* in: *Osnovniye napravlieniya strucktluralizma,* Moskva, 1964, pp. 44–45.
7. Paul M. Postal, 'Limitations of Phrase Structure Grammar', in: Jerry A. Fodor and Jerrald J. Katz (eds.), *The Structure of Language,* Prentice Hall, 1964, p. 141. For a similar, though not so radical, interpretation see Nicolas Ruwet, *Introduction à la grammaire générative,* Paris, 1967, pp. 63–64 and 77–78.
8. On this issue see N. Chomsky, *Language and Mind,* New York, 1968, p. 17.
9. 'The grammar, then, is a device that (in particular) specifies the infinite set of well-formed sentences and assigns to each of these one or more structural descriptions. Perhaps we should call such a device a *generative grammar* to distinguish it from descriptive statements that merely present the inventory of elements that appear in structural descriptions, and their contextual variants.' (Noam Chomsky, *Current Issues in Linguistic Theory,* Mouton, The Hague, 1969, p. 9.)
10. *Ibid.,* p. 11.
11. *Ibid.,* p. 17.
12. Noam Chomsky, *Cartesian Linguistics,* Harper & Row, New York, 1966.
13. Chomsky, *Current Issues, ed. cit.,* pp. 23–24 (italics – A. S.).
14. An explicit reference to this fact is made by S. K. Shaumian, 'Teoreticheskiye osnovy transformatsionnoy grammatiki', in: V. A. Zvegintsev, *Novoe v lingvistike,* Series II, Moskva, 1962, p. 406.
15. 'Thus, in his terms, sentence formation is not strictly a matter of langue, but is rather assigned to what he (Saussure) called parole, and thus placed outside the scope of linguistics proper; it is a process of free creation, unconstrained by linguistic rule except insofar as such rules govern the forms of words and the patterns of sounds. Syntax, in this view, is a rather trivial matter. And, in fact,

198   Structuralism and Marxism

there is very little work in syntax throughout the period of language linguistics' (N. Chomsky, *Language and Mind, ed. cit.,* p. 17).

16. K. Ajdukiewicz, 'Das Weltbild und die Begriffsapparatur', *Erkenntnis,* Vol. IV, 1934; 'Sprache und Sinn', *ibid.*; 'Die wissenschaftliche Weltperspektive', *ibid.,* Vol. V, 1935.

17. See Jarrold H. Katz, *The philosophy of Language,* New York, 1966, p. 116.

18. R. Jakobson (see 'Linguistics' in *Main Trends of Research in the Social and Human Sciences,* I, Mouton/Unesco, 1970) says that priority in this respect goes to the paper by D. Bubrix, 'Neskolko slov o potoke rechi', *Biuleten* LOJKFUN, 5 (1930).

19. N. Chomsky, *Syntactic Structures,* Mouton, 's-Gravenhage, 1957, p. 13. From the point of view of filiations of ideas it is worth noting that such precisely was the standpoint formulated by L. Wittgenstein in his *Tractatus Logico-Philosophicus,* 4.001: 'The totality of propositions is the language.'

20. *Ibid.* See also *Current Issues, ed. cits.,* p. 9.

21. N. Chomsky, 'On the Notion "Rule of Grammar" ', in: J. A. Fodor and J. K. Katz (eds.), *The Structure of Language, ed. cit.,* pp. 119–20.

22. Chomsky, *Current Issues, ed. cit.,* p. 10.

23. N. Chomsky, 'The Formal Nature of Language,' Appendix A in: Eric H. Lenneberg, *Biological Foundations of Language,* New York, 1967, pp. 397–8.

24. *Ibid.,* p. 398.

25. N. Chomsky, *Topics in the Theory of Generative Grammar,* Mouton, The Hague, 1966, p. 11.

26. Chomsky, *Syntactic Structures, ed. cit.,* pp. 49–53.

27. Chomsky, *Topics . . . , ed. cit.,* pp. 13–17.

28. N. Chomsky, *Cartesian Linguistics, ed. cit.,* pp. 31–42.

29. *Ibid.,* pp. 35, 59 *et passim.*

30. N. Chomsky, 'The Formal Nature of Language', *ed. cit.,* pp. 402 ff.

31. *Ibid.,* p. 407.

32. *Ibid.,* p. 401 (italics – A. S.)

33. *Ibid.,* p. 439.

34. N. Chomsky, *Topics . . . , ed. cit.,* pp. 18–19.

35. N. Chomsky, 'A review of B. F. Skinner's *Verbal Behavior'*, in: *The Structure of Language, ed. cit.,* pp. 547 ff.

36. *Ibid.,* p. 548.

37. *Ibid.,* pp. 563–4.

38. *Ibid.,* pp. 577–8.

39. Included in E. Nagel, P. Suppes and A. Tarski, *Logic, Methodology and the Philosophy of Sciences,* Proceedings of the 1960 International Congress. Stanford University Press, 1962, pp. 528–50.

40. *Ibid.,* p. 535.

41. *Ibid.,* p. 536 (italics – A. S.).

42. In extended form published as *Current Issues in Linguistic Theory,* Mouton, The Hague, 1964.

43. *Ibid.,* pp. 17 ff.

44. *Ibid.,* p. 26 (italics – A. S.).

44a. *Ibid.,* p. 27.

45. Chomsky, *Cartesian Linguistics, ed. cit.,* p. 60.

46. *Ibid.,* p. 64.

47. *Biological Foundations of Language,* New York, 1967.
48. *Ibid.,* p. 401.
49. *Ibid.,* p. 416 (italics – A. S.).
50. Chomsky, *Language and Mind, ed. cit.*
51. Chomsky, *Language and Mind, ed. cit.*
52. *Ibid.,* p. 68 (italics – A. S.).
52a. *Ibid.,* p. 69.
52b. *Ibid.,* pp. 68–69.
52c. *Ibid.,* p. 69.
52d. *Ibid.*
52e. *Ibid.*
52f. *Ibid.,* p. 76.
52g. *Ibid.*
53. J. J. Katz, *The Philosophy of Language, ed. cit.*
54. E. H. Lenneberg, *Biological Foundations of Languages, ed. cit.*
55. J. J. Katz, *op. cit.,* p. 247.
56. J. J. Katz, *op. cit.,* pp. 247–8.
57. J. J. Katz, *op. cit.,* p. 269.
58. J. J. Katz, *op. cit.,* pp. 269–70.
59. J. J. Katz, *op. cit.,* p. 270.
60. J. J. Katz, *op. cit.,* pp. 273–4.
61. Lenneberg, *op. cit.,* p. 393.
62. *Ibid.*
63. Lenneberg, *op. cit.,* p. 127 (italics – A. S.).
64. Lenneberg, *op. cit.,* p. 220.
65. Lenneberg, *op. cit.,* p. 221.
66. *Ibid.*
67. *Ibid.*
68. Lenneberg, *op. cit.,* p. 244.
69. Lenneberg, *op. cit.,* pp. 375–6.
70. *Ibid.*
71. Lenneberg, *op. cit.,* p. 377 (italics – A. S.).
72. Lenneberg, *op. cit.,* p. 378.
73. See Eric H. Lenneberg, 'A Biological Perspective of Language', in Eric H. Lenneberg (ed.), *New Directions in the Study of Language,* MIT Press, 1964, p. 76.
74. Francois Jacob, *op. cit.,* pp. 337 ff.
75. Jacob, *op. cit.,* pp. 338–9.
76. Jacob, *op. cit.,* pp. 340–3.
77. Jacob, *op. cit.,* p. 343 (italics – A. S.).
78. Jacob, *op. cit.,* (Monod), pp. 150–1 (italics – A. S.).
79. Jacob, *op. cit.,* pp. 167–8 (italics – A. S.).
79a. Jacob, *op. cit.,* p. 169.
80. Included in *Main Trends of Research in the Social and Human Sciences,* I, Mouton/Unesco, 1970.
80a. *Ibid.,* p. 438.
81. *Ibid.*
82. *Ibid.,* p. 440 (italics – A. S.).
83. Katz, *op. cit.,* p. 274.

83a. *Main Trends,* p. 436.
84. Jacob, *op. cit.,* p. 24.
85. N. Chomsky is right in demanding that the history of ideas and the study of facts be separated from one another (see his paper 'Recent Contributions to the Theory of Innate Ideas', p. 2; the paper is the opening one in the *Synthèse* symposium, mentioned earlier).
86. One of the two is that mentioned in note 85 above, and the other, 'Linguistics and Philosophy', is included in the book edited by Sidney Hook (see note 1).
87. Nelson Goodman, 'The Epistemological Argument', *Synthèse* (cf. note 1), p. 27.
88. *Language and Mind.*
89. N. Chomsky, 'Linguistics and Philosophy', p. 84.
90. Sidney Hook, 'Empiricism, Rationalism, and Innate Ideas', in: S. Hook (ed.), *Language and Philosophy,* pp. 162 ff.
91. Thomas Nagel, 'Linguistics and Epistemology', in: *Language and Philosophy* (cf. note 1), pp. 172 ff.
92. We adopt here the convention that the term *verification* will be used to denote a *testing procedure,* which may result either in verification in the strict sense of the word, or in a failure of disproval (falsification), if an appropriate crucial experiment has been designed. R. Carnap also was inclined to accept the view that the empirical nature of a statement is connected with its verifiability or falsifiability; this compromise formula was adopted following the controversy in positivist circles (with Popper as the main opponent) over the possibility of verification.
93. S. K. Shaumian, 'Teoreticheskiye osnovy transformatsionnoy grammatiki', in V. A. Zvegintsev, *Novoe v Lingvistike,* Series II, Moskva, 1962.
93a. This unwillingness to undertake an attempt to verify the Sapir–Whorf hypothesis was discussed by me on another occasion several years ago.
94. Bronisaw Malinowski, 'The Problem of Meaning in Primitive Languages', Supplement I in: C. K. Ogden and I. A. Richards, *The Meaning of Meaning,* London, 1953.
95. N. Chomsky, 'Linguistics and Philosophy', p. 84.

Name Index

201

Subject Index